**Bluebells
& Bittersweet**

Bebe Miles

Bluebells & Bittersweet
Gardening with Native American Plants

With photographs by the author and drawings (except as noted) by Victoria I. Miles

VNR **VAN NOSTRAND REINHOLD COMPANY**
NEW YORK CINCINNATI TORONTO LONDON MELBOURNE

For
LOUISE STEPHAN PRIORE
and
IRENE PUGH MILES

My favorite gardening mentors

Acknowledgments

My mother started me gardening, and this book is rightly partly dedicated to her. I know now how lucky I was as a child. Early walks with her led to long-ranging trips of my own. The woods that surrounded our home belonged to no one in particular, and I picked up volumes of information about them simply by a kind of natural osmosis.

Such experience is no longer available to many eastern children. New York City's Westchester suburbs, which have swallowed much of my childhood playground, are duplicated everywhere. That is what makes spots like our Bowman's Hill State Wildflower Preserve at Washington Crossing State Park, Pennsylvania, so very important. Not only does it preserve our green heritage, but it also serves as a great continuing laboratory and classroom.

To its staff and volunteer workers I am eternally grateful, but especially to botanist Oliver J. Stark for his patience with an amateur. I have been privileged to know three of its founders: Mrs. Lynwood R. Holmes, W. Wilson Heinitsh, and the great Dr. Edgar T. Wherry, who has done so much to disseminate information about our native flora through his popular guides on ferns and wildflowers. The imagination they showed in instigating Bowman's Hill during the depths of the Great Depression is worth saluting.

Parts of several chapters were originally prepared for *Flower & Garden* magazine, which has kindly given permission to use the material here. Leonie Bell (*The Fragrant Year,* M. Barrows & Co., Inc.) has been generous in sharing both horticultural knowledge and her acute perception of various flower scents. Other authors upon whose experience I have drawn are mentioned in appropriate parts of the text.

As always I am grateful to my family for allowing me uninterrupted hours with trowel and typewriter. I am aware it is not always easy to have a flower child for wife and mother. Special thanks go to Robin, whose help with proofreading has been vital, and also to Hayes Photo Service, New Hope, Pa.

Bebe Miles
Doylestown, Pa.
September 1969

VAN NOSTRAND REINHOLD COMPANY REGIONAL OFFICES: NEW YORK, CINCINNATI, CHICAGO, MILLBRAE, DALLAS
VAN NOSTRAND REINHOLD COMPANY FOREIGN OFFICES: LONDON, TORONTO, MELBOURNE
LIBRARY OF CONGRESS CATALOG CARD NO. 79-110060. ALL RIGHTS RESERVED
PUBLISHED BY VAN NOSTRAND REINHOLD COMPANY, 450 WEST 33RD STREET, NEW YORK, N.Y. 10001
DESIGNED BY MYRON S. HALL III. PRINTED IN JAPAN BY TOPPAN PRINTING CO., LTD.
1 3 5 7 9 11 13 15 16 14 12 10 8 6 4 2

CONTENTS

WHERE DID ALL THE FLOWERS GO? 1

This book describes the best native American trees, shrubs, and plants for use by ordinary gardeners. It is not a wildflower guide nor an inclusive treatment of the flora of these United States. My main target is the casual gardener who wants healthy, colorful flowers without great effort.

I happen to believe our natural history is quite as important as our political history. But somewhere in the course of growing up as a nation we were botanically sidetracked. Our gardens do not feature the wonderful plants which are our natural heritage. Our native bleedingheart, for example, blooms continuously from April to October, but it is a rare sight in gardens. What with the depredations of bulldozers and thoughtless picnickers, it is even rarer in the wild.

Some wildlings are so specialized in their needs that they will soon disappear except in formal sanctuaries, but many others are perfect for gardens. It is these latter which are the substance of this book.

This is not meant, however, as a piece of extreme jingoism. My own gardens are living proof that I heartily subscribe to botanical internationalism. Not one of the thousands of daffodils and tulips I've grown is native to the Americas. A Chinese magnolia stands next to an Atlas cedar from northern Africa. A firethorn from southern Europe climbs the chimney, a Norway spruce hides an eyesore, and a Japanese snowbell shades the back patio.

But keeping company with the snowbell is a sourwood from our Appalachians. The snowbell is taller than I but has yet to flower, while the sourwood put forth a fine crop of blossoms in its first year here, when it was scarcely three feet high.

Except for those in nearby Bowman's Hill, I can show you few other sourwoods in all of verdant Bucks County. We have good local nurseries which offer them for sale in small quantities, but one can drive through dozens of newly

planted subdivisions without spotting a single one among the struggling Norway maples. Yet here is a perfectly hardy tree with a decorative display almost the entire summer. The tiny fingers of its buds begin to show in June, the lovely white flowers light up the dog days of August, and by September its leaves are turning a rich mahogany red. The seed pods are nearly as showy as the blooms, particularly when contrasted with the flaming foliage, and they persist well into winter.

Similar neglect obscures hundreds of other native plants which are hardy, disease-free, and beautifully decorative. Only a handful are commonplace in gardens. Many, like the gorgeous paniced summer phlox and the bright perennial asters, had to make a transatlantic trip before earning admittance. Both these border standbys have been subjected to intensive hybridizing by European nurserymen.

Our history books make much of the cupidity of early European ex-

Facing page: Looking up into the canopy of dogwood blossoms which roofs the spring garden.

9

All franklinias in cultivation are descendants of originals collected by John Bartram in the eighteenth century. Note open seed pod.

plorers who sought gold and quick riches in the New World. Actually, botanical specimens were important parts of reports sent back to the mother countries. Dahlias are mentioned as early as 1615 in a book on the plants and animals of Mexico written by Francisco Hernandez.

It was in England that American plants really came into their own,

however. From the very beginning of the colonial period, English gardeners avidly sought the plants of the New World. Collections of seeds, bulbs, and cuttings often made the long ocean voyage in the special care of the captain. Once safely planted on estates of the wealthy or in botanical gardens, they were tenderly nurtured. Knowl-

edgeable American correspondents and collectors such as Philadelphia's John Bartram were scarce, but English gardeners traded stock back and forth and marveled at each new acquisition.

Meanwhile, back in the colonies, the native plants did not fare so well. Seed and cuttings of plants and trees from Europe to feed the new colony were always a part of a successful expedition's supplies in the early years. Although Indians taught the invaders the benefits of corn, squash, and beans, less useful native plants were too often consigned to fire and ax. To the frontiersman they were weeds or underbrush or unfriendly forest. When living grew easier and there was time to plant flower gardens, they were most apt to be attempts to duplicate the gardens of the mother country.

Perhaps the early colonists wanted plants which reminded them of the homeland left behind as proof they had tamed the wilderness. Thus lilacs still bloom around abandoned sites in New England and the mid-Atlantic states where not even a cellarhole remains as other evidence of some forgotten homestead.

There were a few exceptions, of course. Washington planted many natives at Mount Vernon. Thomas Jefferson was intensely interested in botany and sent naturalists with the Lewis and Clark expedition to the unopened West. Later presidents also encouraged native botany.

For the most part, however, their wonderful discoveries were consigned to dusty herbariums or botanical gardens. It was not until the present century that interest in the nature flora began to reach the common man—and now it is already too late for his children to gather bouquets in wood and field. But far-seeing conservationists real-

ized just in time that without help the native plants would soon be lost as the spread of people reduced the amount of open land. The great value of such sanctuaries as Bowman's Hill is not that they are living museums but that they serve as propagating beds for the dissemination of knowledge, apprecia-

tion, and, more concretely, seed, of the best native plants. Such places are giving us a little extra time to save our native flora.

Since I have always gardened in the East, the plants of that section are featured, but not exclusively. If this book is to serve as even a quiet voice of conservation, these

Redbuds frame entrance to Bluebell Trail, one of 14 separate such areas maintained at Pennsylvania's Bowman's Hill State Wildflower Preserve.

are the plants which need help most. Wild stands vanish overnight as the bulldozer advances. This is tragic for our children. Many do not even know what a live shooting-star looks like.

The great majority of the plants I mention I have either grown myself or observed closely in other gardens. In a few cases, mostly plants native to the West, I quote experts whose opinions I value as a guide to their culture. Such secondhand treatment is given plants that I consider too important or lovely to omit even though I have not had time yet to try them personally. I have been following Dr. Wherry's recommendations on soil acidity requirements for years in my garden and pass them along.

By and large these are plants for the great temperate sections of the country where the most gardeners live. Missing are most species from the Far North and the high mountains, much of the flora of the dry Southwest, and most tropicals. Such very specialized subjects deserve attention by experts from those areas.

Purists may complain about plants left out. Some omissions are intentional. Most of the orchid family is far too difficult for home gardening. Some plants are too invasive for gardens. A few are simply unobtainable through ordinary sources. For any favorites of yours that I have neglected through ignorance, I apologize. This part of horticulture has been so

overlooked that much of my experience has had to be trial and error, and this takes many years. All of us still have a great deal to learn about these charming Americans.

You may be tempted to skip the short lesson on ecology in the next chapter. This is a new word for many people. When you garden with plants which have been long bred for ornamental use, you do not think much about it. But whenever you recognize that a given area has a special problem of shade, aridity, acid soil, or abrupt slope and you choose your plants carefully to meet or overcome these difficulties, you have actually become an amateur ecologist.

One reason plants like chrysanthemums make such popular garden subjects is their ability to adapt to a variety of conditions in many different gardening situations. Many wildlings are not as tractable. A successful gardener achieves his outstanding efforts by matching site with plant. Nowhere is this more important than when dealing with wildflowers.

There was a time when gardening with native plants was confined almost entirely to woodland areas by gardeners interested in raising only plants indigenous to their locality. There is nothing wrong with this approach, but it is too confining. How many people any more own land by the acre? Who can find help to maintain such a sanctuary if they do? Why should wildflowers

be only the province of specialists?

A country three thousand miles wide and containing so many variations of climate, soil, and temperature has much more to offer than a mere woodland selection. There are American plants perfect for dry waste areas, for moist bottomlands, and for ordinary sunny borders too.

If our native plants are restricted to special spots, they will soon be only memories. What this book tries to do is show how you can bring many of them into suburban properties. Let's not treat them any longer as specimens to be exhibited like zoo animals in special habitats (except for those few rarities which have no other chance). Rather let's get them into our gardens, where we can really enjoy them and where they will have a new lease on life and an increased popularity with the general public. I see nothing but beauty about a garden where American bluebells nod happily behind European primroses. Both like the same cool, half-shaded moist soil, and together they make a breathtaking picture.

As I write this the silken parachutes of my butterfly-weed are floating toward a nearby main highway. If this plant begins to bloom along the dusty roadside a few years from now, I shall be much heartened, for it has been a long time since I have seen its gay orange along a Pennsylvania road. Maybe there is something better blowing on the wind than old facial tissue and depressing words.

12

MATCH THE PLANT TO THE SITE 2

A garden, like everything else, accurately reflects whatever effort you put into it. Match plant and site correctly, and you are assured a lovely display, barring accidents. Ignore this basic tenet, and you condemn both plant and site to a constant struggle for survival.

Paradoxically, gardening with our native plants is both easier and more demanding than with garden subjects which have been under cultivation for millenniums. Once established in conditions to their liking, many wildlings can fend pretty much for themselves in your garden just as they have been doing for so long in wood and field. Because they have not been tamed by generations of civilizing, however, most insist on narrower limits than you may have given cultivated plants.

Where you live very definitely decides what you can grow successfully. High and low yearly temperatures, rainfall (or its lack), and soil acidity are basic factors over which you have little control, although I

shall suggest ways to widen your horizons. It is always challenging to try something different or rare, but no matter how clever you are, your best course is to choose most of your trees, shrubs, and plants from among those which normally grow under the conditions of your little part of the globe. A look at neighbors' gardens, local woodlands and roadsides, and nearby botanical gardens or wildflower preserves will give you a fair idea of what to expect if you have moved to a new area.

Most gardeners realize it is rather silly to try to establish a garden of tropicals in northern Michigan or a paradise of woodland plants in the desert. We must use common sense; but we do have considerable latitude. For example, given some shade and moisture and soil to their liking, ferns will luxuriate just as beautifully in your yard as in the wild. Plunked in the wrong soil and exposed to hot sun all day, they soon succumb in any climate. Conversely, the sturdiest sun-loving

composite will pine away in a shaded corner, and a plant like lewisia from the mountain slopes will rot in ill-drained bottomland. Anyone who gardens is quite used to this game even if he has never bothered to define its rules. No one plants roses on the shady side of the house or primroses against a hot, south wall.

Why then should we be less careful when dealing with our native plants? Perhaps because we often equate wild plants with weeds. Many of the most ubiquitous of these, however, are not even American. They are European or Asian plants which have adapted too well to conditions of land subjected to human habitation. Danddelions, chicory, butter-and-eggs, and Queen-Anne's-lace, to name only a few common roadside kinds, are all foreign immigrants which have made themselves very much at home here, often at the expense of more delicate natives. And of course almost any plant growing in the correct spot ought to spread

13

Inexpensive split-log bench is appropriate for woodland setting.

or reproduce itself some. Have you ever counted the increase of a healthy daffodil or iris?

In all your gardening, but particularly when dealing with our native plants, you should become an amateur ecologist. This science, which deals with the relationships between organisms and their environment, has long been a stepchild in man's curriculum. It is now fast becoming the science most important to his survival. If we pollute our water and air, ruin our soil by erosion, poison, or overuse, and otherwise upset the delicate balance of life, we shall soon make our planet unable to support life

even if no idiot ever pushes that fatal nuclear button. Whatever you do on your little piece of property will add to or subtract from the sum total.

By improving and conserving the soil and by planting it with the living organisms it needs, you can do your part toward tipping the scales on the good side. Every ground cover (grass is the greatest) you establish to hold the soil and its water content helps. The roots of the tree you nurture do the same. But a big plant like a tree also mitigates the force of the wind and makes the surrounding air appreciably cooler in summer. Moreover,

every plant, from the tiniest right up to the forest giant, takes carbon dioxide from the air and actually manufactures the life-giving oxygen we all need to breathe. Without greenery, our planet would soon revert to something like the moon. That barren, apparently lifeless orb may be an interesting place to visit, but even astronauts are glad to get home.

We are particularly concerned with native plants, but the factors we are to consider in this chapter are part of all horticulture, and agriculture as well.

As a first step, study your own land. Then draw up a rough plan of what you might do with it. A quick summary of my own family's new property will illustrate how you can go about this. It allows us enormous scope because it was formerly farmland, and there was virtually nothing planted when we moved in.

We have a slight slope where the original topsoil was somehow overlooked by a rapacious contractor. Here we are establishing the New Forest. So far we have planted white pines, Douglas fir, and hemlocks along one edge to give privacy and protect us from the worst of the prevailing winds. Groups of thick-growing native shrubs will add to this windbreak. In its lee (away from the wind), native deciduous trees are being added, picked for various reasons ranging from flower display to brilliant fall leaf color. This slope ends in a poorly drained hollow where swamp maples and tupelos are thriving.

As all these trees begin to grow, we pile grass clippings around their bases. This will eventually kill the meadow grass and add humus to the soil. It also protects small tree trunks from being nicked by power mowers. In time the shade of the trees will (I hope) allow me to have a veritable Eden of woodland plants.

Starts of some shrubs and wildflowers which like sun are harbored in the large saucers surrounding some of these trees. By the time we have real shade there, these little things will have grown into big plants or colonies which I can move to the sunny periphery, but meanwhile I at least can see where some day I shall have my woodland.

One edge of the property ends in a deep culvert which drains enormous quantities of storm water from road and surrounding fields. The head of water at its opening is fearful, so that area is being planted with things like spiderworts and bergamot because their far-reaching roots will hold the banks against the force of the water. None of these is allowed in the garden because of their invasiveness, but they will do well in the culvert, look more sightly than rough weeds, and solve our erosion problem.

At its far end the culvert levels out to a mere trickle but keeps one corner quite moist much of the year. Here go Fraser firs and more swamp maples as well as elderberries, cardinal-flowers, fringed gentians, and all the other plants which should revel in a wet-ground situation. I have taken compass readings so that I know the firs must go at the back in the eventual shadiest section while the gentian will be on the sunny edge to the south. My neighbor's willows will give the cardinal-flowers the touch of shade they like.

Above the culvert is a patch of the worst soil you have ever seen. It is sandy, almost devoid of humus, full of rocks, and very dry as well as being in full sun. On its flat, northern edge I have planted a staggered line of dogwoods, each in a big hole of improved garden loam. In their future shade I will be able to grow more of the woodland plants I love if I can improve the topsoil layer during the waiting period. To the south of the dogwoods various sun-loving shrubs are already taking hold, and on their sloping sunny side is my wild dry garden. Here I need not wait for conditions to improve. Already thriving are colonies of butterfly-weed, asters, evening primroses, and other sun-loving plants of waste places.

On the southern and eastern sides of the house weather conditions are less severe. Here I am planting species from the South, which need some protection from the worst of our winter.

Meanwhile my heath garden is taking shape. Here, in a large area

Rampant root growth of *Monarda didyma* (red bergamot) makes it ideal for holding culvert bank.

15

Liatris thrives in dry, sunny spots. White one here contrasts with perennial gaillardia and dwarf marigolds at top of slope in nearly pure clay.

which faces northeast and thus gets no hot sun at all because of shade cast by the building, we are digging in huge amounts of sphagnum peat. This will loosen the clay soil and ensure high acidity for rosebay, pieris, leucothoe, zenobia, and other allied plants. As soon as the shrubs are in place there, acid-loving ground covers like gaultheria can go in too. By growing all these plants that require highly acid soil together, I am also reducing the amount of maintenance this garden will need.

So you see that even on little more than an acre I shall soon have very varied plantings merely by using to their utmost the natural contours of the land and the situation of the house. On even the smallest property there is always some variety of habitat. By taking advantage of the smallest hollow or the slightest elevation, you can multiply the different kinds of plants you can grow. But certain factors must always enter into your planning.

Sun and shadow

An interplay of sun and shade makes the most interesting kind of garden, and these two types of condition are the easiest to obtain. Even if your house is slap-dab in the woods, there should be one little spot to the south that gets more sun than other places. Older homes where giant trees cast too much shade can be gloomy. I would personally find it hard to cut down a tree, but it is sometimes necessary if the original planting was done incorrectly. If you must, clear away one or two to give yourself more light and air. Be selective about which tree goes. A diseased elm, a willow full of aphids, or a maple whose shallow roots are prying up the pavement is easier to lose than a mature sweet-gum or a beautiful flowering tree.

Conversely, shade is where you find it. It was hard to move to this barren place with nary a decent tree. But on the northern and eastern sides of the house there is less sun, and so it was there we tucked starts of woodland treasures brought

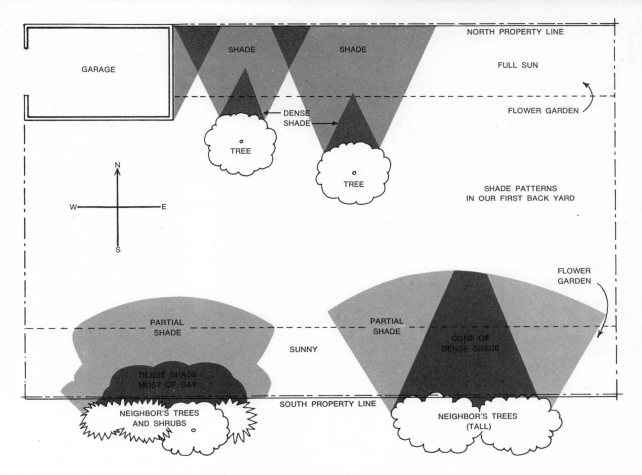

NORTH PROPERTY LINE

FULL SUN

SHADE

SHADE

GARAGE

DENSE
SHADE

FLOWER GARDEN

TREE

TREE

SHADE PATTERNS
IN OUR FIRST BACK YARD

N

W——E

S

FLOWER
GARDEN

PARTIAL
SHADE

PARTIAL
SHADE

CONE OF
DENSE SHADE

SUNNY

DENSE SHADE
MOST OF DAY

SOUTH PROPERTY LINE

NEIGHBOR'S TREES
AND SHRUBS

NEIGHBOR'S TREES
(TALL)

Fig. 1: A careful study of the shade patterns on any property makes for better gardening. (Courtesy *Flower & Garden* magazine)

from our old house. And of course we began planting trees and bushes immediately.

There is not much shade on the north side of a small tree, but there is enough to begin. The tiny start of *Dicentra eximia* which I moved is now a great healthy fountain, colorful from April to October, but its shade so far consists of the pedestal and the top of the birdbath!

This spring I had two small spleenwort ferns from the Christmas terrarium, and no place to give them a permanent home. But there was a big boulder which we had pried with great engineering skill from the bottom of a tree hole. There was no better place to put it than in the front garden. Placed close to the rock on its northeastern side, the ferns got some

morning shade from a nearby birch, and were protected from the worst afternoon scorch. Each has grown astoundingly in one summer. Two baby eastern heucheras hug the rock on its northern side, getting just enough shade to prosper so that each is now a huge rosette.

Fig. 1 indicates shade patterns at the house we bought as our first baby was due. You can see what

17

Left: Small boulder makes a shady microclimate for spleenwort fern and *Heuchera americana.*

Below: Tiny pocket between big tree roots collects enough moisture to provide damp microclimate for spring beauties.

latitude even such a small back yard allows. Fig. 12 shows the general outline of my favorite pocket woodland. Such a shady garden can be made by anyone; you may have to use trees which stay small because of property limitations, but you'll still be able to grow some woodland treasures. And of course there's the encouraging thought that the smallest sapling casts more and more shade as it matures, so the plants in its shadow can increase nicely from even a small start.

Water, water everywhere

If yours is a climate with scanty rainfall, I can only sympathize, for I am not a desert lover. In such a situation I would somehow circumvent the local sanitary codes and use bathwater and dishwater to keep something green.

Here in the East we are more likely to have too much water, at least in some places some of the time. If you have a stream or pond on your property, you are the luckiest of mortals, and the possibilities for natural landscaping are endless. The moisture lovers in Chapter 7 are for your special pleasure. It may pay to consult your county agent about hazards like washouts, muskrats, and high and low water.

More likely you have some poorly drained spots. I do not mean real bogs, which are virtually impossible to maintain without a source of natural water; most plants indigenous to such places are beyond the scope of this book. Rather I refer to the low spot beneath the main drainspout from the roof or the area which gets all the water collected in the drive. These are always a nuisance because grass may not do well, but they offer a wonderful opportunity to grow a tree like the tupelo or a shrub like clethra which need extra moisture. One or two ferns and a few perennials which prefer wet feet, and you have transformed a problem area into an unusual picture.

If you decide to establish a wet garden in a low spot, try to situate it near your water source against a time of drought. In an absolutely dry summer month, it is a real undertaking to drag a hose to the rescue of the panting plants at the end of our culvert. Adding extra peat when you plant such places helps retain moisture.

If you have a large poorly drained area on your property, the easiest solution is to plant it with genera which like their feet wet rather than trying to sow and mow grass. Drainage can be improved with extensive regrading or with tile beds, but both are major undertakings. An auger deeply inserted every few feet will help in some soils, but in heavy clay this measure is at best only temporary. Small explosive charges can break up underlying hardpan, but that is hardly a do-it-yourself job.

We are working on drainage in one section in many ways. One is by planting trees on the periphery. We dig enormous holes for even a small tree, each time going down however many feet are required until we hit the impervious hardpan layer that is our main bugaboo. We then dig a small hole into the hardpan as deep as our muscles will allow on any one day. This hole is filled with small rocks before the tree is planted. The rocks should help keep the break in the hardpan open many seasons, and of course we hope the tree roots will in time work their way into the bad layer too. We know that the hundreds of feeder roots each tree will produce in the good soil in which it is planted will also help hold the earth open and absorb much of its water. Such expedients take some time before they begin to show, but everything helps.

If you want to raise some of the plants from alpine or dry regions, the need for perfect drainage is paramount. Any elevation means better drainage, and so does deeply dug soil with sand content. If your lot is absolutely flat, sogginess can be a problem, but raised beds are not hard to fashion with today's materials. Such a site can be used as a focal point in your landscaping. Its size and location depend only on your desires and pocketbook.

With a bulldozer (they can be rented), all sorts of changes in terrain are possible. One clever stratagem I've seen did double duty. The soil excavated for a small pool was used to make a low mound behind it. Several trees behind this gave the illusion of a real break in the flatness. The possibilities for interesting grading when a swimming pool is added to a property are even greater.

Soil condition

Topography may be difficult to transform, but you can do much to improve the tilth of the soil in your garden area. There is a special place in hell ready I hope for the indiscriminate bulldozer. What these heavy machines do to ruin the structure of soil is unbelievable, and nothing will grow well in it until the damage is repaired.

Plowing and harrowing help but are not often feasible on small places. Having laid out the site of a garden (start small!) or even for a group of trees, there is nothing for you to do but dig it over. Even if the original soil is good, packing by heavy equipment will exclude all the life-supporting air that fertile soil must have.

A few years ago there was advertising for chemicals which would break up the soil. They don't work. Once compacted, the soil must be physically broken up again. You'll have to dig down several feet to do the job right. I did this recently for a new garden and actually had to cart dirt away because mixing air with the adobe the builder had left raised the bed just too much above the surrounding lawn.

If the original soil isn't very good, you can replace the whole bed with topsoil or spent mushroom soil, but

Dredging changed marshy low spot into attractive pond.

it is an expensive proposition, so the next best thing is to mix lots of peat moss into the top foot. By all means learn to compost, for this black gold will do wonders for poor soil. No one ever has enough compost. All these organic conditioners open up clay soil, making it more porous, and they enable too-sandy soil to hold water, as well as making it more fertile.

I dig selected green garbage into new beds, bury grass clippings lightly, and scrounge whatever kind of organic matter I can to help raise the fertility and porosity of the soil our builder left. Pulled weeds go on the compost heap or are piled around plants, where they keep other weeds down and decompose into a kind of duff which is mixed back in every spring. Surprisingly, although natural topsoil takes many years to form, you can hurry things along immensely by mulching constantly with natural materials like pine needles, pine bark, grass clippings, buckwheat hulls, leaf mold, ground corn cobs, or whatever is handiest and cheapest.

If you are starting a woodland garden from scratch, the soil is not likely to be what the plants want, but great quantities of peat moss will do a lot to remedy things. Use more whenever you plant something, keep such an area deeply mulched with something porous like wood chips, and you'll soon begin to have soil that really looks and feels like the good earth again. It is back-breaking labor, but unless you tend to this basic chore first, all the subsequent work and planting is in vain.

Go easy on inorganic fertilizers. Most native plants will do better without any, some will die with very little. It is much more important to have soil of good tilth containing plenty of organic material. Trees and shrubs that like rich soil may benefit from slow-acting fertilizers, but the little plants usually want nothing but the autumn leaf fall and whatever other natural materials come their way. Many eastern soils, however, are deficient in phosphates; it may pay you to test yours and apply remedial phosphorus if necessary.

Acid or alkaline

All of which leads us directly to the next important point: what is the acidity of your soil? This is an important consideration when dealing with the vast majority of native plants.

Many gardeners sprinkle lime haphazardly over lawn and garden because they've heard it's a good thing. It is true that a little lime on acid soils may help release other nutritional elements of the soil. Moreover, many agricultural and ornamental plants with European origins prefer, or do not mind, soil with neutral or even slightly alkaline reactions.

But by far the greatest number of decorative American woodland plants want soil on the acid side. Some of the orchids and members of the heath family require it to be so very acid that nothing else will do well in their natural habitats. Until American botanists and growers realized this point, the vital statistics for native plants transferred from their wild homes to gardens were depressing.

Soil and water acidity are determined on a pH scale. With pH 7 considered to be neutral, higher figures reflect alkaline or "sweet" soil, while lower figures indicate acid or "sour" soil. You should remember that individual numbers represent multiples of 10. Soil with a pH of 6 is 10 times more acid than the neutral pH 7; that with pH 5 is 100 times more acid than pH 7.

Inexpensive, easy-to-use home soil-testing kits are readily available, and if you have not had good luck with your gardening or are embarking on a sizable program of planting, they are a worthwhile investment. Directions come with the kits. There is even one tiny type which can be conveniently carried in purse or pocket on field trips to test the ground where a wild colony is obviously healthy.

Pine-needle mulch helps maintain acid soil for *Goodyera pubescens.*

When you obtain your kit, the first thing to test is your water. Much city water is in the neutral or alkaline range. Continued hosing of acid-loving rhododendron or azaleas with such water can be fatal if other factors are unfavorable too. No matter how carefully you prepare the soil for the plants, the water will eventually leach out and neutralize the acidity. If you know your water has such an effect, you may be able to combat it by adding fresh acid mulches periodically.

Our well water tests out at pH 6, which is murder on copper tubing but wonderful for our native plants. It also means, however, that I must collect neutral rainwater to wash out the testing equipment, and certain house plants are out of the question.

Do not, incidentally, be led astray by believing moss-covered earth is acid. Such appearance indicates truly only that the soil in question is poorly drained. Except for an actual soil test, the only valuable gauge is the type of plant naturally thriving on land. If it supports blueberries, wild azaleas, or gaultheria, you can be sure it is definitely acid. A meadow where fringed gentian or mertensia thrives probably is neutral.

Plants which are indicated in this book as wanting acid soil need a pH count of about 6; those indicated as wanting very acid soil need a pH count between pH 4.5 and 5. When we say trailing arbutus needs soil with pH 4.5, we are talking about a very acid condition indeed, and this is why so many plantings of it fail. It is not easy to maintain such a level artificially. Species native to our Plains states are more likely to want soils on the neutral or even alkaline side.

What all this means to you is that there are definite limitations on what will easily thrive in your soil. Much of the eastern half of the country, which once supported great forests of mixed evergreen and deciduous trees, tends to be acid, but there are limestone areas everywhere. Land on which evergreens have grown for some time turns quite acid.

Again let's use my property as an example. Most of our soil tests at pH 6 both on the surface and below. Tons of Michigan peat have been used to condition the clay because it is cheap and easy to obtain and spread. This peat invariably tests at pH 6. Combined with water of equal acidity, this means that anything which desires light to medium acid soil does fine.

Plants such as dodecatheon, clematis, and *Hepatica acutiloba,* which do not like acidity, are placed close to the house, where lime leaching from the foundation and tonics of wood ashes from the fireplace help them overcome the natural acid soil. Lilacs, incidentally, even when given massive doses of limestone, prosper only near the house for the same reason.

So far I have not successfully supported plants which want a very

Hepatica acutiloba, which prefers limy soil, nestles close to foundation on shady eastern side of house.

acid soil. But under the little white pines which have been in only three years, the soil is already testing slightly under pH 6. Wood chip mulch tests around pH 5.5 when fresh. Some sphagnum peat brings a reading of pH 4. Cottonseed meal, fresh oak leaves, pine needles, and tanbark are other highly acid soil conditioners. Obviously if you mix lots of these materials into a soil like mine, you will be able to maintain a pretty acid condition, especially if you plant oaks and pines to add acid duff to the top layer of soil.

If you want to raise plants with definite pH preferences contrary to your natural soil, group them all together in one spot. Make it at the highest elevation you have, or even in a slightly raised bed, so that

water from surrounding soil will not constantly invade the area. Use limestone rock to support earth being kept neutral or alkaline. Sandstone seems to test out acid, but your local stone quarry may have a more durable acidic rock to suggest for an acid garden. Avoid any mortar for the latter type. And make tests of such soil twice a year to make sure that it is staying in the range you want.

Where you are making an acid bed in an alkaline soil, it will pay to dig down several feet and line the bottom of the pit with highly acid sphagnum peat first, to prevent earthworms from bringing alkaline subsoil up into your special plantings. Lining the opposite kind of bed with large pieces of crushed limestone might help keep things alkaline.

At Bowman's Hill we make special plantings like this in discarded bathtubs. Sunk into the ground, they are filled with soil of the desired type and the edges are disguised with rocks or plants. Surface water must not drain into the tub, of course.

Some authorities suggest merely applying lime to sweeten the soil and aluminum sulphate for the opposite effect. Gardeners whose experience I trust highly say these are at best stopgap measures, that correct quantities are always hard to determine. I prefer to try to build up the soil in the ways previously suggested. If you do opt for either of these chemicals, bring the soil to the desired reading in small doses and make periodic checks.

Obviously it is far easier to garden with plants which prefer the kind of soil you have. Luckily a great many of the most decorative natives do quite well in soil that is only slightly acid. If you use plenty of Pennsylvania or Michigan peat with a pH of 6 when planting

(this helps the roots get a good start anyway), you should be able to raise the greatest number without trouble. Stay away from plants with strict wants at either extreme. If your soil is already highly acid or alkaline, limit yourself to those species which want what you have, except in very special beds where you can try juggling things.

Hardiness

Geography also limits what you can grow successfully. It works both ways. Some plants may want cooler conditions than you can give them; others from warmer regions may not be able to cope with your winters.

Even here in temperate Penn-

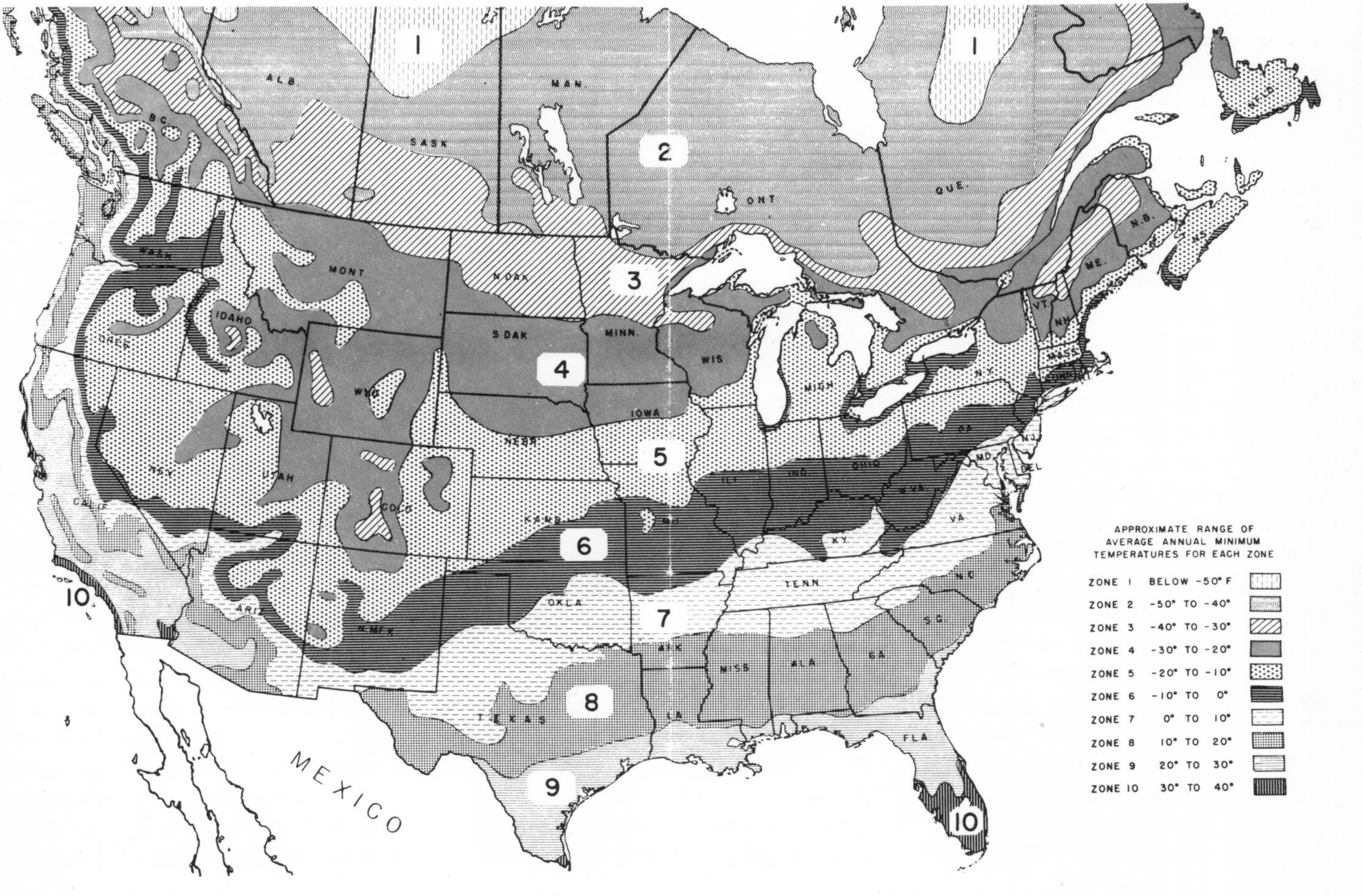

Fig. 2: Hardiness map of the United States allows comparison between zones. (Courtesy U.S. Dept. of Agriculture)

APPROXIMATE RANGE OF AVERAGE ANNUAL MINIMUM TEMPERATURES FOR EACH ZONE

ZONE 1	BELOW -50° F
ZONE 2	-50° TO -40°
ZONE 3	-40° TO -30°
ZONE 4	-30° TO -20°
ZONE 5	-20° TO -10°
ZONE 6	-10° TO 0°
ZONE 7	0° TO 10°
ZONE 8	10° TO 20°
ZONE 9	20° TO 30°
ZONE 10	30° TO 40°

sylvania many alpine plants cannot survive our hot summers, while subtropical species must be brought in before frost to winter in cellar or laundry. Additionally, many plants which come from the dry Plains area or southern California do not like our wet summers.

Up and down are just as important as latitude and longitude. There are spots in the southern Appalachian mountains with much more severe winters than along the temperate northeastern coast at Boston, for example. All this finagling is part of a fairly new kind of gardening: the fashioning of microclimates.

Again start out with plants native to your own area. They will almost always be the most successful, and your gardening will be more pleasurable if you are not spending all your time trying to outwit the weather. Eventually all of us, however, lift our eyes beyond our own fence to what appear to be greener pastures.

If you like such challenges, it can be immensely satisfying to introduce strangers from other sections. Many times one succeeds beyond all belief, for our natives are mostly a sturdy crew if given half a chance. A few pointers are gleaned from my own experience. Rock gardeners are especially adroit at this sport. Much of it is still a matter of trial and error plus intelligent guesswork, and your experience may add to what is still a largely untried field.

Fig. 2 is a hardiness map of the United States put out by the U.S. Department of Agriculture. You will notice the zones wiggle all over. This is because it is colder at higher elevations, warmer along river valleys and large bodies of water. I live on the southern border of Zone 6, so I am constantly trying species recommended only for Zone 7—with considerable success.

After you locate yourself on the map, you have a handy way of comparing your conditions with those of anyone whose opinions or suggestions you come across. If you live in the part of Kansas designated Zone 5, you can be pretty sure that anything which is hardy in Maine will take your climate, other conditions being equal. Notice, however, that part of Maine's coastline is in Zone 6 because of the ocean. There are actually many more of these small divergencies than appear on the map, but it is at least the best point ot reference we have when dealing with such a large and diversified country as ours.

Species considered to be trees and shrubs have been much more thoroughly researched for hardiness than the smaller plants. For zone hardiness in those chapters I have relied heavily on recommendations given by Donald Wyman of the Arnold Arboretum in Boston (*Trees for American Gardens,* Macmillan), Arthur T. Viertel of the New York State College of Forestry at Syracuse (*Trees, Shrubs and Vines,*

Bulletin 43, State University College of Forestry at Syracuse University), and Isabel Zucker (*Flowering Shrubs,* Van Nostrand Reinhold).

When dealing with other plants, the natural range gives some hint, but until more of us have gardened extensively with plants from other sections, much of this is guesswork. We know that galax and shortia from the Appalachians survive up into New England because someone has succeeded in doing just that, but whether my *Campanula divaricata* from North Carolina will do the same, I do not know. With such dubious plants, play it safe. Give them some protection until you have enough plants to experiment with. Remember too that one winter doesn't prove much; the next may may be worse. Nevertheless, microclimate gardening is a most interesting diversion.

North vs. South

Since this is the kind of juggling I know best, we will start with how to stretch your climate north and south. It is definitely harder to do the first than the last, oddly enough.

Northern plants (this includes alpines from high elevations) not only prefer cool weather, they are used to weak, short winter light or none at all because of snow cover, and they cannot adapt well to a climate with alternate freezing and thawing. My hot, often dry summer simply stops many in their tracks even if they can put up with the vagaries of our winter. In addition, alpines almost always demand perfect drainage.

To make these at home south of New York City (except in mountainous regions), give them a spot which has afternoon shade both summer and winter and mulch well with rocks to keep the roots moist and cool. If the location faces northish, it will tend to freeze up and stay that way all winter, thus fighting the evil of heaving roots. Where temperatures seldom go below freezing, you're foolish even to try them. Never let them lack for water in summer. Extra shade and moisture often help northern things survive south of their natural haunts.

Since warm air rises, it is always cooler at the bottom of a hill, even without shade. We have a dry, warm slope at Bowman's Hill which ends in a deep ravine clothed in hemlock along a stream. One often actually shivers on entering the hemlock grove, so great is the difference in temperature on a summer day.

These lower spots will also tend to be snow traps. This is terribly important in climates where snow cover is sporadic, for the stuff is a wonderful insulator. So notice such sites next winter on your property, for they will be particularly good choices for northern plants.

Wind helps keep things cool too, so exposure to such air conditioning may help your northerners in the summer, but it is not always a friend in winter. If there is no snow cover, high wind can be incredibly drying. A thick screen or covering of old evergreen branches is one of the best and least unattractive protections from wind and sun burn.

When trying to acclimatize a more southern plant to our winter, I utilize these tricks in reverse. Such plants, but most especially any broad-leaved evergreens, are never situated where the prevailing winter wind can ravage them. Buildings, windbreaks, stone walls, or a south-facing slope all give protection from the howlers of our winter. Even an evergreen tree or a large, dense bush may give shelter.

Several choice plants from North Carolina are grouped to the south of a large boulder in my garden. I am not sure they need its slight protection, but until I have more plants to try with, that's where they stay, safe in the lee of the rock in a warm pocket. To find the location of such tiny southern oases in your garden, watch for spots where the snow melts first and fastest.

Sunburn in winter when the roots are frozen wreaks havoc on broadleaves like holly too, so give them some protection from the worst of the afternoon sun. This can be merely the broken shade cast by bare branches of deciduous trees. Sun reflected from white buildings in winter is very strong, so keep such evergreen plants away from these areas. The south side of your house is likely to have the kindest winter climate, incidentally.

Wrapping in burlap is a time-tested technique for half-hardy shrubs but so unsightly I try to find them a sheltered spot instead. A good covering of leaves or straw held down by evergreen branches aids many tenderer perennials. Paper bark wrap is an excellent protection for the first few seasons for trees exposed to high winds or intense sun.

The late Mrs. J. Norman Henry of Gladwyne, Pennsylvania, made a specialty of adapting southern species to our harsher winters. She insisted it was important to situate them so that the first rays of the morning sun did not hit plants while they were still deeply frozen from nighttime temperatures, and I have followed her advice with my choicest things. She also suggested keeping such plants as dry as feasible during the winter. Thus good

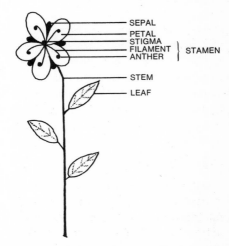

Fig. 3: All flowers have essentially the same parts.

25

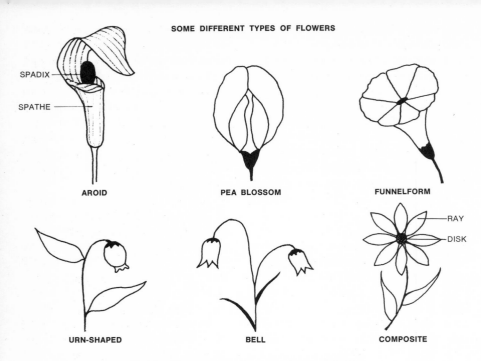

SOME DIFFERENT TYPES OF FLOWERS

SPADIX

SPATHE

AROID

PEA BLOSSOM

FUNNELFORM

RAY

DISK

URN-SHAPED

BELL

COMPOSITE

Fig. 4: Flowers come in many shapes and sizes.

drainage enters again; put them on the top part of a slope if you can, facing toward the south but out of the worst wind. So situated and protected at back and side by an ell from the north wind and the eastern dawn, my baby *Magnolia grandiflora* kept all her leaves last winter and doubled her height this summer.

East meets West

When a handbook tells me a plant is from California, I get a bit miffed, for those western states have great extremes of climate. "Mts." helps, for then one may assume the same treatment afforded eastern alpines may be all that is needed to make them at home here in Pennsylvania.

Coastal southern California is getting into tropical weather, while northern Pacific Coast areas enjoy nearly frost-free winters plus cool, humid summers I cannot duplicate. I try very little from these regions, simply because it is asking the impossible. But anything which grows in mountainous sections or the Plains states is fair game.

Sharp drainage is one problem. Summers in the West are much drier than here. Situate such plants where no water ever collects around them and where you will not be doing artificial summer watering.

Sandy, rocky soil is best, and don't give them the humus peat moss beloved by our easterners. South-facing slopes here have the double advantage of winter warmth and summer dryness, so if a Californian is doubtfully hardy, that's where it goes.

Plants from the Plains do not need winter protection, but summer dryness is a good idea. No humus goes into their planting either, and those which I know or suspect want alkaline soil are kept in a special area between the cement sidewalk and the house foundation where the clay soil is as nearly non-acid as I can provide.

Western plants are not nearly as available as eastern natives, perhaps because they are not yet threatened with extinction. I wish someone would remedy this lack, especially among bulbous plants.

If you live in the dry West and want to try some of our easterners, particularly woodland plants, go over again the section on soil acidity. And add lots of peat moss and compost to the soil, no matter what it tests. Until you have felt one of our woodland soils, you cannot believe its porosity. Often in the top layer where the little plants are growing, there is as much humus as earth. It is like digging into cake!

Summer shade is a must too. Plant them under deciduous trees just as they grow in the wild and let the fall leaf drop pile up to protect them from both winter's cold

26

and summer's drying. Use pine bark mulch rather than peat as a top dressing. Peat is a notorious robber of moisture and in heat makes an impermeable crust which absorbs every drop of water for itself, letting none penetrate to the plant roots. Peat moss is for mixing with the soil, not frosting it.

Finally, remember that our spring and summer is usually a time of adequate rainfall. By that I mean several inches at least every month. The humus you mix into your soil will help keep it acid and moist, but our plants expect water. To make them at home, keep them all together near a source of water so it is easy to give them a deep drink every week or so.

And good luck to you all.

PLANTS FOR PROBLEM PLACES

Windbreaks

Trees (•=evergreen)
Crataegus mollis (downy hawthorn)
•*Juniperus virginiana* (red cedar)
•*Picea glauca* (white spruce)
　　glauca densata (Black Hills spruce)
•*Pinus strobus* (white pine)
　　rigida (pitch pine)
•*Ptseudotsuga menziesi* (Douglas fir)
Quercus (various oaks)
Sassafras albidum
•*Thuja occidentalis* (American arborvitae)

Shrubs (all good for game too)
Cornus stolonifera (red osier dogwood)
Corylus americanus (hazelnut)
Eleagnus commutata (silverberry)
Ilex glabra (inkberry)
Juniperus (prostrate junipers)
Myrica pensylvanica (bayberry)
Prunus maritima (beach plum)
Shepherdia argentea (silver buffaloberry)
　　canadensis (russet buffaloberry)
Symphoricarpus orbiculatus (coralberry)
Viburnum acerifolium (dockmanie)
　　cassinoides (swamp viburnum)
　　lentago (nannyberry)
　　prunifolium (black haw)
　　trilobum (highbush cranberry)

Wet Sites

Trees
•*Abies balsamea* (balsam fir)
　　fraseri
Acer rubrum (red maple)
Betula nigra (river birch)
　　populifolia (gray birch)
Carpinus caroliniana (hornbeam)
Liquidamber styraciflua (sweet gum)
Magnolia virginiana (swamp magnolia)
Nyssa sylvatica (tupelo)
Quercus bicolor (swamp white oak)
　　palustris (pin oak)
　　phellos (willow oak)
•*Thuja occidentalis* (American arborvitae)
Tilia americana (linden)
•*Tsuga canadensis* (hemlock)

Shrubs
Cephalanthus occidentalis (buttonbush)
Clethra alnifolia (sweet pepperbush)
Euonymus americanus (brook euonymus)
Hamamelis virginiana (witch-hazel)
Ilex glabra (inkberry)
　　verticillata (winterberry)
Itea virginica (Virginia willow)
Lindera benzoin (spicebush)
Rhododendron nudiflorum (pinxterbloom)
　　viscosum (swamp azalea)
Salix discolor (pussy willow)
Sambucus canadensis (elderberry)
Staphylea trifolia (bladdernut)
Vaccinium corymbosum (swamp blueberry)
Viburnum cassinoides (swamp virburnum)
　　lentago (nannyberry)
Xanthorhiza simplicissima (yellowroot)
(For perennials check appropriate section in Chapter 7; ferns, Chapter 10)

Very Dry, Sunny Sites

Trees
Betula populifolia (gray birch)
Castanea pumila (chinquapin)
•*Juniperus virginiana* (red cedar)
Ostrya virginiana (hop hornbeam)
•*Picea glauca* (white spruce)
•*Pinus banksiana* (Eastern jack pine)
　　pinaster (cluster pine)
　　rigida (pitch pine)
　　strobus (white pine)
　　virginiana (scrub pine)
Quercus coccinea (scarlet oak)
Robinia pseudoacacia (black locust)

Shrubs
Ceanothus americanus (New Jersey tea)
Comptonia peregrina (sweetfern)
Eleagnus commutata (silverberry)
Juniperus (various prostrate forms)
Myrica pensylvanica (bayberry)
Potentilla fruticosa (cinquefoil)
Prunus maritima (beach plum)
Shepherdia argentea (silver buffaloberry)
　　canadensis (russet buffaloberry)
Vaccinium angustifolium (lowbush blueberry)
(Perennials recommended include:
Anaphalis margaritacea, Anemone patens,
antennarias, arctostaphyllos, *Asclepias tuberosa,* asters, baptisias, *Callirhoe involucrata,* coreopsis, echinaceas, epilobiums, gaillardias, *Hesperaloe parviflora,* liatris, lupines, oenotheras, opuntias, penstemons, rudbeckias, ruellias, *Silene caroliniana, Verbena bipinnatifida,* yuccas.)

3 YOU MAY HAVE TO GROW YOUR OWN

If it were easy to obtain many of the plants in this book, there would have been little reason to write it. Sadly, supplies are limited and suppliers hard to find for far too many of the species listed.

At the end of this chapter are addresses for a few of the best sources. Write first to those nearest your home, since their offerings will more closely approximate what your climate supports best. Nearby botanical gardens may also have seed available or know of local sources.

In many cases it is wiser (and very much cheaper) to start your own plants from seed. This is particularly true where you wish to use herbaceous perennials in quantity. Many ground covers spread by creeping roots, so a small piece will in time give you many plants. Almost any shrub or tree can be reproduced from cuttings, but you must be patient.

I have never had as good luck with plants sent by mail as with trees and shrubs, but this is partly due to poor local delivery. Even if packed properly, small perennials dry out dreadfully if left in a hot place over the weekend; other shipments have been badly molded or rotted. This is another reason to use the nearest possible supplier for growing material. Seeds and bulbs can be delivered from almost anywhere by ordinary mail. For cross-country orders of plants, rely on air freight.

Strangely enough the botanical preserve I know best obtains some of its seed from overseas, where our American plants are treasured as rarities. As we stimulate more interest in our native plants, these conditions will improve. Make your needs known, and the seed houses and nurseries will find it profitable to stock more kinds.

A question of names

For the beginning gardener, botanical names are a nuisance. He shrinks from acknowledging their existence as long as possible. "Dogwood" is a friendly term which conjures up nostalgic pictures for all seasons. When he discovers it is cataloged under "Cornus" instead, he is understandably annoyed; it seems like needless hairsplitting. I know, for I stood at the same crossroads once.

Grow even the least bit discriminating in your gardening, however, and you cannot escape the necessity of using these scientific guideposts. For one dogwood is not like another, and even "pink" or "white" or "red" are useless if you become enamored of Cornus florida plena. Catalogs or nurseries where you will be able to locate a specimen of this unusual dogwood will use botanical names for the same reason I have done so in this book: it is the only sure way to find one's path in the bewildering horticultural maze.

I have learned to be leery of the nursery which does not so label. Too often one does not get what one wanted. To the confirmed gardener, mislabeling is a cardinal sin.

Once you accept scientific names

as a necessary evil, you will find them endlessly useful and often amusing. To make the transition easier, I have included in the index as many of the more common names and nicknames as possible. In the chapters, however, all plants are listed alphabetically by their generic Latin name.

A brief description of the system called binomial nomenclature will help you find your way. Before its adoption, there was far too much rhyme and reason to the scientific names given plants. To differentiate each, long lists of Latin adjectives were appended. The great Swedish botanist Linnaeus brought order to this chaos, and our modern plant and animal worlds are now classified in essentially his system.

To avoid language barriers, Latin was adopted worldwide. Elaborate ways of registering new introductions or discoveries prevent the same name being used for two different items.

Each plant (tree, bulb, etc.) has two names. They are usually written in italics. The first shows its genus (plural: genera) and is capitalized. The second is the species name and often gives details of origin, habit, height, color, or other detail which distinguishes it from others of its genus. Without such guides we would be completely lost in understanding each other. Handbooks defining the specific terms are fun to leaf through.

Getting back to our dogwood: the eastern species is *Cornus florida*.

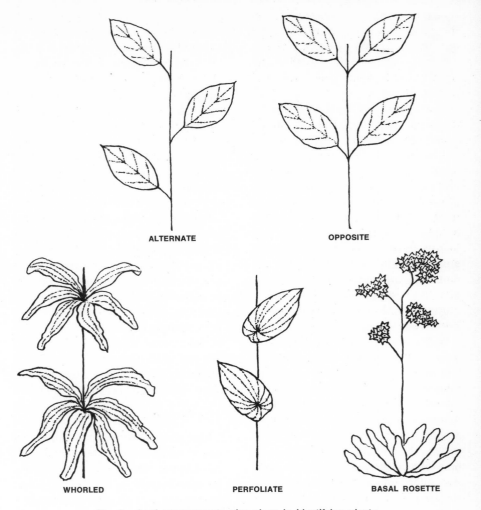

Fig. 5: Leaf arrangements give clues in identifying plants.

Add the word *plena,* and you are speaking of its double-flowered form, a variety rather than another species. It is a fine point whether a system of binomial nomenclature should allow this, but it is certainly useful. It may also be written *Cor-* *nus florida var. plena.* In a three-part name, the third name is always for varietal differentiation.

A nurseryman who has developed or discovered a special form vegetatively reproduces his special plant (cultivar) so that each of its progeny is exactly like the parent (which he considers superior to the type). He may then list it as *Cornus florida* Cherokee Chief (a red-flowered form). Such selections are often called clones.

Out West we have the Pacific flowering dogwood, *Cornus nuttalli.* Seeing one, it is not hard to understand its close kinship to its eastern cousin. But if you order *Cornus canadensis,* you will receive a low-growing ground cover rather than a tree. There are dozens of shrub dogwoods too, some with bad habits. So we must go further than merely saying "dogwood" when we consider this genus, and to get exactly the dogwood for a specific purpose, we must be careful which we choose.

Since we are considering Americans, there is one odd quirk to mention. As the white man explored the New World, he sent back a continual stream of plants never before seen. These were classified as best they could be by the overworked Old World botanists. There was then no United States of America, but merely a loose collection of colonies under different flags. Thus such words as *floridus, carolinianus, pensylvanicus, virginica,* and *canadensis* do not refer to present geographical divisions. When used as the species part of a plant's name, these words almost always indicate American origin, but the plant may be much more common and quite hardy in the climate of the Mid-Atlantic states than in Florida, as in

the example of the eastern dogwood. *Canadensis* tends to be attached to more northern species, but that is the only safe generalization. Even to explorers our geography was a pretty uncertain thing in those early days, so we cannot blame the stay-at-home botanists for natural mistakes.

Reproductive organs are often the determining factor in botanical classification, so it is not safe to jump to conclusions that members of the same genus are similar in growth habit. Plant families are even more loosely organized. Trailing arbutus, blueberries, and the sourwood tree are all heaths, for instance, but no one would substitute one for the other in a garden.

In this book, unless I have indicated otherwise, I use L. H. Bailey's *Manual of Cultivated Plants* as the authority for names of genera and species except for capitalization.

Hybrids and selections

Some of our wildflowers have not been as neglected as others. A plant with particularly good flowers or growth habits may have been found in the wild and vegetatively propagated by an alert nurseryman. Or formal hybridization may have produced a highly desirable form. Such varieties are usually sold under trade names such as *Phlox stolonifera* Blue Ridge, *Dicentra* Bountiful or *Rudbeckia* Gloriosa Daisies. There are excellent choices for garden use.

Purists will immediately complain

that such are not wildflowers. This hair-splitting is permissible only in botanical gardens where pure strains are important for scientific purposes. One of the treasures of every such preserve is its collections of varieties within a species. These are often found by sharp-eyed collectors because their superior form or color captures his attention within a colony of flowers.

If you could go with me to Bowman's Hill in April I could show you pure white, lavender-gray, and rosy-pink forms of the common bluebell *(mertensia).* Another section of the sanctuary has *Phlox divaricata* in shades from snowy white through every tint of lavender to the purest tone of the sky. There are spring-beauties *(claytonia)* with double flowers, larger blossoms, pinker or whiter forms, even one with yellow blooms!

Given enough time nature experiments with almost everything. A sport or a mutation or a natural hybrid may occur anywhere. That it is more lovely than its brethren will not stop the hungry rabbit or the equally voracious bulldozer. Anyone who finds such a different form should do all he can to save it, at least until an expert can decide whether it is an improvement worth perpetuating.

Few gardeners have enough time, knowledge, or opportunity to tramp the woods in search of improved forms. It is a real bonanza when one locates a start of some such glorious mutation as the double-

Double bloodroot is one of choicest natural mutations.

flowered bloodroot. The nurseryman who is willing to devote the extra energy involved in propagating superior forms is a genuine hero— much more to be commended, incidentally, than the dealer who merely plunders wild stands to fill his orders.

In a way the professional hybridizer plays God when he develops a new form. I see no reason not to encourage him. Recalling some delicately colored double California poppies I saw not long ago in the Burpee Seed company's trial gardens, I cannot wait for color selections to be available so I can add a great bed of the pink ones to my dry front garden.

All this is not to discourage anyone from tending a strictly wild garden in some form. Our wildlings need all the help they can get. As special habitats grow scarcer, some species will not survive unless someone takes the extra care to provide a haven.

But increased interest in American plants is bound to stimulate hybridizers and encourage nurserymen to offer stock or seed of special forms. This is all to the good, and our gardens will be the better for it. One intent of this book is to inspire American gardeners to grow more American plants, whatever their origin.

Can you collect?

Please don't try to fill your garden with plants collected in the wild. Raping the few remaining natural stands only makes a bad situation worse. But trips to observe wildflowers in their native habitats can be useful, as well as very pleasant. You will begin to notice beautiful combinations of plants with common requirements which you can duplicate in your garden. But let it stop there.

In the first place all land belongs to someone, and there are laws to protect it. I would quite cheerfully jail anyone caught digging plants from my own little acreage or a sanctuary.

Some of the best of our wildflowers are being raised in nurseries specializing in them. Plants from these sources are actually the best way to begin a garden of natives. Root systems of specimens thus grown are better adapted for transplanting than plants collected in the wild.

Happily, many of these finest subjects for gardens increase well by division, offsets, or creeping roots. If placed in the right environment, they may begin to seed themselves too, so one or two plants will be all you need to start your own colony. Prices for most wildflowers are comparable with other garden plants. Seed of many of the most decorative is also available, and will be more so if the demand for it increases. Costs in either case are much less than a fine for trespassing.

Even if you can get permission from the owner, a hillside full of blossom is one of the worst places to get plants. Far better to mark those you want and wait until they go dormant. You'll have to keep a close check, because many of the prettiest spring things disappear entirely by the time hot weather comes. Their chances of surviving the move are much better if it is done during their dormant period, but don't do it at all unless you know you can match their needs. It breaks my heart to think of how many lovely stands of pink lady-slippers have been denuded by people who know nothing of their special wants. As a rule of thumb, spring-blooming plants are best moved after seed ripens or in late fall. Summer- and fall-flowering types are ideally transplanted in early spring.

Check the soil acidity, shade, and

exposure of the original colony. Then if you really think you can duplicate it and if there are plenty of specimens, mark some of the smallest. There is a temptation to move the biggest and best-flowering plant, but a less mature one is a much better choice. For one thing, its root system is not yet as extensive, so it will be easier to dig without undue disturbance.

Never pull up a plant. Use a spade and take a big, deep square of soil all around the plant. This not only means less root loss but also helps the plant get acclimated to its new home. Many wildlings have special soil fungi without which they cannot survive. A portion of the original soil may contain enough to establish the fungi in your garden.

Pick a cool, preferably overcast day for any collecting trips. Take wet newspaper or burlap to wrap around each plant's roots the moment it is dug. Even neater are plastic bags and a jar of water. Slip the plant into the bag, sprinkle it with water, and tie the bag around the root ball. Ice chests with ice are fine too. Never leave any transplants even a minute in the hot sun.

Be prepared to plant them as soon as possible, for you must fight both drying out and rot, either of which is quite likely (depending on the weather). Water well after you plant and at frequent intervals if there is no rain for a week or two. Plants still in the growing state (with green leaves) may also need shade for a few days to help them

get over the shock of transplanting.

Many landowners are understandably loathe to have you take their plants but may give permission to collect seed. This is usually a better strategy anyway, for seed-grown plants prove much stronger and thriftier than collected specimens. Leave some seed to help perpetuate the wild stand.

Here too you'll be marking plants while in blossom. (Short strands of thick red yarn are easy to spot later.) Again you'll have to keep a close check, for often seed matures quickly after spring flowering. You can tell it is ripe by the condition of the pod or container, which tends to turn dry as the seed is ready, and also by the color and feel of the seed itself. Immature seeds are often white or green and soft to the touch; ripe ones are usually dark-colored hard capsules.

Take along a piece of white paper and shake the seed container over it to find out what it looks like. The tiniest seeds come from the most unexpected places. While nature lets much of this seed fall when it is ripe, in the north temperate zone many species do not germinate until the following spring. Unless you know differently, seal your seed in envelopes after the husks are removed and store it in airtight containers in a cool spot. A home refrigerator is ideal.

Land marked for clearing is one great exception to all I have just written. If you know an area that will soon be under water, develop-

ment, or asphalt, you can help the cause of conservation by collecting, since the original plants will soon be dead. But concentrate on those which have some chance in the environment you can give them.

Even knowing the bulldozer is soon to come, you had best get permission somehow. If you cannot provide a home for the plants of a particular ecological grouping, you may still act constructively. Contact the nearest garden club, wildflower preserve, botanical garden, or university. They may be able to benefit even if you can't. The real winners will be the native flora you save plus the future generations who will enjoy it.

The main thing I want to stress is that you must not let an interest in native plants delude you into creating a graveyard of dead transplants all over your garden. There are much better ways to do it.

To propagate your own

Nursery stock (and its shipping) grows more expensive each year. Often it will pay you to buy a mother plant and raise additional specimens yourself by some method of propagating. Many kinds are easily raised from seed. Others which are difficult to germinate increase well by division, layering, or cuttings, and these vegetative means of propagation are the only ways to reproduce a choice mutation or selection which may not come true from seed.

Where a species is dioecious

(having male and female flowers on separate plants, like the hollies), only the female will produce fruit, and then only if there is a male plant close by. If you plant these seeds, the progeny will be both male and female, and you will usually have to wait until they flower to differentiate between them. If you desire one or the other, it is better to pay more for a plant of certified sex or raise a cutting from a specimen of known sex and species. In the long run it pays great dividends in both plants and personal satisfaction to be able to do some of your own propagating.

Propagating from seed

Seeds are basic to reproduction, and many wildlings cannot be obtained any other way. Given the right combination of soil, moisture, temperature, and light, almost anything can be raised from seed, but trees and shrubs often take many years to come into maturity. Annuals, biennials, and perennials, however, are almost always reproduced from seed, especially if desired in quantity.

Since they have been so neglected, many wildflowers contain unknown qualities. Raising them from seed, you may find considerable variation in color and size of flowers, height of plants, and even hardiness. By selecting the best for further reproduction, you may get yourself an outstanding strain. This is exactly what seedsmen have done with cultivated species.

Male holly cuttings bear wool yarn markers. New growth indicates cuttings have rooted.

Wild seed is not always true to type. If you come across a white sport of the common bluebell *(mertensia),* for example, its seed may not produce plants which all give white blossoms. There may not even be any in the first generation, but such plants will contain genes with a white tendency. Continued selection plus patient cross-fertilization of plants with the whitest flowers will in time, perhaps, give you a strain which will breed true whites. Generally, however, white sports breed true. All this is the work of the plant breeder. Many of our wild-

33

flowers have not yet been given such treatment, but there is no reason why they shouldn't respond just as more popular garden plants have. That is, however, the postgraduate part of what is essentially a very simple process.

The one important rule in raising plants from seed is to see that they never suffer a setback. Tiny seedlings cannot take any kind of shock. Once they germinate they must have light, and good air circulation is always important. They should neither drown nor lack for water.

If you buy wildflower seed from a reputable source, it ought to be fresh and true to label. Scattering it in unprepared ground is pretty much a waste of time. Only the most rampant kinds can compete with grass or weeds, and these are seldom what one wants in a garden. Popular mixtures of wildflower seed are equally senseless. The wants and habits of different kinds are too variable. After you have plants, you can make all sorts of combinations, but start out with packets of single kinds.

Many annuals should be sown in the bed where they are to flower. For those which need cool weather for germinating or growing, earth prepared in the fall makes early sowing easier.

There is no reason why other wildflower seed cannot be sown directly in place in the garden also, but I seldom do except with plants with which I am very familiar. For one thing I am afraid I will not rec-

ognize a new one's cotyledon leaves (the first to appear when the seed sprouts). More importantly, such seed is often difficult or expensive to obtain; I do not want it completely at the mercy of wind, weather, and animals. Lastly, the germination periods of many wildflowers are yet unknown; I have had some germinate the second year after sowing. So I raise almost all perennial wildflower seedlings in special containers.

The containers may be wooden flats, flower pots, or whatever is handiest. After Christmas I collect half-gallon cardboard milk cartons. With one side removed and holes punched in the bottom for drainage, they make splendid seed flats. Most windowsills will hold them,

each species may be kept separate. When it comes time to transplant, nothing could be easier. Simply peel away the front of the flat, and each little plant may be removed with little damage to its roots.

Of foremost importance is the growing medium. Special potting soils are sold in many garden centers, but anyone who raises seed in quantity should make up their own. A good general mixture is 2 parts good garden loam, 1 part peat moss, and 1 part coarse sand. My soil is clay, so I use only 1 part soil. If yours is on the sandy side, use equal parts of peat and soil instead. With species requiring very acid soil, use either peat moss or sphagnum peat mixed with an equal amount of sand to aid drainage.

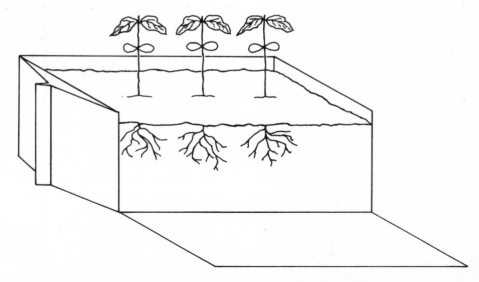

Fig. 6: Milk carton makes a simple seed flat. (Charlotte Prudhon Meyers)

34

Wheelbarrow acts as mixing bowl for potting soil.

Whatever the mixture, germination will be better if you have a uniform, fine soil. Pressing it through a screen of hardware mesh before adding sand and peat is an excellent idea. I prepare large batches of the mixture in a wheelbarrow, using a small shovel as a stirring tool.

When filling containers, press the soil down around the edges firmly and level well to prevent excess settling. Don't quite fill containers; leave space for later watering. If you have no special labels, use popsicle sticks or pieces of cut-up white plastic bottles. A crayon or grease pencil makes a good waterproof marker. Note name and date of sowing, for memory can be a tricky thing.

For ordinary seed I make shallow trenches with a pencil, tap seeds out of the envelope, then carefully just cover from sight, either with more of the mixture or with pulverized peat. Very fine seed must not be buried too deeply. It is better simply sprinkled on the smooth surface of the flat. Sometimes I cover it with a powdering of sand. Large seeds, like those of the pea family, usually germinate better if soaked overnight in a saucer of water before sowing. Poke a hole for each with your finger so they won't be too close.

If you collect seed which is contained in a soft berry, depulp it by soaking a day or two in water, then rub out the seed in an old dish towel as best you can. Sow it at once, or if you want to store it, wait for several days until it is thoroughly dry.

After seed is in place, water the flat thoroughly once with a fine mist sprayer. It must not be soaking wet, but soil should be definitely moist. Many species take three weeks or more to germinate. All during that time, the soil must remain moist but not wet, so check and water accordingly, always gently, so as not to wash the seed away. If you cover the flat to conserve moisture, check every day, for once a seed germinates, it must have light and air.

Plants from warm climates (garden marigolds, for instance) will not germinate until the soil warms up in spring and the nights have no frost. Sowing it too early can mean failure. Most of the perennial wildflowers in this book, however, germinate best with a touch of cold; some need long exposure to lower temperatures before dormancy of the seed can be broken.

You have two choices of action. With very rare or tricky seed, use half each way. Your discoveries may well aid other gardeners, for there is still far too little known about the behavior of many of these wildlings.

Method No. 1. If fresh seed is available, many botanists suggest sowing our wildflowers after November 15 in most parts of the country. (If you live in far northern states, you can push that up to October 15.) By then it is cold enough to prevent any immediate germination. The seeds will get whatever cold they particularly need and will begin to germinate whenever temperatures the next spring reach the required height. This can range from 40° to 68°.

You can put the seed directly into special beds or use containers. The latter will stay more uniformly moist and cold if buried about half their height in soil. Protect them with evergreen branches to mitigate extremes of wind and weather. Animals, especially mice, can decimate such plantings over a snowy winter. If they are a problem, cover on all sides, top, and bottom with hardware mesh. Such a bed is best located out of high wind and should not face south to prevent too early germination, but it should have light.

35

Make sure it is not in a low spot where moisture will collect.

Method No. 2. This is my favorite; I have had much success with it. New seed is ordered as soon after New Year's as possible. Collected ripe seed has been put in labeled envelopes, sealed in airtight glass containers, and stored in the refrigerator. (Most refrigerators maintain just the right temperature to keep seed viable, but make sure it never gets wet. Don't store any seed in the freezer.)

Meanwhile, back in the fall I mixed up a good load of potting soil, which has been stored in the garage. Sometime in February or early March, I begin sowing perennial seed, and the containers are then put outside on an open porch where they have some protection from weather and animals but get all extremes of temperature. Since they are more or less covered, I do have to check from time to time to be sure they are sufficiently moist. I have had marvelous success with this method. Adjust sowing times earlier or later, depending on whether you live south or north of Philadelphia.

Most seed houses indicate on the seed packet whether a species needs cool germination temperatures. Those for which fall or winter sowing is suggested (and most hardy wildflowers fall into this category) are the first to be sown. There is a constantly changing selection of my little milk-carton flats from February until May, when the last few biennials are started. Delaying these latter ensures that the plants will not try to bloom the first season and be caught by frost.

As each type germinates, it is brought out to a picnic table where the light is good until midafternoon. A constant check is necessary to make sure nothing dries out in those first crucial days of root growth. Flats dry out very quickly, and this is sure death to tiny seedlings.

Some sowings do not respond to either of these treatments, but these flats are not discarded. During their first summer and the following winter, such flats are stored in an out-of-the-way open spot and left to their own devices. Some seed, especially that of trees and shrubs, needs alternate periods of heat and cold to break dormancy. These may germinate the second spring, hence the need for good labels.

It is possible to sterilize your soil before sowing seed, but in most gardens such care is hardly necessary. I have never done it since the first time I stunk up the entire house by putting soil in the oven! With seed sown indoors, damping off and mildew can be a problem. Overwatering and lack of air circulation are the main culprits. There are sterilizing powders you can mix with the seed before sowing to prevent damping off, but with outdoor sowing these are not often necessary.

If you are growing seedlings inside at a window, they must have good light after germination or they will grow spindly and weak. And if you are sowing seed outside later where it is to grow, do not let it suffer from drying out either by wind or sun. It may be necessary to put a fine spray from the hose on such beds several times a day in dry weather even though it is quite cold. What you want is uniformity once the germination process is started by your first watering.

Transplanting seedlings and nursery plants

There is always excitement when a new species germinates. What lovely planting will arise from these tiny seedlings? Sometimes there is only a single plant from a whole sowing. I have even treasured a stranger for weeks before I discovered it was only a stray weed!

Granted germination is crucial, transplanting of the seedlings requires even more care, if only because the weather is bound to be warmer by then. A shock at this point may result in death of the whole crop, but a modicum of care solves everything.

The cotyledon leaves are usually quite different from the second set, which are the actual plant leaves. After there are two pairs of true leaves, you should think of getting seedlings out of the flats so they can get down to some serious growing. It is possible to thin them right in the flat so each is about an inch apart and let them grow on a bit longer there.

Old Christmas tree branches act as sun and pedestrian barrier while tiny seedlings get foothold.

If you want lots of a particular variety, you will do best by picking the tiny seedlings out one by one and planting each carefully in a small flower pot or old paper cup. Avoid disturbing roots more than necessary and use the same friable soil mixture to fill the pots. Shade all transplants for a day or two and never let them lack for water until they begin to perk up. Plants grown on in pots for a few weeks can be knocked out carefully and transplanted almost anywhere without extra care. But keep a check, for these tiny pots dry out incredibly fast too.

It is less work if you can transfer seedlings directly from flat to garden, but you cannot control conditions nearly as well. So choose a cool, overcast day for this task. Many's the spring sniffle I've con-

tracted from a day of transplanting in fog and drizzle, since that kind of weather is perfect for the plants.

Have the site well dug over and raked level before you begin. Disturb the roots as little as possible, and never let them dry out through sun or wind. Firm the soil around the roots, setting each plant a bit deeper than it was in the flat. Give each a small depression to make watering easier.

If it turns hot or windy the next few days, you must mist the new transplants often if they are in a sunny spot. But one morning, you'll see they are each standing firm and growing new leaves. That's the signal they've taken, and you can begin to relax.

With perennials this transplanting can either be done directly into permanent homes or into a special

nursery bed where they may be left a year to form thrifty clumps. Since most of these plants will have been started fairly early, the first choice is entirely feasible because they will have all summer to get a good root system as an anchor for their first winter.

Potted plants from a nursery do not need detailed nursing the first few days after transplanting because the grower has already done that step for you. But plants which arrive with bare roots or wrapped in damp peat must have care until they get a good system of feeder roots growing again. You cannot move anything without breaking some of these roots, but bare-root stock faces the greatest danger. Often I pot such plants (trees and shrubs too) for a few weeks, then transfer them to permanent homes when

Small start of Leucothoe Rainbow, planted temporarily in gallon milk carton for easy nursing, produces good growth in one summer.

new growth shows they have recovered. Losses are almost nonexistent with such care.

The transplanting of larger trees and shrubs which are bagged and balled is only the same process, but on a larger scale. There is one really important difference: these larger plants have bigger appetites. No matter how much fertilizer, spraying, or water you give them afterward, their business end is deep in the earth, and you want those roots healthy. It is not absurd to make a hundred-dollar hole for a ten-dollar tree.

For a tree only 3 feet high I dig a hole nearly 3 feet deep and at least twice the diameter of the tree's burlapped ball. In the bottom 6 inches go stones which came out in the digging. Then the best dirt we have (mixed with lots of peat moss) is shoveled in so that the new roots will have that to grow into, and this is stamped down gently. This is your only chance to do something about the dirt the tree will grow in; don't muff it.

More peat is shoveled in around the ball of roots themselves. I lower a big tree into the hole carefully, then cut away as much burlap as possible on the sides but leave the scraps beneath to avoid breaking the root ball. This allows us to arrange any lengthening roots so they will grow outward rather than around the root ball. Sometimes such girdling roots will strangle and kill a plant.

Make sure the tree sits at about the same depth as it did in the nursery. You can gauge this by measuring the height of the root ball with your shovel before you lower it in. After enough earth and peat is shoveled back in so that the tree is partially anchored, the hose is run until the soil is fairly well packed around the root ball. Now more soil and more water if necessary to eliminate any air holes. You may have to add a bit more soil as it settles. A top mulch of stones or wood chips looks neat and conserves moisture.

When you do the original measuring, always place a new tree or shrub so that it ends up with a shallow depression around it an inch or two lower than the surrounding soil. This makes deep watering easier later on. Support if

38

needed with a stake and guywire. Run the latter through an old piece of hose to protect the bark.

Again, if it turns hot and dry, get out that hose. With evergreens or trees coming into leaf, water the tops at the same time to cut transpiration. Do this several times the first week if there is no rain and once a week thereafter during the first summer whenever there is drought.

I used to refrain from fertilizing new trees and shrubs until their second season. You want a good root system before you begin to encourage top growth. This last

Three stakes anchor new oak tree against winter wind. White rags on guy ropes prevent accidents. Young bayberries around base are beginning to spread.

year, however, I used one package of a new slow-acting, five-year fertilizer under each of some small dogwoods, and I am delighted with the results. Never feed newly planted stock with quick-acting nitrogenous fertilizers.

If this were a perfect world, that is all there would be to transplanting; but our planet supports roaming animals, children whose parents don't care, and other hazards. So I place old evergreen branches (I collect the neighbors' discarded Christmas trees just for things like this) over spots where I have put in new little plants. This prevents many walking disasters until plants are big enough to call attention to themselves.

A mower can wound a tree trunk badly enough to kill it, so all my trees have big clear mulched areas around them. This also allows tree roots to get all the available food and moisture without competing with the grass. Very small living sticks get a white rag tied to the top to remind the mower to be careful. Trees in the path of the hose (I have nearly 200 feet of it in the back to struggle with) get additional protection in the form of a short stake on either side so the hose can't burn off the bark as I am pulling it from far away.

Deer and rabbits adore young trees and shrubs. Even when they don't eat them, rabbits sharpen their teeth on the lower branches, so after raging in vain I now protect new ones a few years with a

winter basket of chicken wire around the first few feet. Anchor the basket with a stake against the wind.

Division

It is often much quicker to increase plants vegetatively than by seed. If you fail to raise a wanted species from seed, buy a plant or two and see if you can divide it.

Anything which increases by stolons, runners, or basal rosettes alongside the mother plant is ideal for such treatment. With those which bloom in early spring, do the dividing after flowering. With later types, get it done as early in spring as possible. Often you need only dig down gently on the side, then pull or cut the daughter plant away without ever disturbing the mother plant. There are even trees and bushes with stoloniferous habits you can take advantage of.

In mild climates you can do the dividing in late summer after the worst heat is over, but I much prefer spring. Here it is cool and rainy then, and the new plants need a minimum of shade and watering to take hold and soon make thrifty new specimens.

Any time a perennial has grown into a good-sized clump, it is ripe for division. A big phlox, for example, can be dug out in early spring and cut into chunks with a sharp spade. As long as a chunk has some roots of its own with the new shoots, it will make a new plant.

39

Plants with sparse wandering root systems are a different problem. Often a piece of root cut off the mother plant and set shallowly in a shaded, moist medium will send up new shoots in a few weeks. A plant with a thick creeping root or a surface rhizome may be divided in early spring before growth is far advanced. Each piece of root with an "eye" to indicate a new shoot can be planted separately with fair success. Keep damp but never wet until new feeder roots develop.

Any bulbous or cormous plant will produce new plants either atop or alongside the original in time. These are best removed and replanted while the plant is dormant. For most species this is just after the foliage browns off. With liatris, which flowers in late summer, the corms may be pried apart successfully as soon as they show their first green shoot in spring. Replant immediately.

Layering

This is surely the easiest way of increasing anything and may be tried with any tree or shrub which has pliable branches near the ground. In the spring, preferably, wound a branch at a point where it will easily reach the ground. With very small twigs it is enough merely to scrape the top layer of bark off the underside with a fingernail. Larger branches may need a small notch cut out of them. Either wound is best treated with a

rooting hormone powder. Then bury the wounded portion in an inch or two of earth and anchor with a stone, leaving it attached to the mother plant and with the far tip of the branch out in the air.

Depending on the genus, in a season or two you will have a new plant with its roots growing at the point of the wound. You can tell if it begins to put out new growth there. I usually sever the new plant from the mother but leave it to grow in place another season before disturbing it by transplanting.

Some plants will layer themselves whenever a branch tip touches the

ground, but these are often rampant spreaders that shouldn't be encouraged.

Many perennials which have sprawly branches or runners may be layered too. Just place a clod of earth over one of the branches and leave it alone for a year. It will then stool out into a new plant at that point.

Air layering is a bit more difficult, but possible for trees and shrubs with upright growth which cannot be bent to the earth without damage. In the spring, a wound is made a foot or so from the end of a handy branch. You can scrape

Fig. 7: Simple layering is the easy way to increase a shrub.

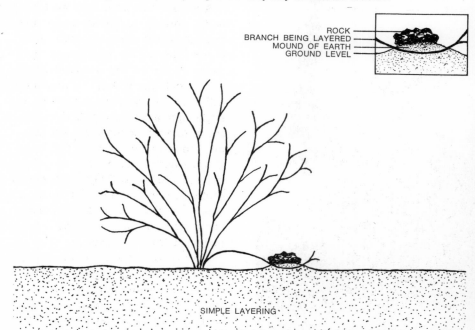

ROCK
BRANCH BEING LAYERED
MOUND OF EARTH
GROUND LEVEL

SIMPLE LAYERING

40

Air-layering package is sealed well at both ends.

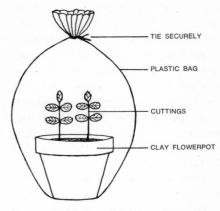

TIE SECURELY

PLASTIC BAG

CUTTINGS

CLAY FLOWERPOT

Fig. 8: Plastic bag ensures proper humidity for rooting cutting.

bark, cut a notch, or slice halfway through the branch and hold the cut open with a matchstick. Treat with rooting hormone, then wrap with a wad of damp sphagnum moss. Wrap this in turn with a piece of strong, clear plastic large enough to cover it completely, and secure the plastic at both ends with waterproof tape.

The package is then left alone one whole season. The second spring, unwrap and see what has happened. The wounded branch may have already rooted, in which case cut it from the mother plant just below the newly rooted section, pot it, and nurse it until it appears to be growing on its own. Often the wound will have callused over, but the roots are not yet formed. In the latter case, dust again with rooting hormone, rewrap, and wait another season.

Cuttings

Suppose you covet a tree or bush just like one from a source where you cannot layer it. Try to root a cutting. If you must transport it any distance before potting, wrap the cut end in wet tissue and insert the whole thing in a plastic bag. Keep out of hot sun until you get it safely home.

Hardwood cuttings are the easiest. Take them 4 to 6 inches long from a terminal shoot of the tree or bush in late fall. Make a clean cut and then remove any leaves off the bottom 2 inches, cutting carefully so as not to strip the bark.

Dip this part in rooting hormone and insert in holes poked with your finger in a thoroughly moistened medium composed of equal parts of peat moss and coarse sand. A clay flower pot at least 4 inches deep will allow decent formation of roots. Space the cuttings several inches apart in the pot. Now put the whole pot into a plastic bag, tie tightly at the top above the plant, and place in a cool, shaded spot inside for the winter. You want a site out of direct sunlight, but not dark; in the coolest room of the house, but not where it will freeze.

Check periodically. The pot should not need anything, for the plastic bag acts like a miniature terrarium. Often by early spring

41

new shoots will begin to form. Water only if and when the plastic bag no longer has steam inside or the surface of the soil feels quite dry. When you see the new growth, bring the pot gradually to good light but keep cool. After the heat is turned off in the house in spring is time enough to remove the plastic bag gradually, leaving it open a few hours longer each day until the plant has accustomed itself to being born.

Once the plastic bag is off, you must not let the soil dry out. Transplant the rooted cutting to a sheltered spot where it can be nursed along for a season. The following year or so you'll have a well-rooted tree or bush to put in its permanent place.

I have started this whole process

successfully as late as Christmas with many evergreen kinds.

Softwood cuttings are taken earlier in the summer, but they are more difficult because they are more apt to rot. You can even do this with perennials. Again you want tip shoots, and they must be mature enough to snap rather than very soft new growth. Treatment is much the same except that the plastic-covered pot is usually put in a cool, shaded spot outside. You want to strike a happy medium so that the cutting neither wilts nor rots. If roots form in time, you can plant it for the winter in a nursery bed or cold frame or you can winter it inside in a cool room.

I have had better luck with shrubby softwood cuttings by using the old mason-jar technique of our

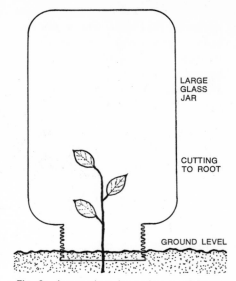

Fig. 9: Large glass jar makes a miniature greenhouse to root a cutting outside.

grandmothers. Here the treated tip is inserted in the earth outside, and a big glass jar is inverted over it with its mouth pushed down firmly into the soil. Water around it as necessary in hot weather. This is then left in place until the following spring, when a new plant is often the happy result. When doing this make sure you choose a shaded spot, or the sun striking your miniature greenhouse will steamcook your cutting long before it roots.

Sources for native plants

The following list is far from complete. It represents houses which I have done business with successfully or whose current catalogs have impressed me. You are always advised to order as close

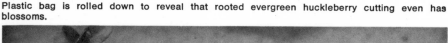

Plastic bag is rolled down to reveal that rooted evergreen huckleberry cutting even has blossoms.

to home as possible. Small local nurseries may know where you can obtain certain types of plants even if they don't handle them. Early spring copies of gardening magazines are treasure troves of advertisements by wildflower specialists.

You can learn a lot about an unknown plantsman just by studying his catalog. The nurseryman who uses Latin names to help the customer find exactly the species he seeks probably pays attention to important details. If you cannot find a plant you want, don't hesitate to ask one of these good firms, but confine your queries to the winter off-season when they have more time, and enclose a stamped, self-addressed envelope. There is a happy camaraderie among most native plant growers and their customers, but the relationship should not be strained. The nominal sum charged for many catalogs is a worthwhile investment.

Mostly Seed

Prairie Gem Ranch Seeds
Smithwick, S.D. 57782

W. Atlee Burpee Co.
Philadelphia, Pa. 19132

Seed and Plants

George W. Park Seed Co.
Greenwood, S.C. 29646

Leslie's Wildflower Nursery
30 Summer St.
Methuen, Mass. 01844

Clyde Robin
P.O. Box 2091
Castro Valley, Calif. 94546

Harry E. Saier
Dimondale, Mich. 48821

Mostly Plants

Arthur Eames Allgrove
North Wilmington, Mass. 01887

Gardens of the Blue Ridge
Ashford, McDowell Cty., N.C. 28603

Green Bush Gardens
Charlotte, Vt. 05445

Jamieson Valley Gardens
Rt. 3-E
Spokane, Wash. 99203

Lamb Nurseries
E. 101 Sharp Ave.
Spokane, Wash. 99202

Lounsberry Gardens
P.O. Box 135
Oakford, Ill. 62673

Mincemoyer Nursery
Rt. 5, Box 379
Jackson, N.J. 08527

Putney Nursery
Putney, Vt. 05346

Savage Gardens
P.O. Box 163
McMinnville, Tenn. 37110

The Three Laurels
Marshall, Madison Cty., N.C. 28753

Vick's Wildgardens, Inc.
Box 115
Gladwyne, Pa. 19035

Woodland Acres Nursery
RD, Crivitz, Wisc. 54114

Mostly Bulbs

Charles H. Mueller
River Road
New Hope, Pa. 18938

International Grower's Exchange
P.O. Box 398
Farmington, Mich. 48024

P. de Jager and Sons
188 Asbury St.
South Hamilton, Mass. 01982

Walter Marx Gardens
Boring, Ore. 97009

Rex Bulb Farms
Box 145
Newberg, Ore. 97132

Mostly Trees and Shrubs

Adam-Brainard
654 Enfield St.
Thompsonville, Conn. 06082

Brimfield Gardens Nursery
245 Brimfield Rd.
Wethersfield, Conn. 06109

Dauber's Nurseries
P.O. Box 1746
York, Pa. 17405

Fiore Enterprises, Inc.
Prairieview, Ill. 60069

Mellinger's, Inc.
2310 W. South Range Rd.
North Lima, Ohio 44452

Musser Forests
Box 73, Indiana, Pa. 15701

Squirrel Hill Nursery, Inc.
2945 Beechwood Blvd.
Pittsburg, Pa. 15217

4 ALL-AMERICAN TREES FOR SHADE AND COLOR

Nothing enhances a property more than a stand of healthy trees. Our own flora offers an entrancing variety of fine ones, many perfectly tailored for today's smaller homes and properties. At the end of this chapter is a list of deciduous trees primarily recommended for shade purposes. Evergreen trees have a chapter of their own.

Our main interest is the wonderful sequence of native flowering trees which unfold from early spring to late fall. The gardener smart enough to select these trees gains a display of flowers, fruit, and/or autumn color as well as cooling summer shade.

If you have not had experience or success with planting trees, review the suggestions in Chapter 3. Remember always that the health of a tree depends on its roots. You will have only one good opportunity to do something about that, so make sure the best dirt goes in the bottom of the hole before you plant the tree.

Nurserymen, aware of the in-creasing sophistication of their customers as well as the requirements of smaller properties, are offering a wider variety of forms of trees than ever before. In any genus there may be pendulous (weeping), dwarf, or fastigiate (narrow columnar) forms as well as the type described in this chapter. Each has its place. In addition there are selected variations in the color and shape of flowers or leaves.

All such abnormal forms must be vegetatively reproduced to retain the characteristic which makes them different. They will almost always be more expensive than the type, but if your planting scheme calls for a weeping tree, you will not mind paying the piper. Imaginatively used, such forms make stunning focal points in a design. Beware, however, of using too many; it is easy to lose your emphasis.

Also resist the temptation to plant one of everything. If you have a favorite tree, work in several specimens to lend continuity to your planting. Some trees—dog-woods are a notable example—look best in groups anyway. Place trees together rather than creating extra work by making many separate holes, which need hand trimming, all over the lawn. A triangular grove at the corner of a property helps define your line and creates a much more spacious-looking lawn. A small yard sprinkled helter-skelter with trees in no particular design looks just that much smaller as well as being difficult to care for. Combine the group of trees with a few shrubs, set some bulbs and plants along the edges, and you have a real garden.

The trees on your property are the backbone of its planting. Get them in as soon as possible so they can begin growing, for many transplant best in small sizes. It is surprising how fast they mature once they get acclimated, given good planting to begin with. I have had small trees outstrip a larger specimen of the same species in a few years, probably because they underwent less transplanting shock.

By the same reasoning a mistake in placing a tree can be a costly process. Better to draw up a general planting scheme before you begin than to have to sacrifice a grown tree later. Include in your planning whatever trees you already have; then determine your most pressing needs.

You may want summer shade for west or south windows, privacy or general screening on one side of the property, or the tempering effect of a windbreak. Trees will do all these things as well as soften the landscape, hold eroding soil, and offer homes and food for the birds which police the insect population.

My family are wont to laugh mightily at the "living sticks" I plant. Many of the more unusual trees can be easily obtained only bareroot through mail-order firms, and my chances of success are best with young specimens. Even I admit they do look foolish surrounded by many square feet of empty space. But the sticks grow into trees with height and spread, and these two important factors should be considered when you decide what to plant where. You can always fill in with annuals for a few years while the tree is growing.

Nothing appears so woebegone as a house with shrubbery grown over every window. Nor do the trees look or grow as well when crowded. Allow for maturity when you plan, remembering that many species put forth more than a foot of growth every year.

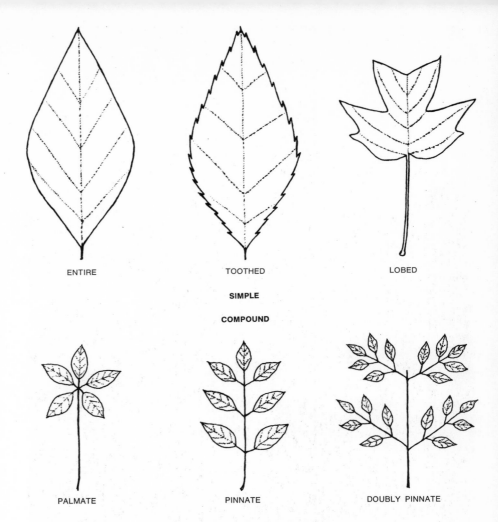

ENTIRE   TOOTHED   LOBED

SIMPLE

COMPOUND

PALMATE   PINNATE   DOUBLY PINNATE

Fig. 10: A leaf may be many things.

One other consideration needs attention in your planning. Flowering trees have personalities all their own both in bloom and autumn color. If your house is barn red, you should avoid a redbud or a pink dogwood against it, and the gorgeous scarlet of the autumn sourwood will be quite wasted. Use evergreens or trees with green foliage to set off those with raucous color. A pink dogwood surrounded by several white ones at a distance from a red house will look quite at home.

Depending on your family's

45

Mature flowering halesia is springtime picture beyond compare.

tain-ash, dogwood, and the hawthorns light up the fall with fine berry displays. The sourwood is decorative into winter.

Many fine flowering trees are hardy into Zone 3, which covers most of the northern states, but some of the most beautiful cannot survive fierce winters. These latter you should plant on the lee side of buildings or windbreaks where the weather is mitigated. Microclimates (discussed in Chapter 2) can successfully carry trees and bushes through at least one zone colder than they normally grow. Smaller sizes need more nursing than well-established trees. When possible, buy stock locally or as far north as you can find a supplier. These strains may be just a tiny bit hardier.

Through some as yet unexplained phenomenon, many American trees and shrubs are closely related to species native to Asia. There was a time when everyone wanted one of these exotics instead of a home-grown product—not because the Asiatics were any more decorative, but just because we are a quirky animal. So nurseries concentrated on producing the Asiatics.

Like any industry, these producers change their habits slowly. If you want the American species, insist and keep on looking for a more up-to-date supplier. This advice is particularly important for gardeners in the northern states, for many times the American species is hardier than its Asian cousin.

schedule, it pays to think about a sequence of bloom. Everyone has springtime color, but summer can be enlivened by trees too. In June

the swamp magnolia perfumes the air with its white chalices, and the flowering year is extended by adding a stewartia or franklinia. Moun-

46

With all these factors in mind here are the cream of the American crop. Zone numbers indicate hardiness (see Fig. 2). Maximum heights are for optimum conditions. Bloom dates are for Philadelphia; adjust north or south.

ACER RUBRUM (red or swamp maple): Zone 3; 120 feet but usually medium-sized, semi-oval shape, rapid grower; low damp soil.

A perfect tree to start the growing year, for its gay clusters of tiny red flowers in March before the leaves appear are a happy harbinger of delights to come. If you can, put it in a spot where you can see its flowers against the sky from a favorite window. This tree transplants easily, even in big sizes, is widely available, and is neater than many maples. A bonus is the deep red of the fall foliage. Found from Newfoundland to Florida and Texas.

AESCULUS (horse-chestnut or buckeye): mostly Zone 3; medium-sized, palmately compound leaves cast heavy shade; fruit and husks may be a nuisance; rich moist soil.

A. glabra (Ohio buckeye) has erect clusters of greenish-yellow flowers in May, prickly 2-inch fruits, a broad round top, and tends to stay under 50 feet. A. octandra (yellow buckeye) is a taller tree with erect yellow clusters of flowers and smooth fruits. A. pavia (red buckeye) is tender (Zone 5), grows only about 20 feet, bears long dark red

or purplish panicles of flowers. A better choice for northerners (Zone 3) is A. carnea, a hybrid between the last and the European species. It grows to 40 feet, has fleshy to deep red blooms. Its variety briotti, with scarlet blossoms and little or no fruit, is easily found and the only aesculus I'd consider planting on a small property.

AMELANCHIER (Juneberry, shadbush, shadblow, sarvistree, serviceberry): Zone 4; medium-sized trees tend to be narrow; adaptable to soil and shade but best-suited as understory trees on edges of woodland or groups of other trees.

In early April when spring is still an elusive season, the first of the amelanchiers light our woods with their airy white flowers. The display may not last long if hot days arrive early, but it is something to look forward to each year. Forty-three species of birds revel in the edible purplish-black berries which ripen in June and July. Never buy one without ascertaining its species, for many are nondescript shrubs. All have yellow to red autumn foliage.

Tree forms include A. laevis (Allegheny serviceberry), which can reach 40 feet, has bronzy spring foliage, and the very similar A. arborea (shadblow). A. canadensis (downy serviceberry), with silvery young leaves, likes swampy ground. A. grandiflora (apple serviceberry), a fine, widely available hybrid which ranges from 10 to 25 feet, is the best bet for small properties,

since its flowers are larger. Pink forms are advertised, but it is a pallid shade.

ASIMINA TRILOBA (pawpaw): Zone 5; 40 feet, short trunk with dense, round head; rich moist soil.

Here is a conversation piece. Large, drooping leaves give this a tropical look, and solitary dark-purple, bell-shaped flowers about 2 inches across in May are followed by strange cylindrical fruits 3 to 7 inches long and an inch thick. They are first yellow, then brown and edible, tasting "sort of like a poor banana," according to my most trustworthy informant. Since pawpaws are difficult to move, start either with seed or very small trees. They can be a nuisance, however, with stolons coming up everywhere.

CASTANEA PUMILA (chinquapin): Zone 5; to 45 feet but usually less and shrubby; does well on dry rocky slopes.

Fluffy creamy-white catkins in June and July are quite decorative, but the smell is revolting, so place away from patios and windows. The light-green burs which follow contain a small edible nut; plant at least two trees to ensure fruit. Some dieback is to be expected.

Our wonderful true American chestnuts (C. dentata) which once covered the eastern woodlands and gave such delicious nuts are only hearsay to my generation, but I recall my father describing the adventure of bringing home pillow-cases full of goodness in the fall. These mighty 100-foot giants are all dead, victims of an Asiatic blight. In his memory I intend to plant two from a recently discovered source of Oregon-grown trees. In all probability they will succumb too, but it is worth trying. Sprouts still spring from the dead stumps in our forests and sometimes grow large enough to bear nuts before they too die; foresters keep hoping a resistant strain will appear. The little chinquapins, however, are resistant.

CERSIS CANADENSIS (redbud, Judas-tree): Zone 4; to 45 feet but seldom lives that long; open habit, branching low; fertile, well-drained loam.

Often used as a lawn specimen, the redbud grows naturally as an understory tree, so I suspect it prefers some shade. It is often found on the edges of woodland with amelanchier and dogwood. The latter blooms at the same time as the redbud and is a perfect foil since its whiteness helps take the curse off the redbud's near-magenta. Many nurseries offer pure white and pink forms of redbud which are easier to work into the homescape.

Clusters of small pealike flowers appear to spring directly from the tree because they are borne on the tiniest of stems and are found along the branches and even the trunk rather than at the tips of twigs. Heart-shaped leaves which appear after flowering are graceful and flutter in every breeze. Since the new ones have bronzy tones and the undersides of the others a milky cast, the tree is always decorative.

Hardier than the Asiatic and European species, our redbud also throws seed freely from the flat pods of fall. If you grow to love it, allow some of these volunteers to develop so you will always have a tree or two coming along as re-placements. Though short-lived, redbuds die hard. Sprouts arise from cut stumps, and by judicious pruning you can keep a tree a long time. Note this picture of a fall-cut limb that was used to line a path but produced clusters of flowers on schedule the following spring!

CHIONANTHUS VIRGINICA (fringe-tree, old-man's-beard, graybeard-tree): Zone 4; to 30 feet but tends to be shrubby in north; at least half sun and moist sandy soil.

Few plants are lovelier than chionanthus in bloom. The long fluffy panicles of fragrant white flowers appear in May with those on male plants larger; females bear long-stemmed, dark blue berries in fall. Nurseries seldom indicate sex; either is a choice plant. Place where you can enjoy the scent, always remembering that it leafs out late so remains wintry-looking most of the early spring. Autumn leaves are yellow. If grown as a

Cersis leaves flutter in every breeze.

Downed cersis tree produces flower cluster one last time.

OPPOSITE:
TOP
(l.): dogwood berries and clethra seed heads in autumn
(r.): framework of dogwoods in spring garden
MIDDLE
(l.): swamp azalea flowers show prominent stamens
(r.): franklinia flower in fall
BOTTOM
(l.): *Dicentra eximia* and *Phlox divaricata* to north of dogwood
(m.): Douglas fir in winter attire
(r.): oxydendrum in September dress

shrub, allow plenty of room; I know one 10 feet high and nearly as wide. Again it is hardier than its Asian cousin but susceptible to scale.

CLADRASTIS LUTEA (yellow-wood): Zone 3; to 50 feet, short trunk and broad, open head; any good soil.

Like many of the choice plants of the southern Appalachians, cladrastis is hardy far north of its native haunts. Though a slow grower, it is well worth planting as a specimen tree. Compound leaves are decorative, and racemes of fragrant white, pealike flowers in June are most beautiful even if they tend to come only in alternate years. Short seed pods contrast with the yellow autumn leaves and grayish bark. There is a rare rose-flowered form.

CORNUS FLORIDA (dogwood): Zone 4; to 25 feet, spreading branches; any good soil but use peat moss, takes partial shade.

By all odds our most outstanding native tree for home use, the dogwood is ornamental all year. Its horizontal twigs tipped with the button buds of next season's flowers are graceful in winter, its spring flowers are superlative, and its fall dress is dark crimson leaves and fine red berries. The latter are quickly eaten by enterprising birds. Because of its branching habit this is also an ideal perching tree for near a birdbath.

A single specimen is breathtaking but in the wild dogwood tends to grow in groves, and it is somehow just that much lovelier with company. If you want a small shaded garden, nothing is quite so perfect for the overhead canopy as three dogwoods set on the points of a triangle. In good soil with some acidity and sufficient moisture, dogwoods grow quite quickly once the roots take hold after a year or so. Even though it may look foolish at first, allow at least a 12-foot distance between the trees, more if you can.

To ensure bloom for the next year, don't let your dogwoods lack for water during summer drought. Along the northern extremes of its range, plant the trees in the lee of evergreens or buildings to provide a milder microclimate; otherwise bloom may be scarce. Too much shade also cuts down on its floriferousness.

Next year's dogwood buds are formed by late summer.

There are yellow-berried and pendulous forms as well as many with pink or reddish bracts. Particularly long-lasting in bloom, the double-flowered form may be cataloged as either *C. florida plena* or *C. florida pluribracteata.* These variations are all grafts and often not as hardy or fast-growing. Moreover, off-color dogwoods range from delicate flesh pink to near magenta. A mixture can be somewhat weird. Pick these in flower to see; they can be moved well then. To my taste, one red dogwood goes a long way and lacks the chaste delicacy of the white. If you must have one, give it a background of evergreens or white dogwoods.

On the Pacific Coast *C. nuttalli* (Zone 7) may reach 75 feet under favorable conditions. It does not do well in the East, and a touted hybrid between it and *C. florida* died here its first season. *C. alternifolia* (pagoda dogwood) is extremely hardy but not nearly as decorative since it does not have the big bracts which are the showy part of the blossom.

CRATAEGUS (hawthorn): Zones 3 to 5; medium-sized with dense, twiggy, picturesque shape and thorns; most will take poor clay, even wet soil, like lime.

There are dozens of native hawthorns. As a class they have glossy foliage which colors well in fall, clusters of white or pink flowers in May, and bright fruit which may be red, orange, yellow, blue, or black.

Only a handful are described here, selected mostly for their hardiness or a long-lasting fruit display. Many nurseries offer fastigiate forms for narrow places.

Cedar-apple rust and fireblight both attack hawthorns. To lessen chances of infection never plant them near red cedar trees, and avoid overwatering and too much fertilizer.

Perhaps the best is *C. phaenopyrum* (Washington hawthorn), with white flowers in late May or June and bright-red fruit which persists all winter; may grow to 30 feet and hardy in Zone 4. It is a fine nesting tree; finches, pine grosbeaks, and thrashers like the fruits. *C. crusgalli* (cockspur thorn) is even hardier, has white flowers, all-winter red fruit, and good orange to red fall foliage and is often used for impenetrable hedges. Its persistent fruit often saves hungry birds in March when food is scarce. *C. nitida* (glossy hawthorn) has similar habits but is native to the Midwest. *C. succulenta* (fleshy hawthorn, Zone 3) seldom tops 15 feet. Its clustered white flowers are followed by red fruits which drop in the fall. *C. mollis* (downy hawthorn, Zone 5) also has white flowers, but its early-dropping fruit is larger. *C. viridis* (green hawthorn, Zone 5) of southern and central states produces its white flowers late and has long-lasting red-orange fruit.

DIOSPYRUS VIRGINIANA (common persimmon): Zone 4; to 50 feet, round-headed with contorted winter silhouette; succeeds in most soils.

The small whitish flowers of the persimmon are too inconspicuous to be decorative, but the good dark-green, shiny leaves in summer are followed by small orange pomes which hang long into the winter to provide interest at a time when most needed. Wait to taste them until after hard frost unless you want an unpleasant puckering. Varieties differing in fruit size and flavor are available at many nurseries, but plant several since the sexes are usually on separate trees.

FRANKLINIA ALATAMAHA (franklinia or gordonia): Zone 5; to 30 feet and usually shrubby; prefers acid soil.

Named for Ben Franklin, this gorgeous tree was found in Georgia by his friend John Bartram, our first native botanist. Since 1790 when collected specimens were brought back to Philadelphia, it has never been found growing in the wild. All trees in commerce are believed to be descendants of Bartram's originals.

This is a good candidate for the best place on your property. North of Philadelphia I would definitely give it a protected site, but it is worth any trouble you take. Small specimens seem to need more care than those several years older. It has fine shiny green leaves which make perfect foils for the large white camelia-like flowers of late summer. As fall nears, the leaves

Franklinia makes a shrubby tree in North. Below, its old seed pods give it an interesting winter silhouette.

51

take on red and orange tints, and often there are flowers still opening, a stunning combination. Bees almost drown in the cluster of yellow stamens centering each bloom.

Along its northern limits it may not produce fruit, but those in milder climates get a bonus from a healthy tree: its winter silhouette is enlivened by the brown wooden roses of old fruits. Tiny green apples take two years to ripen, then open to drop the seeds and remain on the branches for several seasons unless removed by flower arrangers who wire them for dried pieces.

Use plenty of peat when planting and never let franklinia want for water in summer. It is often late to leaf out and sometimes dies back in small sizes over the winter but eventually becomes a shrubby tree.

HALESIA (silverbell, snowdrop-tree): Zones 4 and 5; may be shrubby in north; rich, well-drained soil.

Few late April treats equal the pleasure of standing under a mature silverbell at the height of bloom. Thousands of inch-long white bells festoon each branch, and in the breeze they flutter like a cloud of butterflies. The show does not last overly long, but it is worth waiting for. Come autumn the tree sports strange winged fruits which persist far into winter. Watch out for scale infestation.

Best of them all is *H. monticola* (mountain silverbell), which can reach 100 feet in its southern Appalachian home. Zone 5 is its limit,

Halesia: in flower above, in fruit below.

and it will need a sheltered spot there. Here at Philadelphia I have seen a majestic tree at least 50 feet high. *H. carolina* (*H. tetraptera* or carolina silverbell) is another zone hardier and smaller in flower, in fruit, and overall. It throws suckers from the base and will grow into a large shrubby tree unless they are removed. Place it near a path where passersby can enjoy the show overhead.

LIRIODENDRON TULIPIFERA (tulip-tree): Zone 4; to 200 feet with a straight trunk, high branching; rich, moist soil.

Few people realize that this is a flowering tree closely related to the magnolias, for its big tulip-like flowers usually are borne high above the ground. Lower branches tend to die off as the tree matures, so it is rare to see a flower up close unless a windstorm sends some plunging earthward. They are greenish-yellow cups with bright-orange markings inside. Fall sees the foliage a blaze of gold, while in winter the ripening seed packages resemble brown flowers high in the tree.

Tulip-trees transplant poorly, so buy only in small size and bagged and balled if possible. Once established, they grow quite rapidly; thus this is not a tree to put next to a small house. Rather place it at the

Ripening seed pods dress up tulip tree in winter.

far end of your property where you can view its nobility in best perspective.

MAGNOLIA: Zones 4 to 7; varied shapes and sizes; rich, humusy soil.

Our native magnolias have been sadly neglected in favor of earlier-flowering Asiatic species. This is a shame, for not only do the Americans grow into beautiful shade trees, their flowers (with one notable exception) are impressively fragrant during warmer weather when people are more likely to be outside to enjoy them. All should be moved with a ball of earth in early spring for best results.

Best known is *M. virginiana* (*M. glauca,* sweetbay, swamp magnolia, Zone 5). Evergreen in the South, it holds its laurel-like 6-inch leaves here at Philadelphia until close to Christmas, when I often weave some into wreaths. It will grow to 70 feet, but often is shrubby in the North, likes acid soil. Mine sits near the front porch in a depression where rainwater collects and the hose can be left dripping in time of drought, for this is a swamp-loving tree. Its white 3-inch chalices open sporadically from late May to late June. Each lasts only a day or two, then turns brown like a gardenia. Their fragrance is pure delight. Bright red late summer fruit, green winter stems and the summer effect of the fluttering leaves with their silvery undersides are all extra attractions. Mine added 23 inches in height last year.

Young growth of swamp magnolia is shrubby.

Even more magnificent is *M. grandiflora* (bullbay, Zone 7), a great southern tree which can reach 100 feet, has evergreen foliage, and bears fragrant white flowers 8 inches across in June. Here is a good example of how one can stretch the range of a tree. I know of several healthy trees here in Zone 6, one of which is at least 30 feet high. It flaunts its leathery foliage at the winter wind and appears to have little extra protection except that afforded by some nearby decid-

uous trees. It may be a form of the variety listed as *gallissoniensis,* supposed to be very hardy but never appearing in nursery lists; in any event I covet a cutting and someday shall get up the courage to beg one.

Much hardier and faster-growing is *M. acuminata* (cucumber-tree, Zone 4, to 90 feet), which with its 10-inch leaves makes a fine tall shade tree. The greenish-yellow, bell-shaped flowers in May are not conspicuous, but the red knobby fall fruits are often 3 inches long. Its variety *cordata* has canary-yellow blooms.

Away from the house where their sickening odor cannot intrude, the flowers of *M. tripetala* (umbrella magnolia, Zone 4) are striking even if appearing in late spring after the leaves. They are creamy-white and as wide as 10 inches, borne at the ends of the branches, which make an irregular, open head up to 40 feet high. Fall fruits are rosy-red and may reach 4 inches.

M. fraseri (ear-leaved umbrella-tree, Zone 6, to 45 feet) has fragrant white flowers nearly 10 inches wide, rosy fruit, and leaves as long as 20 inches. If it's big leaves you're after, though, try *M. macrophylla* (bigleaf magnolia, Zone 5, to 50 feet), which produces leaves some 3 feet long as well as fragrant cup-shaped white flowers. Shelter it from the wind, which can rip those immense leaves into unsightly shreds.

MALUS (crab apple): Zones 2 to 5; medium-sized trees to around 25 feet; adaptable to varying conditions.

American crab apples tend to have greenish fruit and are much more susceptible to cedar rust and fireblight than Asian species. Since the family supplies some of the most ornamental flowering trees, it has been highly hybridized. With the exceptions noted below, the small property owner is better advised to buy one of the fine Asian-named selections or hybrids. They

are widely available, bloom young, transplant easily, and have blossoms which may be white, pink, red, or magenta. If you are combining crab apples, see them in flower first because some shades are not complimentary. Fruits vary from pea to walnut size and feature either yellow or red shades, depending on variety.

Now for the American exceptions. Bechtel's crab at peak bloom is the most beautiful pink tree in the world. It is a double-flowered form of *M. ioensis* (prairie crab, Zone 2). The 2-inch flowers, which resemble little roses, literally cover the tree in May. I know one fifteen years old and 25 feet high. As its owner says, "Looking into the tree from a

second-story window is like a glimpse of Heaven."

Equally charming, I'm told, are Charlotte and Nieuland, double forms of *M. coronaria* (wild sweet crab or garland crab, Zone 4). The variety Prince Georges, a hybrid between *M. ioensis* and *M. angustifolia* (southern crab, Zone 5), is less disease-prone and considered by many the best choice of all.

OXYDENDRUM ARBOREUM (lily-of-the-valley-tree, sorrel-tree, sourwood): Zone 4; to 60 feet but slow-growing, narrow; acid soil.

Here is a true tree member of the great heath family, and American gardeners should be ashamed that it is not more widely planted, for

Fingers of white bells are sourwood's summer decoration.

54

it has everything. Best of all, it blooms when it is still very small. Its clean, shiny green leaves resemble those of a peach and in dry situations often begin to turn orange in mid-summer. The little urn-shaped white bells hang in drooping panicles, which remind me of delicate fingers, at the very ends of the branches, so they are quite noticeable. Even the buds are decorative, and the flowers develop over a very long period. In a recent year I noticed the first opening on the Fourth of July. Bees are crazy over them (there is a slight fragrance), and I am told that sourwood honey is something very special. Nor is this the end. The seeds which follow are almost as ornamental against the scarlet fall leaves and remain on the tree until December. Oddly, they sit erect along the flowering stem.

Often sourwood produces suckers at the base; they are better removed unless you wish a shrubby tree.

PRUNUS AMERICANA (American plum): Zone 3; to 35 feet with crooked, picturesque growth; rich moist soil.

If your main interest is fruit, you will want one of the named selections found in a good nursery catalog. Many different native plum trees have played a part in the development of superior fruit. But if you want one just for the artistic effect, this eastern species is hard to beat. White flowers come in April or May, and the late-summer fruits are red-skinned with a yellow pulp. It tends to form basal sprouts, so keep it pruned or you'll usually have a thicket. *P. nigra* (Canadian plum) is similar, hardy into Zone 2.

ROBINIA PSEUDOACACIA (black or yellow locust): Zone 3; to 80 feet and fast-growing with contorted branches and rugged, furrowed bark; adaptable, will take poor soil.

This American is popular in Europe but has lost ground at home because it often suffers from leaf miners and borers. So be it. Try one of the new systemics if you're a perfectionist. It has two reasons for being considered: its rapid growth and the wonderful jonquil fragrance of its long clusters of white flowers in June.

Compound leaves cast light shade, and the brown seed pods remain most of the winter. Since the branches have stout thorns, it could be a nuisance around barefoot areas, but for rapid, screening effect, few trees can match it. Sometimes there are root suckers.

There are many other native robinias, many of them shrubby and spreading widely by stoloniferous roots. Most have insipid pink flowers and lack fragrance; I do not recommend them.

SORBUS AMERICANUS (American mountain-ash): Zone 2; to 30 feet but often shrublike in north; will take partial shade and moist soil.

A smaller tree than its European counterpart *(S. aucuparia), the* American mountain-ash will also grow better for far northern gardeners. White flower clusters in May and June are followed by bright red berries in fall. Essentially the two trees are much alike except that the American's winter buds are sticky and smooth, while the European's are hairy but not sticky. The related *S. decora* has larger berries but is hard to find. Trunk borers can be a problem with all sorbus.

STEWARTIA OVATA (*S. pentagyna*, mountain stewartia): Zone 5; to 24 feet but tends to stay smaller; rich, acid soil.

Audubon's plate of the Carolina turtle doves shows the ethereal quality of the stewartia's white flower which closely resembles a camelia, to which it is in fact related. He chose *S. malacodendron* for his illustration, but that 20-foot tree is tender north of Washington, D.C.

Northern gardeners wisely prefer this hardier sister. It too has beautiful blooms 2 to 4 inches across with prominent yellow anthers on white stamens in the center during July. If you can find it, the variety *grandiflora* has flowers a bit larger and purple stamens which merit its being called the showy mountain stewartia. Both forms are hardier than the more often advertised Japanese and Korean stewartias, but north of Baltimore I would definitely give them all a warm, sunny position to ensure best growth. Like all late-flowering trees, they must not lack for water during early summer.

TILLA AMERICANA (basswood, American linden): Zone 2; to 120 feet and a rapid grower into a round-topped tree; any soil with sufficient moisture.

In July clusters of very fragrant creamy flowers attract bees by the flocks where basswood is grown. Although the heart-shaped leaves are often 6 inches long, the flowers show because they hang downward from a straplike bract. Deep, furrowed bark is another feature, as is the fine yellow autumn foliage. There is a variety, *macrophylla,* with even larger leaves. Either is a good choice for the suburbanite in a barren development who needs quick shade, but the leaves are a bit coarse.

Sassafras has three different types of leaves and puts on one of the most colorful fall displays.

RECOMMENDED AMERICAN SHADE TREES

Botanical name	Common name	Zone	Max. height (in feet)
Acer saccharum	sugar maple	3	125
sturdy tree; dense, round head; brilliant fall foliage; the source of maple sugar			
Acer pensylvanicum	striped maple, moosewood	3	35
good for woods planting in cold areas; bark striped white; yellow fall foliage			
Betula lenta	black or sweet birch	3	80
rounded mature head, shiny black bark, yellow fall foliage; not for hot climates			
Betula nigra	river birch	4	100
long catkins; ovoid head, graceful twigs; wet sites; yellow fall foliage; weak wood may break in storms			
Betula papyrifera	canoe or white birch	2	120
superior tree; brown bark turns creamy white as tree ages; yellow fall foliage			
Betula populifolia	gray birch	3*	40
white bark; short-lived but gives graceful quick effects; dry or wet sites			
Carpinus caroliniana	ironwood, American hornbeam	2	40
fluted dark blue-gray bark, odd seeds; understory tree; red, yellow fall foliage			
Carya ovata	shagbark hickory	4	120
open growth, picturesque bark; edible nuts; takes dry, hilly site; golden brown fall foliage			
Fagus grandifolia	American beech	3	120
smooth, silvery gray bark; wide-spreading branches; surface roots; yellow fall foliage			
Gleditsia triacanthos inermis	thornless honey locust	4	100
quick-growing; casts light shade			

RECOMMENDED AMERICAN SHADE TREES (continued)

Botanical name	Common name	Zone	Max. height (in feet)
Gymnocladus dioicus	Kentucky coffee-tree	4	110
	beautiful doubly pinnate compound leaves; picturesque open habit; can be dirty on lawn		
Liquidamber styraciflua	sweet-gum	4	150
	star-shaped leaves turn red, purple in fall; ball-shaped seeds hang on long; damp rich soil; transplant in small sizes		
Nyssa sylvatica	tupelo, sour-gum, black-gum, pepperidge	4	100
	slow grower; transplant in small sizes; likes wet soil; scarlet fall foliage		
Ostrya virginiana	hop hornbeam	4	60
	shreddy bark, rounded head; odd seeds; takes poor, dry soil; understory tree; yellow fall foliage		
Quercus alba	white oak	4	150
	broadspreading and majestic but slow-growing; transplant as small tree; deep red-purple fall foliage		
Quercus bicolor	swamp white oak	3*	100
	bark on branches peels; will take wet site		
Quercus borealis	northern red oak (*Q. rubra*)	4	80
	easy to move and moderately rapid grower; round head; dark red fall foliage		
Quercus coccinea	scarlet oak	4	100
	harder to move; glossy bronze-scarlet fall foliage		
Quercus falcata	Spanish oak	5	100
	spreading branches		

* Probably will need some protection within the zone.　　　　(Continued on next page)

RECOMMENDED AMERICAN SHADE TREES (continued)

Botanical name	Common name	Zone	Max. height (in feet)
Quercus imbricaria	shingle oak	5	75

laurel-like leaves persist long into winter, turn russet; can use for hedges

Quercus macrocarpa	bur oak, mossy-cup oak	2	170

big acorn, almost enclosed by fringed cup

Quercus palustris	pin oak	4	100

rapid grower, easy to move; requires moist soil; lower branches sweep downward; deeply lobed leaves turn bronze in fall, drop late

Quercus phellos	willow oak	5	60

easy to transplant; takes poorly drained soil; willow-like leaves turn pale yellow in fall

Sassafras albidum	sassafras	4	115

usually stays much smaller, forms thickets; mitten-shaped leaves turn orange, red in fall; takes poor soil; transplant when small

Ulmus americana	American elm	2	120

easily transplanted; graceful vase-shaped crown; give rich moist soil; subject to disease

* Probably will need some protection within the zone.

EVERGREENS FROM COAST TO COAST 5

Probably no other country in the world has evergreen trees in the variety found here from one ocean to the other. Even excluding those hardy only in subtropical areas, there are far more that I personally have not grown than vice-versa.

If you have a local favorite, that would be an ideal choice for your climate and soil. Herein are listed only the best and most readily available for home gardens. I make no claims for completeness, nor can I do more than suggest the wealth of selections offered by many nurseries.

A few famous variations are mentioned by name, but today's high interest in special forms has inspired many nurserymen to the extra work involved in vegetatively propagating evergreens with fastigiate (columnar), globe, pendulous (weeping), and dwarf characteristics. Houses specializing in rock-garden plants are particularly good sources for these variations, but many garden centers offer some of them. Dwarf forms are useful for foundation plantings and entrance gardens for today's smaller houses, creating nearly maintenance-free areas.

Except in the case of small seedlings, never buy an evergreen unless it is balled and bagged or in a container. Even the littlest seedlings should never be left with their roots exposed to drying wind or sun. Avoid evergreens with many rusty or browning needles, a sign of disease or neglected watering which often means a weak tree. Most evergreens do not replace all their needles every year, thus the loss of too many in a short time is a serious factor.

The best time for moving evergreens is early spring or late summer. In either case if the weather is hot and dry, give them deep frequent watering the first week and once a week thereafter until it turns cool. Chapters 3 and 4 give hints on planting trees.

No evergreen should go into the winter in a dry condition, for winter sun and wind rob the needles of moisture which the roots are unable to replace if soil water is locked up by frost. During rainless hot summer periods all evergreens benefit once in a while from a forceful hosing of the foliage during daylight hours. This lowers the temperature, cleanses the needles, and discourages infestations of mites, which flourish in hot, dry weather.

Except to make a thriftier, shaplier tree, most evergreens do not need pruning and look pretty silly if kept too formally clipped. Many types do not produce new needles or shoots on old wood, but tip pruning usually encourages new shoots. I do any remedial work just before Christmas, using the greens for indoor holiday decorations. This is not only a handy source of greenery, but is an ideal method of stimulating new growth in the spring. Trimming done late in the summer, especially if combined with heavy rainfall, may push a tree into putting out soft new shoots which are unable to harden off before severe weather.

Young white pine shows effect of several dry years on its growth. Time will erase distorted shape.

American holly is included in this chapter because it is primarily grown as a foliage plant, while evergreen magnolias are found in the chapter on flowering trees. Although I knew a gardener who wintered both a palm and a live oak successfully for some years at Philadelphia, these types of trees are not for home gardeners in the north and are not described. Bald cypress *(Taxodium distichum)* is a tree for swamps. Missing also are the cypress *(cupressus)* of the Southwest and deciduous larches *(larix).* Few of the first are reliably hardy in the north, while the larches to my mind are too ugly for the average property; they lose their needles each fall and spend the winter looking like a dead tree. After all, the chief charm of an evergreen for your home is its attractiveness all year round.

ABIES (fir): although popular as Christmas trees, the firs are the least desirable evergreens for the home property.

A. balsamea (balsam fir) and its counterpart from the southern mountains *(A. fraseri)* are hardy in Zone 3, but they do not do well where the cool, moist conditions they want are missing. *A. concolor* (white fir, Zone 4) is more adaptable, even withstanding moderate city conditions. Wyman terms it reliably hardy at Boston and says it will grow as fast as 18 inches a year. It makes a dense pryamid of silvery green, can reach 120 feet.

CHAMAECYPARIS (false cypress): sometimes cataloged as cypress or retinospora, these evergreens are often confused with arborvitae since they have similar flat, scalelike foliage.

Most offered are hardier oriental species. The so-called Atlantic white cedar *(C. thyoides)* is a tree of the coastal bogs and seldom commercially grown. *C. lawsoniana* (Lawson false cypress) is native to only a small part of Oregon and California but hardy in Zone 5. It likes a mild, moist climate. The type grows into a majestic pyramid, often reaching more than 100 feet, but numerous slow-growing dwarf forms have been developed as well as some with silvery or bluish foliage. Even hardier is the dark-green *C. nootkatensis* from Alaska, but again it does not do well in dry weather. Both dwarf and silvery forms of it exist also.

ILEX OPACA (American holly): few trees are more beloved than this native symbol of Christmas with its shiny red berries and equally decorative spiny leaves.

Hardy into Zone 5, it is worth your fashioning a small windbreak just to give holly a sheltered spot from winter tempests. It is much hardier than English and many of the oriental hollies.

Here at Philadelphia we often see mature hollies reaching toward 30 feet, and in Delaware, where it is the state tree, holly sometimes tops 50 feet. Farther north they

60

Left, American holly lights up barren winter landscape. Below, even baby holly is decorative against the snow.

Impressive new growth after winter trimming of *Ilex opaca*.

will never attain such stature, but often spread quite wide. So much the better for a small house if they merely make a 10-foot green beauty spot.

Unlike English holly, our native thrives on pruning, so that once you get a good bush going, you do it no harm to cut all the greens you want within reason. Bloom (and berry) comes on new wood, and the December trimming merely increases the number of side shoots next spring and helps form a thicker mass of foliage.

Older hollies resent moving, so choose smaller sizes and do all transplanting in early spring. Use lots of peat, since they want a

moist though well-drained site on the acid side. Never let them lack for water. They will take considerable shade, but wind protection is the main consideration.

An established holly near my porch put forth 30 inches in height in one season (a wet one). You can keep them in bounds somewhat by pruning, but a vigorous specimen wants to grow. So don't plant even a tiny sprig without allowing plenty of room for eventual spread; 10 feet is a minimum. In mild climates hollies are also used for hedging.

There are more than 600 named varieties of American holly, some varying only minutely from many others. Leaf size, color, shape,

spininess, plus size and color of the berries as well as hardiness account for most varieties. Your country agent is the best source of information on which do best in your locality.

He will also suggest which male to plant, for this holly is also dioecious, and by far the greatest number of named forms are females. One trick if you are planting many females is to remove a flowering branch from the male and place it in a jar of water near each group of females, thus ensuring good fruiting. Or you can plant a male nearby and keep it trimmed down as a small shrub while giving most space to the more spectacular females.

61

Sometimes a male and female plant are put in the same hole, and the male is then kept pruned back so that the bush growth is mostly female.

American holly is very susceptible to the disfiguring leaf miner. Your garden center will have a suitable spray to recommend, and if timing directions are followed closely, you can keep this pest fairly well controlled. Healthy trees which do not suffer from a lack of water are much less apt to have a bad infestation. There are new systemic poisons on the market to combat leaf miners, but birds eat the holly berries in late winter when food is scarce; one risks killing them too.

Columnar red cedar stands sentry duty on edge of woods.

JUNIPERUS VIRGINIANA (red cedar, Zone 2): by far the most popular and easily available of tree-form junipers, this species will take poor, dry soil.

While it may reach 90 feet, it is a slow grower, and it retains always a thin, columnar form, fine for windbreaks in confined quarters. It is also good for seashore plantings. An aged single specimen has a rugged, picturesque look, but it moves best in small sizes.

Much is made of the cedar-apple rust, a serious pest in the northeast which spends part of its life on junipers and part disfiguring apples, hawthorns, and related trees. There are sprays to fight it, but if you have cedars, it is easy enough to spot the telltale orange galls during a wet spring. Carefully cut them off into a paper bag and burn them, and you have broken the cycle.

Apart from their decorativeness, red cedars have another peculiar characteristic: they are very prone to being struck by lightning. After the bolt struck the giant which stood about 20 feet from the front door of my childhood home, we considered this a sort of natural protection. The downpour pretty much put out the fire on the tree, but we went out after the storm had passed and wet the trunk down well anyway. That tree was still

going strong 25 years afterward, and I have also found live ones in the woods with the telltale zigzag burn. Never camp under cedar trees or any other free-standing kinds, for that matter.

Two widely offered forms of eastern juniper are *canaerti*, a rich green, and *burki* with bluish foliage. *Crebra* has a very narrow growth habit. I have a dwarf called Silver Spreader which is making a nice bluish ground cover on a dry slope, and there are others with various foliage shades of green, blue, and yellow.

It is worth noting that most junipers have two kinds of foliage. One is needlelike and most often found on immature branches, while the older ones may have scalelike foliage. The shredding bark of most varieties is a helpful identifying mark if you're in doubt.

This is another native with the sexes on separate trees, so if you crave a specimen which will bear the little bluish berries, inspect those for sale until you find one with berries present. This is almost the only way to get one; many birds dote on the berries. With the native kinds you ought to be able to count on a nearby wild male for pollenizing.

J. scopulorum (western red or Rocky Mountain cedar, Zone 5) is quite similar to the eastern form, but it does not attain the same heights. It is reputedly better able to take the dry weather of the plains and western states.

JUNIPERUS HORIZONTALIS (creeping juniper): prostrate junipers are the ideal cover for dry, sunny banks, and our native kinds are rock-hardy everywhere. Nomenclature and origin of many of the dwarf and creeping types now being sold is very mixed up, but the following five Americans are widely offered and usually correctly labeled.

The Waukegan juniper (var. *douglasi)* has steel-blue foliage, and the Andorra juniper (var, *plumosa*) is gray-green. Both spread horizontally, seldom reach even 2 feet high, and turn purply in winter. Bar Harbor is a famous clone with blue-

Prostrate junipers vary from groundhuggers to those with somewhat upright growth.

Dwarf Alberta spruce displays almost perfect conical shape.

green fronds only a few inches high. It puts out long fingers in a single season and is lovely either as a ground cover or at the top of a slope or wall. It may be kept in bounds by pruning, but it will also root if earth topped with a stone is placed on one of those fingers. That way you can have large patches of this fairly rare variety in quicker time. Blue Horizon and *wilsoni* are similar but much slower-growing.

There are dozens of other low prostrate junipers from all over our country and the rest of the world. All have their points, but do use them in broad patches of a single variety for greatest effect.

PICEA (spruce): with two exceptions, the spruces have been over-planted on home properties, often to the dismay of the hopeful home owner.

Just about the time a specimen attains respectable height, it begins to lose its lower branches and hence the perfect pyramid it displayed as a younger tree. This natural tendency can sometimes be hidden by a foreground planting of some sort, and for this reason the big, very hardy spruces (Zone 2) are ideal to use as screen or windbreak plantings where their stiff habit is softened by smaller trees or shrubs.

What is more horrifying is that the cute little evergreen suddenly takes hold and grows into a huge tree which blocks paths, doors, and windows with its great spread. When placing them, do allow for the fact that the blue and Engelmann spruces grow into trees in the 100-foot range, while the white spruce is not far behind.

Let's consider the recommended exceptions first. The Black Hills spruce (*P. glauca densata,* Zone 2) is a variety of the white spruce and ranges from 20 to 40 feet at maturity, but it is a very slow-growing tree with dense foliage, making a fine pyramid. Color can range from green to blue, depending on its antecedents.

The related dwarf Alberta spruce (*P. glauca conica,* Zone 3) is the perfect answer for the spot where an evergreen must never outgrow small size. After at least 25 years the one in my mother's garden was scarcely 6 feet tall. The tiny needles are borne so profusely and symmetrically that the tree presents an almost perfect cone. Make sure you are buying the true dwarf, however, for the regular Alberta spruce is a 150-foot giant at maturity.

P. glauca, the white spruce itself, is a quick-growing tree with foliage which is less stiff and a prettier bluish-green than the much-touted dreary, dark-green Norway spruce. Although cheap and easily obtained, it is not nearly as good as its two preceding varieties for discriminating gardeners. In western states *P. engelmanni* is somewhat similar but slenderer. Both are hardy in Zone 2.

There was a time when everyone wanted a Colorado blue spruce (*P.*

pungens, Zone 2). It is true that the silvery blue of a good variety makes a lovely specimen until old age begins taking its toll. Since it is often given the most conspicuous site, its unsightly maturity simply shrieks for attention. Moreover, many a "blue" spruce grew into a green tree. If you must have one, pay the extra to get a grafted plant of one of the outstanding selections such as Moorheim or Hoopes, since cheaper seed-grown trees have a wide variation of color. Then put it where you can hide its awkwardness with shrubs when the lower branches begin to die.

PINUS (pine): fine ornamentals, the native pines exhibit a remarkable flexibility for survival in many different kinds of situations. Described here are only a few of the most beautiful and easiest obtained. They are outstanding for their informal grace.

Why is the eastern white pine (*P. strobus,* Zone 3) so important for home gardeners? First, its beauty: the long, soft green needles which never discolor and boughs with a delicate informality no matter what their age. Second, it transplants easily and grows quickly; a potted baby here grew 5 inches in every direction its first year after planting, while slightly older trees average at least a foot each season, often much more. Third, it is adaptable to many different soils and sites. It will also take almost any gale, bending even in hurricanes, so is good

for a wind screen. The clean scent of the foliage is a bonus.

Although white pines may reach 150 feet under optimum conditions, they seem to slow down their growth after the first few years. Allow for some spread, however, since they make a more rounded tree than the stiffer spruces. Lower branches which interfere with traffic can be removed without ruining the picturesque silhouette. If pruning is necessary or when choosing boughs for indoor decoration, cuts made in portions of a branch which carry needles will stimulate new growth buds. Those made on needleless spots may cause that branch to die back. There are several dwarf forms in the trade.

P. resinosa (red pine, Zone 2) is

Long needles of white pine add to its gracefulness.

65

an even hardier tree with reddish bark and glossy, dark-green needles. They are often as long as those of the white pine but have only two in a bundle instead of its five. Equally good for ornamental use and tolerant of poor soil, this pine does not grow as tall as the white and has a more nearly pyramidal growth. It may need spraying against insects.

Lately the bristle-cone pine (P. aristata) of the western mountains has been offered in eastern catalogs. Aged specimens in Arizona are thought to be among the world's oldest living things—more than four thousand years young. Wind and weather in the mountains keep them dwarfed, but the kinder climate of the East may help them grow to their mature 50 feet, so I am dubious about putting them in confined quarters even though they are reputedly very slow growing.

We are sometimes also offered the ponderosa or western yellow pine (P. ponderosa, Zone 5). It will take dry soil and grows to 150 feet in a narrow pyramid. While it is a fine lumber tree and may have merit in midwestern and central states, it is hardly as lovely as our white and red pines for the East.

There are also a number of pines which grow only on the Pacific Coast. Many more are not decorative enough for home grounds except where they are the only tree which will take an inhospitable environment. These include the eastern jack pine (P. banksiana) for dry,

sandy banks; the cluster pine (P. pinaster) for southern beaches; the pitch pine (P. rigida) for dry, windy, rocky sites; and the scrub pine (P. virginiana) for poor, dry soil.

PSEUDOTSUGA MENZIESI (P. taxifolia, Douglas fir): if you can use only one evergreen, this is my suggestion. It is a tree that is beautiful, fairly fast growing, healthy, and very hardy in some forms. In recent tests it has also proved to survive the polluted air of cities better than most evergreens.

The one usually offered in the East is the variety glauca, which has a bluish tinge to the foliage and is hardy in Zone 4. Another selection is rugged enough to survive in Canada.

Even young trees present a dense pyramidal effect, and I am told will take the pruning necessary for a hedge, although this seems a shame when it is so lovely left to its natural form. My largest tree is exposed to the very worst winter wind imaginable and loses neither color nor needles no matter how tough the season. I do give it extra water in times of drought. Last year it made 10 inches of annual top growth.

If you have empty land to support it, Douglas fir makes the best Christmas tree of all since its form is so good and needles do not drop quickly. It commands much better prices than the ugly Scotch pine so many of my neighbors are growing for market.

This state tree of Oregon was honored in 1969 on a stamp as representative of our great northwest.

TAXUS CANADENSIS (Canadian yew, ground-hemlock): not nearly as neat or as good a winter green as imported varieties, our native eastern yew is nevertheless hardy in Zone 2, hence a boon to far northern gardens. It makes a straggling shrub 2 to 4 feet high, grows in shade, has a reddish-brown tinge to the foliage in winter. You can prune it to encourage better appearance.

There is a hybrid, T. hunnewelliana, which is reputedly just as hardy but has neater pyramidal growth. It too browns in winter. When you consider the other yews are not hardy beyond Zone 4, you can see that our plain Jane has her place.

The western yew (T. brevifolia) is a tall 45-foot tree, but dwarf forms are sometimes offered. I do not know if they suffer the same foliage discoloration as the type.

THUJA OCCIDENTALIS (American arborvitae): as in so many cases the native arborvitae are hardier (Zone 2) than the oriental species. Many, unfortunately, particularly those with foliage color variations, turn brownish in cold weather, but they are still rugged trees. If you should ever locate forms of T. plicata (giant arborvitae) from the West, they do not have this habit, but they are hardy only into Zone 5.

In the wild the typical American arborvitae can reach 60 feet and prefers moist soil and air. Most forms offered in garden centers are dwarf or slow-growing and much overused for foundation plantings. Make sure any you buy for that purpose are true dwarfs or they will grow out of bounds. The scale-like foliage is usually quite dense, and there are pyramidal, globe, and spreading forms. In dry weather give them a strong hosing frequently to cut red-spider infestations.

If all that sounds like faint praise, let's end by admitting that aborvitae will grow in almost any awful soil, even one mishandled badly by a cheap builder, as long as it has sufficient watering. It also withstands wind and sea salt, so makes a good narrow windbreak. It can even be formally pruned as a hedge.

TSUGA CANADENSIS (northern hemlock): there need be no qualifications to name the hemlock one of our most beautiful and useful native trees except to note that it should not have a position exposed to strong wind. Although hardy in Zone 3, it will drop needles on the windy side. It is incidentally the official tree of my adopted state, Pennsylvania.

Although in the wild hemlock will make a green pyramid some 75 feet high, it can be judiciously pruned to a specimen around 25 feet. Or it can be kept clipped carefully into a formal hedge a few

Closeup of hemlock to show fine needles.

feet high. It seems to like to grow in groups. I remember a triangle of three where we used to play as children. The needles made a soft floor completely free of weeds and snakes, and the low, sweeping boughs quite hid us from nosy passersby.

Hemlock should never suffer from lack of water and is often found toward the bottom of moist, shaded ravines. It grows quite happily in sun too. Once you have some old

enough to bear the tiny cones, you're almost sure to have visiting chickadees; they love the seeds.

My test tree has averaged about a foot of growth annually. Because its foliage is so fine and the branches are so supple, it never suffers any ice or snow loss. Nor do the lower branches die back, so it is one of the very best subjects to screen an undesirable view. And the dark green of its foliage makes the perfect backdrop for white-

67

řáplovík   sluncovka   trojlist

hořec   lobelia   rozchodník   zavinutka   vlčinec

blossomed trees like dogwood or amelanchier. It harmonizes even with the magenta of redbud. Its only drawback is that the needles drop almost immediately after picking, so use any prunings for mulch instead of decoration.

Slightly less hardy, the hemlock of the southern mountains *(T. caroliniana)* has all the same fine characteristics but is a darker green. In addition it is said to withstand the dirt and pollution of city condi-

tions better. Since it is a slower, denser tree, it is recommended especially for hedges.

No one speaks well of the western hemlock *(T. heterophylla)* under drier eastern conditions, but in its moist Pacific homeland it can reach 200 feet and must be a magnificent sight.

There are literally dozens of selected hemlocks in dwarf and prostrate forms quite lovely for special plantings. One merits mention:

the famous Sargent weeping hemlock *(T. canadensis pendula)*. Set in the right spot, it is spectacular with its dark, drooping branches almost like a fountain. Never cram it into a small corner. It wants to grow to about 15 feet high and has a very wide spread. It will be small and expensive when you buy it, but arrange just the right place and be patient. One day you'll have a crowd stopper.

Heavy snow does not bother the supple hemlock.

OPPOSITE:
TOP (l. to r.):
Helenium autumnale Bruno, mixture of escholtzia, *Trillium erectum*

MIDDLE (l. to r.):
Gentiana andrewsi, Lobelia cardinalis, Asclepias tuberosa, Monarda didyma, Lupinus perennis

BOTTOM (l. to r.):
Oenothera fruticosa, Arisaema berries with Christmas fern, *Coreopsis verticillata*

6 STAR-SPANGLED SHRUBS FOR ALL SEASONS

In a sense this chapter is an adjunct to that on trees, for most of the planting techniques are similar. The one great difference is time. An old man plants beeches and oaks for his grandchildren, but he can put in azaleas and blueberries for himself. Since the lower-growing shrubs come to maturity sooner than their towering relatives, they help give your property a finished look sooner.

While every shrub has an intrinsic beauty of some sort (and there are plenty of Americans which can compete with the rest of the world on this score), our natives are also important for their diversity. They reflect the great differences in climate, topography, and soil of our great country.

European and Asiatic bushes which have long enjoyed popularity tend to thrive with tender, loving care only in the conventional temperate garden. Indeed, that was the reason they were cultivated, hybridized, and encouraged in the first place. America stretches from the cold, bleak northern border to subtropical climes—dipping into moist hollows, climbing windswept mountains, and reaching over long deserts. Its people live in all these places.

Even a suburban property in the kindest Mid-Atlantic state may have a low damp corner or a border where the winter wind roars in with desiccating intensity. In such extremes of locale one must choose shrubs to fit the land. This is the great strength of our native bushes: there are some for almost any position and condition.

If you choose them with discrimination and imagination there are also American shrubs to provide decoration the whole year round. Some bloom late into fall or in earliest spring. Many have persistent, striking fruit. A few retain their leaves to brighten the landscape during the bleak months. For your convenience these latter are grouped together as evergreens in the second half of this chapter.

All the admonitions about proper planting of trees apply when placing bushes, but your mistakes are easier to correct. It is possible to move large shrubs. Should you find it necessary, remember you cannot possibly get all the roots when you move the plant. To make up for this, prune severely when transplanting established shrubs. By cutting down on the amount of top which must be supported by the disturbed roots, you give the bush a better chance of recovering.

Ideally you plan where a bush is to go just as carefully as when placing a tree. Exposure, sun or shade, soil preference, and eventual height and width are all important. If you are adding new shrubs to established plantings, it is easy to pick areas of shade or sun as needed.

New properties are often so barren and the small trees look so lonely that one is tempted to plant dozens of bushes to overcome the desert look. Before long one needs a machete to get through the yard. You can achieve a finished look for a new property with a minimum of later work if you keep several things in mind when placing shrubs.

First, and most important, is to allow enough space between tree and bush or between the bushes themselves. A small sprig of a bush grows very quickly into a specimen, especially if it does not have to compete with the tree's roots or with its neighbor's. Two shrubs which each have an eventual spread of 6 feet should not be set much closer together than that vital 6 feet unless you want a thicket. They will make lovelier specimens farther apart.

Another good rule of thumb: plant shrubs which require some shade on the northern and eastern sides of a young tree, and place those which do best in sun on the southern or western edge of where the tree will cast its shade. The latter types will need no protection while young, but don't put them too close to the tree since its eventual shade will be considerable.

Those which must have shade for proper growth will benefit from some artificial shadow until the tree begins to take over the job. You can do this very easily with a small starter shrub by inserting old evergreen branches in the ground and bending them over the plant on the sunniest sides. Or you can make a temporary lath shade.

Attention to such details saves untold hours of work, and years of shrub growth need not be sacrificed through needed future transplanting. Be especially careful about a shrub in front of a window. Most kinds look loveliest when allowed to grow into their natural shape rather than being bobbed every few years. I have listed maximum heights in the descriptions of species to give you an idea of

what to expect. A window is, after all, to be looked through. There is room to quarrel about whether some genera belong here or in the tree chapter. There are shrubby trees and bushes which can be encouraged to grow into small trees. The maximums will give you some insight into the possibilities.

Some shrubs (and trees) lend themselves well to hedges and formal clipping. Others look butch-

Big planting hole gives a small shrub a good start; cloth tie will not rub bark.

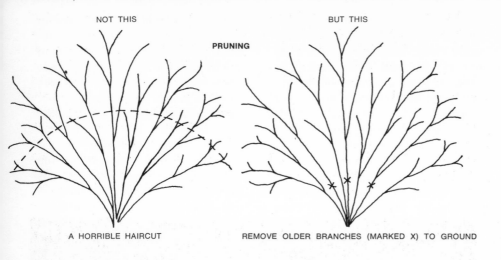

NOT THIS · BUT THIS

PRUNING

A HORRIBLE HAIRCUT — REMOVE OLDER BRANCHES (MARKED X) TO GROUND

Fig. 11: Perfect pruning doesn't really show.

ered unless allowed to grow into their natural shape, whether it be vaselike, arching, or a round mass. Personally I think most hedges are prettiest when grown naturally, and this is much less work than the formal type. Natural hedges require more width, however.

Most shrubs benefit from some pruning every few years after they reach maturity. If done correctly, this renews the plant by encouraging the growth of vigorous new branches. But there is a world of difference between an intelligent thinning and a haircut. See Fig. 11.

Never cut a specimen shrub uniformly into a lollipop shape. This does more harm than good and usually a year or two of regular blooming is lost. Instead, drop on your knees and make your pruning cuts at ground level. Remove a few

of the oldest branches entirely. They will be thickest and darkest, while newer branches often still have a green tinge.

Auxiliary branching can be fostered by cutting back new shoots once in a while to varying lengths. If done at the wrong season, however, this nipping process (which is different from pruning) may deprive you of maximum bloom, since many shrubs flower only on old wood. If you don't know, you're always safe to do this kind of trimming when the shrub is in blossom.

DECIDUOUS SHRUBS

Please note that many of the following shrubs spread by suckers. Such types can be trained by pruning into fine specimen groupings, but they are poor choices to use in the background of a border or

in spots where the wandering underground roots compete with neater plants.

AESCULUS PARVIFLORA (bottlebrush buckeye): Zone 5; to 12 feet and spreads by suckers into wide thickets; any good soil; takes some shade but better in sun.

White flowers with pink stamens on foot-long panicles during July and August are the outstanding characteristic of this cousin of the horse-chestnut. Seed heads are yellow, turning brownish-orange, and quite decorative. Best used behind a smaller shrub since lower branches not very pretty.

AMORPHA FRUTICOSA (indigo bush, false indigo): Zone 3*; to 20 feet but blooms better if pruned to ground every few years; spreads by suckering; adaptable to many soils; sun.

Many varieties with flowers from dark purple through blue to white exist. The common type bears 6-inch purplish-blue spikes of flowers with prominent gold stamens in May and June. *A. canescens* (lead plant, Zone 2, to 4 feet) has the same compound leaves but in a gray shade.

ARALIA SPINOSA (Hercules-club, devil's-walking-stick): Zone 4*; to 30 feet; rich soil, will take part shade.

* Probably will need some protection within the zone.

72

Not a graceful bush, but can be used for bold effects. Bare, spiny trunk and branches are topped by fans of doubly pinnate compound leaves. Large terminal clusters of white flowers in August are followed by black berries. Bees love the flowers, birds the fruit.

ARONIA ARBUTIFOLIA (red chokeberry): Zone 5; to 10 feet; spreads by suckers; adaptable but good for low moist spots in full sun or light shade.

Showy long-lasting red fruits are the main attraction of aronia. Flowers are white or pinkish in May. Available are a columnar variety as well as the form *brilliantissima,* which has brighter berries. Hardier (Zone 4) are *A. melanocarpa* (black chokeberry, to 4 feet) and *A. prunifolia* (purple chokeberry, to 12 feet).

AZALEA: These deciduous members of the rhododendron tribe are still often listed in nursery catalogs as azaleas. They are included here rather than under *Rhododendron* in their proper alphabetical place for your convenience. Moisture needs may vary among them, but except where noted, these members of the great heath family want high or partial shade and must have acid soil.

In areas where the soil is not strongly acid, azeleas are a poor choice for foundation plantings since lime may leach from the mortar. They have shallow roots and benefit greatly from a *loose* mulch of acid material like oak leaves or wood chips. Because the roots do not go too deep, it is possible to grow azeleas in areas where the soil is not suitable if you are willing to remove the earth to a depth of 18 inches and replace it with soil well laced with acid humus. Check the notes in Chapter 2 on soil acidity for further information.

Many of the native azaleas are notable for their fragrance. They have also played an important part in hybridizing since they are decidedly hardier than Asiatic species. These hybrids have a wide range of color plus immense heads of large flowers. Generally speaking, the hybrids are heavier and more formal-looking. The natives give an airier effect and are particularly lovely when used among large trees where there is high shade. Here too the legginess of many does not call attention to itself as it might in more formal plantings.

There is much natural variation among the natives, and colors of any one species may range from pure white to many shades of pink and rose. If you are going to use several of the same kind in one place where coloration makes a difference, it is wise to buy them locally where you can see them in bloom first. The same admonition can be made about hybrids offered by color rather than name; I have seen some jarring combinations of purple-red and orange-red bushes.

All azaleas should be moved bagged and balled in the spring for best results. Since they do not mind being moved in blossom, it is no hardship to pick the ones you want by their flowers. This way you can check on fragrance too; there is considerable variation among strains.

There is a decidedly greater range of colors available among the hybrids, and there are hundreds in the trade, many little different from their brothers. I do not pretend to be an expert on them. I must confess, however, to a certain boredom with the big trusses of flowers of certain highly touted (and expensive) hybrids. Many are literally smothered in bloom so that the effect of a single flower is quite lost; these azaleas are important only as blobs of color.

You will notice many of the native species have open heads of long-tubed flowers with prominent stamens. They are just more graceful though not always as showy as the hybrids. Most also have colorful fall foliage. To show you the sequence of bloom possible, I am listing them in the order of flowering here near Philadelphia. Maximum heights are seldom attained in cultivation, but are a handy means of comparison. Most benefit from light pruning right after flowering, so can be kept lower than in the wild. Thus treated, they become much fuller bushes. Tall types like the flame azaleas are an exception to this; let them grow treelike.

Southern and West Coast gardeners have additional species; I have confined myself to those hardy at least to Zone 6. These are also the ones most easily located in the catalogs.

Rhododendron canadense (rhodora, to 3 feet) is not only the first to bloom (early April here) but by far the hardiest (Zone 2). It demands acid, moist soil and cool temperatures, so give it a spot in an airy, low frost pocket. Small clusters of rose-purple flowers are valuable more for their earliness than their color.

R. canescens (southern pinxterbloom or Piedmont azalea, Zone 6, to 15 feet) comes in late April with "clusters of rosy-tubed white or pale pink flowers . . . before the leaves, with a bouquet of spice and honeysuckle," according to Leonie Bell. Unfortunately it is not widely available.

Much easier to locate is *R. nudiflorum* (pinxterbloom, to 10 feet), which may even grow in Zone 3 and will take full sun. Its pink or white flowers have narrow tubes with long, protruding stamens. Similar but with a heavenly spicy fragrance is *R. roseum* (downy pinxterbloom or roseshell azalea, Zone 3, to 15 feet). Strains of this latter vary from pale pink to crimson, and it wants some shade, particularly in warmer states. It may spread slowly by stolons. Both these last two bloom in early May and are reputedly less demanding about the acidity of the soil, but give them plenty of peat.

Mid-May finds *R. vaseyi* (pinkshell azalea, Zone 4, to 15 feet) at its height. Appearing before the leaves, its bell-shaped pink flowers are spotted orange. It is fairly adaptable to soil and sun but is found in wet woods in its native Carolina. There is a fine white strain in the trade called White Find (LaBar), which is well worth hunting for.

A little later come the bright flowers of *R. calendulaceum* (flame azalea, Zone 4,* to 15 feet). Preferring light shade in dry woods, it may have blooms in any shade of yellow, orange, or red. Coming upon it in a shadowed spot, one catches one's breath, and it is in such a setting you should put it rather than next to a building. Try to see it in bloom before you buy if color makes any difference to your design.

One of the natives I covet but have not yet found in the trade is *R. atlanticum* (coast azalea, Zone 5,* to 2 feet), which blooms in early June. Typically it has fragrant white flowers flushed crimson, stays low, and spreads into clumps by stolons. It sounds a wonderful bush for the front of an azalea planting.

R. arborescens (smooth or sweet azalea, Zone 4,* to 25 feet) is easily located. It too blooms in early June with fragrant white flowers and red stamens. Petals may be flushed pink and have yellow blotches. It wants moist soil

* Probably will need some protection within the zone.

and makes a dense, wide-spreading large shrub.

Latest of the hardier azaleas is *R. viscosum* (swamp azalea, Zone 3, to 15 feet). Where it has plenty of moisture, it will grow in nearly full sun, but you can put it in your garden by giving it light shade and extra water in dry times. The long-tubed white flowers have a lovely spicy scent, may be tinged pink.

In Zone 6 you can prolong the show into July with two more natives both from Georgia. *R. serrulatum* has very fragrant white funnelform flowers and grows to 25 feet in the south. *R. prunifolium* bears startling orange-red blooms with prominent stamens and can reach 10 feet. Some remarkable hybrids between them (*R. gladwynansi*) were developed at Philadelphia by the late Mrs. J. Norman Henry. They have flowers ranging from white through yellow and pink to salmon and point the way to future possibilities for hybridists.

Northwest Coast gardeners will be interested in *R. occidentale* (western azalea), which has large white or pink funnelform flowers with a yellow blotch and prominent stamens. I have never seen it, but it is reputed to have a far-carrying perfume. Coming from Oregon and northern California, it apparently dislikes hot eastern summers. It has been used in the famous Knap Hill hybrids.

CALYCANTHUS FLORIDUS (sweetshrub, Carolina allspice): Zone 4;

to 10 feet; rich, well-drained soil in partial shade.

All old-fashioned gardens had at least one bush of what was commonly called just "shrub." Its reddish-brown flowers 2 inches across in May and June look a little like everlastings and have a fruity odor when bruised or warmed in one's palm. Crushed twigs also give off the fragrance. The fruits which follow and the bush itself are not particularly decorative. Usually grown mostly for sentimental reasons, it is stoloniferous.

CEANOTHUS AMERICANUS (New Jersey-tea): Zone 4; to 3 feet; takes poor soil.

Along the west coast there are glorious blue-flowered types of ceanothus, but I have never seen one. Reputedly there are white forms too, and they like a sunny, well-drained, light soil. Here in more vigorous climes we must be content with the poor relation of the family. It has dense heads of tiny white flowers in June and July and is useful because it will grow almost anywhere. The nursery trade ignores it, probably because it does not transplant easily. Try to obtain seed and sow in early spring.

CEPHALANTHUS OCCIDENTALIS (button-bush): Zone 4; to 20 feet but usually shorter; likes swampy ground.

In my refrigerator now are seeds of this little-known native which bears fragrant globes of white

flowers most of the summer. Prominent pink pistils sticking out all over each head look just like pins in a pin cushion. I cannot understand why it is so hard to find a source of plants, for it is a pretty, undemanding plant that deserves wider attention for wet places.

CLETHRA ALNIFOLIA (sweet pepperbush, summer-sweet): Zone 3; to 10 feet and spreads by suckers

into thickets; wants moist, slightly acid soil and partial shade.

One of the first things we did at the new house was cut out a deep bed beneath the downspout at the back of the house for a clethra bush. Here it gets a thorough soaking whenever it rains, and here it sends its wonderful sweet anise fragrance over the summer evenings. The little fluffy flowers in July and August are

Clethra makes a fine summer decorative in wet spots.

generously borne on terminal spikes about 6 inches long and last well when picked. The type is white, but bushes with varying tones of pink flowers are also widely offered.

Summer-sweet's shiny green leaves often have bronzy tints and supply grand foliage for bouquets all season. In fall they turn yellow to orange while the seed capsules remain all winter to give the bush an interesting silhouette against the snow.

Clethra wants only partial shade for good blooming, but it must have extra water. Every house has a roof gutter, and the hollow below it will keep this all-star native happy if there is a tree or building to give it some shade. You can always hose in drought. Don't be without this one any longer.

COMPTONIA PEREGRINA (sweet-fern): Zone 2; to 5 feet; good ground cover for dry, sandy, acid soil.

The catkin flowers of the sweet-fern are unimportant, but its leaves are fernlike and have an aromatic fragrance so that it makes an interesting focal point among lower-growing plants which thrive in the same site. Keep it out of the garden, however; it is too invasive.

CORNUS STOLONIFERA (red osier dogwood): Zone 2; to 10 feet and spreading by stolons; adaptable to almost any situation.

While the dogwood tree is surely one of our best natives, its shrubby

relatives are really not worth cultivating. There are many, but only one is included here and that for two specific reasons: it makes a quick, cheap screen for new properties and it is known to attract 100 species of birds. It has clusters of whitish flowers in May and June, which are followed by pea-size fruits which turn from white to shades of blue and are eaten quickly by the birds. The red autumn foliage and the red twigs against the snow are neither of them good enough to be important of themselves. Many branches are nearly prostrate and tend to layer, so a planting makes a surprisingly thick screen in little time. Varieties with yellow twigs and dwarfer habits are sold.

CORYLUS AMERICANA (hazelnut, filbert): Zone 4; to 10 feet and spreading into thickets.

When the hazelnut's fruits are ready to eat in early fall, the green sticky husks turn dry and brown. Then country children risk scratched legs and arms to gather the sweet harvest. There are no prickers, but the bushes make close-set wands, and it just isn't possible to emerge without drawing blood. This native is a good selection for the sunny edges of a windbreak, and if you don't gather the nuts, hungry pheasants will be glad to oblige.

Hybrids of American and European filberts yield bigger nuts and are probably a smarter investment for the home gardener, but I shall

always remember our feeling of accomplishment at bringing home the wild ones, which seemed to taste sweetest.

DIERVILLA LONICERA (*D. trifida* or bush honeysuckle): Zone 3; to 3 feet and spreading by stolons; sun or part shade, any soil.

Formerly cataloged as a weigela, these spreading shrubs are useful for holding problem banks but hardly showy enough to gain entrance to a garden. The small clusters of funnelform, half-inch flowers are yellowish-green in early summer. *D. sessilifolia* (southern bush honeysuckle) grows several feet higher, has brighter yellow flowers, but is hardy only to Zone 5.

DIRCA PALUSTRIS (leatherwood): Zone 4; to 6 feet usually with a single trunk and many upcurving branches; damp humusy soil and partial to full shade.

If it bloomed later, we might overlook the dirca, but its very earliness makes it worthwhile for those whose properties are too shady for forsythia. In late March or early April before the leaves appear, it displays little pale yellow bells in small clusters. The fruit which follows is inconspicuous and soon falls, but each year I look forward to the dirca's flowering as a sure sign of spring. The nickname comes from the extremely flexible nature of the branches, a trait which is handy if you use it in a windy spot. Unfortunately it is seldom stocked by nurseries, and you'll have to ask around.

ELAEAGNUS COMMUTATA (*E. argentea,* silverberry): Zone 1; to 12 feet; sunny, well-drained, alkaline soil.

Hard to find in the East, silverberry is more popular with western nurseries, probably because of its preference for limy soil, which is much more common in those states. The yellow flowers in May and June are not showy but have a discernible fragrance. It is grown chiefly for its silvery foliage and fruit and is very hardy, thus good for windbreaks.

ELLIOTTIA RACEMOSA: Zone 7; to 20 feet; sandy, acid soil.

Though I know of no source for this native, it is so lovely with its small fragrant white flowers in narrow terminal racemes that I mention it for southern gardeners who may be able to locate a specimen. I know of a garden at Philadelphia where it successfully wintered over and bloomed for some years, but I would not expect to see it often north of Washington, D.C.

EUONYMUS AMERICANUS (strawberry-bush, brook euonymus): Zone 5*; to 8 feet but may be straggly; sun or part shade in ordinary soil but likes dampness.

American euonymus are mostly grown for their bright fruits. This

* Probably will need some protection within the zone.

one has small clusters of little greenish-purple flowers, which are followed by pinkish warty fruits. In combination with the red fall foliage they are quite startling, and then they open to display orange seeds! An interesting variety is *obovatus* (running strawberry-bush), which grows to only a foot. *E. atropurpureus* (wahoo or burning-bush) sometimes reaches 25 feet and is hardy in Zone 4. Its flower is purple, its fruit crimson and persistent, and its fall foliage brilliant red.

All euonymus suffer from scale infestations. At the first hint of it, get a miscible oil dormant spray and use as directed spring and fall. In some gardens scale is so bad that lilacs, bittersweet, and euonymus of all kinds are impossible to grow.

FOTHERGILLA: mostly Zone 5; well-drained, moist soil and light shade.

These adaptable shrubs from the Appalachians deserve more attention. Their fragrant, petalless white flowers are displayed in 2-inch clusters that resemble bottlebrushes because they are all stamens.

F. major (large fothergilla) may reach 10 feet and has a somewhat pyramidal growth habit. *F. monticola* (Alabama fothergilla) seldom tops 6 feet and makes a more spreading bush. Both flower in May. A little earlier, smaller in every way, and hardy perhaps to Zone 4 is *F. gardeni* (dwarf fothergilla).

All these relatives of the witch-

hazels color yellow, orange, and red in autumn and are fairly slow-growing, so may be used in foundation plantings. With adequate moisture they will grow in full sun.

HAMAMELIS (witch-hazel): adaptable but prefers moist spots with partial summer shade; subject to dieback.

When you have seen a witch-hazel in bloom, you will believe flowers can take almost any shape, for the petals resemble little ribbons tied to the twig. Since there are no interfering leaves, they are indeed showy, but their greatest appeal is their appearance at the two ends of the flowering year when almost nothing else is in bloom. The famous extract as well as divining rods come from the fall witch-hazel.

H. virginiana (American witch-hazel) grows treelike to around 15 feet and puts forth her display in October and November. The small yellow ribbons have a sweet musty odor and are an unbelievable tonic for a soul depressed by a raw taste

Ribbony petals of witch-hazel light up the wintry woods.

77

Witch-hazel seed pods are decorative too.

of coming winter. In protected places it may even survive in Zone 3.

Hardy only to Zone 5, *H. vernalis* (spring witch-hazel) may open her first yeasty-smelling flowers as early as January in a warm spot, but is more likely to bloom in February or March. They vary from yellow to red and yellow. This species spreads by suckers and prefers a sunny home. The yellowish fruits are interesting in the fall.

HOLODISCUS DISCOLOR (mountain-spray, ocean-spray, rock-spirea, cream-bush): Zone 5*; to 15 feet; full sun, humusy soil.

Native to the western states, mountain-spray reaches its peak of flowering in July when colorful shrubs are few. Large fluffy heads

of creamy-white flowers are borne on the ends of arching branches, and the crinkly leaves are pretty also. It is reputedly hard to move from the wild and so far available only from West Coast nurseries. My plant never recovered from its long journey.

HYDRANGEA ARBORESCENS (wild hydrangea): Zone 4; to 10 feet; moist, rich, porous soil and best in full sun.

By far superior to the type is the variety *grandiflora* (Hills of Snow hydrangea), which makes fine clumps and bears large round clusters of showy sterile white flowers which stay on indefinitely and can be used in dried arrangements. In shade this hydrangea tends to get straggly. In any situation it may be trimmed to the ground in the fall, since it blooms in June and July on new growth.

Such treatment keeps them thrifty and shorter.

H. quercifolia (oak leaf hydrangea, Zone 5) also has white flowers, but they form upright panicles and turn purplish as they age. Its distinctive leaves are dark red in fall, and it tends to be stoloniferous, usually staying under 5 feet. It will take shade.

HYPERICUM (St.-Johns-wort): Zone 4; to 6 feet; takes partial shade; adaptable but prefers sandy soil.

While the cheerful golden flowers of the native hypericums are not as large as many of the Asiatics, they are freely produced from July to September on bushes definitely hardier. Blooms last longer if given some protection from the worst of the afternoon sun.

There are some pretty weedy members of this family too, but you will be delighted with two easily found species. *H. kalmianum* seldom exceeds 3 feet and is evergreen in many climates. *H. prolificum* has many forms, most of which are a little taller and may also be evergreen. Even if the tops winterkill, new growth will flower the next summer. Give them room to arch their branches.

ILEX VERTICILLATA (winterberry, black-alder, swamp holly): Zone 3; to 15 feet; likes moist acid soil in the sun but will take drier location.

Never was a nickname apter than winterberry for this deciduous holly.

* Probably will need some protection within the zone.

78

Its leaves turn black with the frost, then drop, making the bright-red berries along the bare branches incredibly dazzling against the early snows. They are often used as winter decorations.

Like most hollies, this one bears male and female flowers on separate bushes. While only the latter yield berries, at least one male must be close by for decent berry production. Unlike other species, this one is seldom offered by sex, which presents a problem. Your best solution if you cannot buy them by sex is to order a number in small sizes (which transplant best) in earliest spring. Get them in quickly and prune back to only a foot or so, since they are usually offered bareroot and need help in getting over the shock. When they are old enough to flower, inspect them carefully. Female flowers have a knob in the center where the berry will be; male flowers have only pollen-bearing stamens. If space is limited, discard all but one healthy male bush. That way you get the most berries for the space.

Winterberry will not grow as tall in drier situations and must be watered carefully its first summer; without a good root system, it is very susceptible to drought.

ITEA VIRGINICA (sweet-spire, Virginia-willow): Zone 5; to 10 feet; sun or shade and any soil but likes moisture.

Although I cannot give you any help in finding a source of this decorative native, it is too fine to ignore. Make a clamor, and perhaps the nurseries will begin to carry it. Fragrant spires of white flowers are carried on wandlike canes in June and July. Autumn foilage is bright-red, and a single specimen will slowly form a good clump. It deserves better shift than it has had.

LINDERA BENZOIN (spicebush): Zone 4; to 15 feet and wide-spreading; grows almost anywhere but prefers moist woods.

Spicebush can be a nuisance, for in its favorite haunts it spreads quickly if not kept under control. If you have room enough not to have to be too selective: its fluffy yellow flowers borne in clusters along the twigs in March are one of the first signs of spring, and its red fall berries are important bird food. Autumn foilage is yellow. Both flowers and leaves give off an astringent odor when crushed.

It is another dioecious shrub, so it is necessary to have plants of both sexes for berry production. It is so common in eastern woodlands, I doubt the need for a male if you can get a certified female for fruit.

PRUNUS MARITIMA (beach plum): Zone 3; 10 feet; poor, dry soil in sun.

Anyone with a New England background ought to know this American, and the fame of beach plum jam and jelly is slowly spreading. It will grow in the driest, windiest spot, hence has long been popular for seashore plantings. Many white flowers cover the bush in May, and the fruits ripen red or purply in late summer.

Rich garden soil is too much for the beach plum, making it blowzy. If you have a barren corner, it is a fine subject, however, and judicious pruning keeps it from getting too straggly. Allow room for suckering and natural layering or train carefully to tree shape.

Some day I shall plant the related *P. besseyi* (western sand cherry, Zone 3) but in its improved form, Hansen's bush cherry. How wonderful to gather my favorite fruit from a 6-foot bush rather than a tree!

As with all fruits, plant at least two bushes of a species to ensure cross-fertilization and best fruit production.

RHODODENDRON. For deciduous species of the genus *Rhododendron,* see AZALEA, above.

SALIX DISCOLOR (pussy willow): Zone 3; to 20 feet; prefers wet site but keep away from any type of plumbing.

Spring would lose something without pussy willows, but they are like all the other members of the family: their roots will go anywhere in search of moisture. Moreover, they attract aphids in the summer, and this can be a messy business since these insects drip sticky juice

Elderberry flowers are like lace.

lacy white flowers in June and July. You'll have to fight with the birds to get the purply-black fruit, for they gobble it almost before it is ripe enough for the most delicious pie in the world. Elderberry wine is another treat if you have enough bushes. Less well known is the fact that the blossom heads can be dipped in fritter batter and fried in deep fat.

To foil the birds, throw a few yards of nylon net from the five-and-ten over each bush as the berries ripen. Removed carefully and stored dry, the net will last several seasons.

Improved forms with bigger fruit are available from many nurseries and are the best choice for the home gardener. If your bushes get straggly, you can cut them down in early spring, and they will come back with renewed vigor, but you will find they are healthy only if given adequate water. There is a variety with yellow foliage in the trade that sounds awful.

SHEPHERDIA ARGENTEA (silver buffaloberry): Zone 2; to 18 feet but usually smaller; takes poor dry soil.

This fall I am sowing seed of this fine native because I have been unable to find a nearby source of plants, and I want it in quantity. Its thorny branches make ideal hedges, and its hardiness is legendary. What appeals even more is that its young twigs and leaves are silver, a wonderful point of interest for the long windbreak we are fa-

underneath the tree. Keep salix far away from foundations, parking areas, and patios, as well as any type of pipes.

If you have a low, out-of-the-way spot where one won't make trouble, you can have a big bush in a few years just from a single fresh wand of furry catkins. Place the branch in water, wait a few weeks until it forms roots, then plant and water carefully until it takes hold. Branches will be easier to gather and much more plentiful if you cut your willow back severely every spring, so don't stint the picking.

They also force quickly if brought in any time after the first of the year and placed in water in a cool dark spot until the buds begin to swell into the beloved "furries." You can utilize many other early-flowering shrubs similarly for an indoor treat ahead of season.

SAMBUCUS CANADENSIS (American elderberry): Zone 3; to 12 feet and spreading by stolons; prefers wet situation and some sun.

If you have the right spot for it, our native elderberry is worth growing just for the beauty of its large shioning. Whether we will ever make jelly from the tart red fruit, I do not know, but I am told it tastes like sour cherries; birds ought to like them. Although this is a plant mainly of the Plains states, it is recommended for seashore plantings because of its hardiness under severe conditions.

S. canadensis (russet buffaloberry) grows wild from Newfoundland to Alaska, so is equally robust. Its twigs and buds are brownish, and it lacks thorns although it has a twiggy growth habit. Fruit on this species is reputedly insipid, and its maximum height is only 8 feet. Sexes are on separate plants, so you will need several bushes to get fruit from either species.

STAPHYLEA TRIFOLIA (American bladdernut): Zone 3; to 15 feet; part shade and moist rich soil.

You'll probably have to start this unusual shrub from seed too, since it is seldom seen in cultivation. Its distinctions include bark usually striped with white and inflated seed pods as long as 3 inches which start out green but turn tan and are useful in dried arrangements. The leaves are bright green, and nodding clusters of little pale greenish-white flowers appear in April and May.

SYMPHORICARPUS ORBICULATUS (*S. vulgaris,* Indian currant, coralberry): Zone 2; to 6 feet; will grow almost anywhere.

If you have a dry bank where

Symphoricarpus comes into its own in late fall with reddish berries against yellow leaves.

erosion is a problem, the coralberry is a fine, suckering subject to hold it in place. The tiny summer flowers are inconspicuous, but the clusters of berries in fall are attractive to birds. Don't put this in the garden.

All children of my generation loved the related snowberry (*S. albus*), which has clusters of waxy white berries that make a delightful pop when stepped on or pinched in late summer. Hardy in Zone 3, it is still often seen in shrub borders where its 3-foot arching branches actually bend with the weight of

the fruit. The variety *laevigatus* is recommended for its larger fruits and may reach 10 feet in time.

VACCINIUM (blueberry): Zone 2 or 3; variable heights and preferences, but acid soil a must.

Nowadays home gardeners plant selections and hybrids of blueberries to get the best fruit, choosing several varieties for cross-fertilization and to get crops early and late. The little clusters of white or pinkish bells are quite pretty in late spring, and of course the fruit is a real dividend, while the glossy

81

green leaves turn bright colors in the fall. In sunny spots the bushes will not be as leggy as in shade. I wonder why more people do not include these in their shrubbery where the soil is suitable. If one doesn't want the fruit, more than 90 species of birds will be delighted with the menu.

It is also possible to obtain the native species for special purposes. *V. corymbosum* (highbush or swamp blueberry, to 15 feet) will also grow on drier ground and makes a good hedge. Lowbush blueberry (*V. angustifolium,* to 2 feet) is useful as a ground cover in dry soil. *V. pallidum* (dry land blueberry) is hardy into Maine and has dense clusters of berries on bushes around 3 feet high.

VIBURNUM: at least to Zone 3; variable habits but most adaptable.

If you want to attract birds to your property, the American viburnums are musts. Although perhaps not as showy in flower as some of the European and Asiatic species, our natives are noteworthy for bright berries, brilliant spring and autumn foliage, and hardiness just about anywhere in the country.

V. acerifolium (arrow-wood, dockmanie, mapleleaf viburnum) is for dry areas with light shade and acid soil. It will grow in more shadowed sites but won't bloom as well. Flowers are small and white in 3-inch clusters during May or June, and fall foliage ranges from pink to purple, setting off the blue-black berries. Maximum height is about 6 feet, and it may be pruned after flowering to prevent straggliness.

V. cassinoides (swamp viburnum, witherod) performs equally well as an understory shrub for the edges of moist woods or in low wet spots. It can reach 12 feet, has creamy-white flower clusters and red autumn leaves. Birds dote on the fruit, which is often present in all stages of maturity from yellow to red to blue-black. Selective pruning will keep the bushes thrifty, although with plenty of sun it may not be necessary.

V. prunifolium (black-haw) can grow treelike in time, perhaps reaching 25 feet, but can be kept as a twiggy large shrub, especially in partial shade. It has odd sharp spurs like many fruit trees. Both spring and fall the clean small leaves are a bold red, and planted in full sun, the twigs retain a reddish tint all year. There are clusters

Blue berries of *Viburnum prunifolium* have a silvery bloom; leaves provide red note far into fall.

of white spring flowers and bluish-black berries which remain a long time. The latter have an unpleasant odor. *V. lentago* (nannyberry) is much like it but likes a moister spot.

V. trilobum (V. americanum, highbush or American cranberry-bush) sports hanging bright-red berry clusters which last most of the winter if you do not gather them. Boiled with sugar and strained, they are said to make a jelly similar to that of real cranberries (which, incidentally are *Vaccinium macrocarpon* and require actual bogs hardly likely on home grounds).

The three-lobed leaves of this substitute have a lovely pink tinge in spring as well as good fall color, and the ribs of the leaves are red all season. It takes both sun and shade, but should have humusy soil which retains moisture for best results. Under such conditions this viburnum makes a neat rounded bush about 10 feet high. The flat clusters of white spring flowers have larger sterile blossoms around the outside much like some hydrangeas.

XANTHORHIZA SIMPLICISSIMA (*X. apilifolia,* zanthorhiza, shrub yellowroot): Zone 5; to 2 feet and spreads by stolons; shady, damp spots, but will take sun.

Another fine ground cover for moist spots, xanthorhiza is much too rampant for garden use. Neither the brownish-purple flowers nor the fruits are showy.

Glossy leaves of highbush cranberry exhibit red tints spring and fall.

83

EVERGREEN SHRUBS

America has some of the showiest broad-leaved evergreens in the world, many of them hardy in the farthest northern states. It is worth repeating, however, that where winters are severe, they should have protection from the wind. In areas without snow cover the winter sun may also burn the leaves of shade lovers, so locate them accordingly.

Almost all of these all-season stars require acid soil. Even in the eastern states where the earth is likely to be to their liking, most benefit from lots of peat moss incorporated into the soil when planting. This helps keep it moist too.

If you live in an alkaline soil area, read carefully the suggestions in Chapter 2. I can sympathize with your longing to introduce some of these beauties to your property, but how successful the attempt may be is up to your own ingenuity. It might be smartest to plant several oaks and pines first since their leaves and needles will help maintain the acidity of the soil. There are a few of these evergreens which will do all right in neutral to alkaline soil, but peat moss always helps.

Since the majority are shallow-rooted, plan to give them all a good acid mulch of woodchips. This keeps the root run cool and moist as well as making disturbing cultivation and weeding unnecessary.

ANDROMEDA POLIFOLIA (bog-rosemary): Zone 2; to 2 feet and creeping; humusy acid soil in sun or light shade.

For all intents and purposes we can consider the related *A. glaucophylla* (downy andromeda) right along with the bog-rosemary. Both are extremely hardy and useful in rock gardens despite their natural moist haunts. They will need water during dry weather, however. Both have small leathery leaves and light-pink spring flowers which are urn-shaped like so many heaths. I suppose they are more of a sub-shrub since they remain so low. There are so few evergreens that stay dwarf enough for rock-garden use that they should be much more popular than they are. You will probably be able to locate plants only through houses specializing in rockery subjects.

CEANOTHUS VOLUTINUS (snow-bush): Zone 6?; to 8 feet; dry, thin slopes.

Every gardener wants plants not hardy or indigenous to his climate. California has more than a hundred different kinds of ceanothus, most of them far too tender for my Pennsylvania garden, but this one is worth trying, so I include it here in case you too like challenge. It grows wild to 8,500 feet in the Rockies, which is one reason I think it might take our winters if given a very well-drained site. The leaves are shiny on top and downy underneath, and the flowers white. Seed is available from western sources, who recommend pouring boiling water on it and leaving it to soak for 24 hours before sowing in sandy soil. I have a spot all picked out for it where it will have some wind protection, but can give no further pointers yet.

CHAMAEDAPHNE CALYCULATA (leatherleaf): Zone 2: to 4 feet; damp peaty soil in shade.

Here is another very hardy evergreen of the heath family. The dull-green leaves are rusty underneath, and the small white urns are borne at the tips of the branches. It is a straggly bush, best kept for half-wild areas or rugged terrain.

CYRILLA RACEMIFLORA (southern leatherwood): Zone 6*; to 30 feet; moist peaty soil in light shade.

In northern states cyrilla will remain a shrub under 6 feet and may lose its leaves during the winter. Racemes of small white flowers in June and July are showy against the bright-green leaves. Bark is grayish. Since it is slow-growing, it can be used where a larger shrub would soon be out of bounds. Flowering is on the current year's growth, so it can be pruned in early spring to prevent its becoming straggly without sacrificing bloom, and moderate winter dieback will do no harm.

GAYLUSSACIA BRACHYCERA (box huckleberry): Zone 5; 6 to 18

---

* Probably will need some protection within the zone.

inches; acid leafmold in sun or shade.

Too choice and expensive for anything except a special spot, box huckleberry makes a superb slow-growing ground cover, spreading by underground runners. Its inch-long leaves have a reddish cast most of the year when grown in sun. Small flowers are pink or white in short racemes. The most famous stand is located in Pennsylvania. Thought to be a single plant many thousands of years old, it extends for more than a mile.

ILEX GLABRA (inkberry): Zone 3*; to 8 feet and spreads by stolons; wet acid soil in shade but takes drier spots.

The severity of the winter will determine whether inkberry remains evergreen or not. While its leaves are smaller and less interestingly shaped than those of traditional holly, its hardiness recommends it to gardeners in climates too severe for the others. Often used for hedges, it can be utilized as a screen to protect less robust hollies from the winter wind. Because this is one holly which has flowers of both sexes on each plant, there is generous production of the black berries, which are sought out by birds in late winter. Dwarf forms are sometimes offered.

KALMIA LATIFOLIA (mountain-

* Probably will need some protection within the zone.

laurel, calico-bush): Zone 3*, to 36 feet but usually around 10; acid soil which does not dry out too much, blooms best with some sun.

There is no time of year when mountain-laurel is not a beautiful addition to any property where the soil is acid enough to support it. It is outstanding in May and June, when it displays clusters of delicate white to pink flowers, but I treasure it almost more for its winter effect. The glossy leaves do not noticeably droop even with bitter cold, and they have red stems. Emerging from the snow as I shovel past them, the sight is incredibly heartening.

Each Christmas I cut a few small branches for the house. Kept in water, they retain their gloss for many weeks, a far more lovely effect than those dead-looking laurel ropes for which the southern mountains are denuded each year. My selective pruning seems to encourage extra branching. Older specimens of *K. latifolia* sometimes exhibit an almost picturesque silhouette.

Mountain-laurel will tolerate quite moist locations but does just as well on slopes if the soil has plenty of humus and does not dry out too much. I have some in almost full sun, and bloom literally covers them, but the bush will grow even into quite deep shade. Under the latter conditions flowers are scarcer and growth somewhat lanky. Don't put it in a badly windswept spot.

Always buy kalmia bagged and

balled in the spring and try not to choose clumps with thick old sawn stumps, since these will have been collected from the wild and may lack a decent feeder-root system for a good start in your garden.

You can use the dwarfer *K. angustifolia* (lamb-kill or sheep-laurel) right in the garden without worrying about its growing too big. Hardy at least to Zone 2, it seldom tops 3 feet and produces good bloom even in lots of shade. Its flowers tend to be much redder than regular laurel but otherwise are quite similar. The branches are more ascending and perhaps stay more delicate-looking.

LEDUM GROENLANDICUM (Labrador-tea): Zone 2; to 3 feet; cold peaty soil.

Although I have no personal experience with Labrador-tea, I include it here for gardeners in far northern states where hardy broad-leaved evergreens are few. You could try it farther south if you have a low, cold spot with acid soil, but it is not recommended and usually suffers badly from red spider. It produces small clusters of white flowers in May and June and often grows as wide as high in favorable locations. The narrow leaves have rusty, woolly undersides.

LEIOPHYLLUM BUXIFOLIUM (sand-myrtle): Zone 5*; to 3 feet; peaty sandy soil in sun or semi-shade.

Here is another good sub-shrub for the acid garden which is equally at home in front of larger broad-leaves as a kind of facer or in the rock garden. The leaves are box-like and clusters of white or pinkish flowers come in May and June. Judicious tip pruning will keep it thrifty, but the related *L. lyoni* (often cataloged as *L. buxifolium prostratum*) from the southern Alleghenies is an even better ground cover since it seldom tops a foot.

LEUCOTHOE CATESBAEI (drooping leucothoe, fetterbush): Zone 4; to 6 feet but usually lower; moist, well-drained peaty soil in shade.

The drooping racemes of waxy white bells the leucothoe displays in early spring are reason enough to treasure it, but the foliage is alluring at all seasons. The leathery leaves turn bronzy in fall and often have hints of color at other times. Easily layered, it should be encouraged to form small colonies in shady acid locations. It is a fine choice for planting in front of leggier broadleaves.

Winter wind is an enemy, so give it a protected spot. Branches damaged by severe winters may be cut back, even to the ground, and new growth will give the bush an even fuller look.

There are dwarf forms available, but the variety Rainbow is my favorite. Its leaves are variegated, showing cream and yellow streaking. Most striking is the new growth, a bright red which looks almost like a poinsettia at a distance. Hardy only into Zone 6, it

deserves the best spot you have—out of the wind and protected from the afternoon winter sun.

L. axillaris (coast leucothoe) is much like *L. catesbaei* but less hardy and reputedly does not have as good autumn color. *L. racemosa* (sweetbells) is a deciduous relative which may reach 12 feet and is hardy in Zone 5. It prefers moist places and has more erect flower clusters. Its autumn leaves are scarlet but fall with frost.

MAHONIA AQUIFOLIUM (Oregon grape-holly): Zone 4*; to 6 feet; tolerant of soil but must not suffer from drought and needs shade at all seasons as well as wind protection.

Tired of hearing about acid-loving plants? Here's a welcome respite. Native to the Pacific northwest, mahonias provide bright-yellow clusters of flowers in April or May followed by bunches of grape-like, blue-black berries. But their main attraction is the dark-green holly-like evergreen foliage.

Pruning just makes them thicker, so you can use all the foliage you wish for indoor arrangements. Come spring there may be some scorching of the leaves, and this should be quickly trimmed out too.

I am told that in its native state mahonia often grows in the sun, but our eastern weather is far harder on evergreens than the mild climate of Oregon's coastland. So I warn you that here we must place

* Probably will need some protection within the zone.

them carefully. One of the most magnificent I've ever seen grew in the east-facing ell of a house. Protected on the south from the sun and on the north from the worst winter wind, it completely filled the area with healthy green.

Since mahonias tend to spread by stolons, give them plenty of room to expand. Where it will not interfere with other things, *M. repens* is a useful ground cover, quickly taking over large areas with foliage that averages a foot high.

MYRICA PENSYLVANICA (*M. caroliniensis,* northern bayberry): Zone 1; to 10 feet and nearly as wide; poor, sandy, dry, acid soil in sun.

If you need landscaping at the seashore or have a windswept barren spot, bayberry will serve you well. Under severest conditions the leaves will hang late and then drop, but the plants will not mind this. In my windbreak they are evergreen but tend to curl on bitter days. Gray berries are borne in clusters along the wandlike branches; they are used to scent soap and candles. They are lovely for winter bouquets but leave some outside for the first hungry migrating birds of spring.

This is another of the shrubs with male and female flowers on separate plants. Since it looks best grown in large masses, it is just as easy to plant the male right alongside the females. It makes me angry that many nurseries will not specify sex when offering it for sale, for bayberry produces lots of root

Young bayberry already displays its proclivity to spread.

suckers, and they could just as easily label them.

One way to solve this is to find someone with old bayberries. They will probably welcome your helping them keep them in bounds by removing some of the outside suckers, but make sure you get some roots and pot in peat until each takes hold. Even in early spring a few berries should remain to help in identification. The bush without any berries should be a male, and you will want only one of those. I have had many people complain that their bayberries produce no fruit;

it's not their hardiness that is lacking but one sex or the other.

M. cerifera (southern bayberry) is hardy only to Zone 6 and likes moisture, peaty soil. *M. californica* reaches 35 feet in mild climates but is not recommended for the North either.

PACHISTIMA CANBYI: Zone 4*; to 12 inches; moist, well-drained soil in semi-shade.

Unless you're sharp-eyed, you'll never even notice the tiny greenish

* Probably will need some protection within the zone.

or reddish spring flowers of pachistima. The clean little leaves, which often have bronzy tones, are its main attraction. It layers well and roots easily from cuttings, so it is simple to have it in quantity as a neat ground cover. I have rooted and grown it in definitely acid soil successfully, but a good authority tells me it does best in limy situations. Bailey says, "any well-drained soil." *P. myrsinites* from the west has slightly prettier, larger leaves and grows twice as high in time. I doubt it to be hardy past Zone 6.

PIERIS FLORIBUNDA (andromeda, lily-of-the-valley-bush, mountain pieris or fetterbush): Zone 4; to 6 feet; humusy acid soil, part shade.

I suppose the clusters of faintly fragrant white urn-shaped flowers in April and May represent the high point of our native pieris, but I find myself attracted most by their winter buds, which are prominently displayed and usually have a pinkish tinge. At all times the glossy foliage is a joy, perhaps no time more than in late spring when the new tip leaves are often bright red.

Considerably hardier than its more popular Japanese counterpart, it also tends to hold its flowers more erect so they are just that much showier. It is simply one of our best native evergreens for shady spots. It benefits from some wind protection too. And do remember that it is a shrub with a naturally arching, spreading growth

Like most of its family, *Rhododendron maximum* develops flower buds the previous summer; don't let it suffer from drought.

habit. It needs adequate room to look most beautiful, so don't jam it between other burgeoning things. It can be one of the most graceful of all bushes.

RHODODENDRON MAXIMUM (rosebay): Zone 3*; to 35 feet; acid, well-drained soil with plenty of humus and shade.

In your garden rosebay will probably seldom top 12 feet and that after years of slow growing. Future growth is often treelike, however,

* Probably will need some protection within the zone.

so give it plenty of room to expand. Its remarkable hardiness endears it to far northerners.

There is much variation in color of the big trusses of bell-shaped flowers, so that if you can, get one locally when you see it in bloom. Blossoms range from white to rose and are spotted green or orange. Part of the charm of this rhododendron is that it blooms in late June so you must make doubly sure it does not suffer from lack of water that first summer after such late planting. Some understanding nurserymen will allow you to inspect

bushes in the growing rows and save the one you mark for the next early spring, but there is usually a charge for such extra service.

The same admonitions given earlier for azaleas (deciduous rhododendrons) should be carefully reviewed if you are not familiar with the family. They will not grow everywhere without extra trouble.

Much shrubbier than rosebay is *R. carolinianum,* which is hardy into part of Zone 4, reaches 6 feet, and blooms in mid-May. It grows naturally into compact round bushes, but color may range from pure white through pink to a rather sickly rose. In the wild it is found on exposed windswept balds. *R. catawbiense,* equally hardy, is a little later to bloom and can reach 20 feet, though usually staying around 6. Its magenta hue I find hard to make comfortable in my limited garden.

Some remarkably hardy hybrids have been developed from these Americans. Some are cataloged as Waterer hybrids. Three that are popular and easy to find are America, with dark red flowers and an open growth habit; Catawbiense Album, with white blooms; and Purpureum Elegans, which is lilac-purple.

VACCINIUM OVATUM (evergreen huckleberry): Zone ?; to 12 feet; peaty soil in part shade.

Everyone knows this Pacific Coast shrub, for every florist uses the waxy-leaved branches as foliage. In a recent year I rooted some from a Christmas-present bouquet. The little plants even produced a few pinky flowers before succumbing to fall drought during a period when I had to neglect my garden. So I have planted several plants from an Ohio nursery, hoping they are a hardy strain. They are in a protected spot, and we shall see. Their new growth is bronzy for a pretty effect.

V. vitis-idaea minus (mountain-cowberry) has no qualms about the cold, being hardy in Zone 2; it is found even on the top of New Hampshire's Mt. Washington. It is really a ground cover, seldom growing more than 3 inches high, with tiny, shining green leaves, big bunches of pink spring flowers, and equally showy red fall berries. A darling that makes dense mats and ideal for under acid-soil shrubs.

ZENOBIA PULVERULENTA (dusty zenobia): Zone 5*; to 6 feet but usually smaller; sandy acid soil in shade.

At the very end of the alphabet, another fine native for the acid garden. Zenobia has grayish leaves which set off the lovely racemes of waxy white fragrant flowers in late spring. In the northern end of its range, it may lose its leaves, so give wind protection. Although hard to locate, it is well worth your trouble. Put it in front of leggy azaleas for a lovely contrast.

* Probably will need some protection within the zone.

7 BELOVED PERENNIAL AMERICANS

Many of the most cherished Americans are in this chapter. Anyone whose childhood memories do not include a favorite wildflower is poor indeed. It is a sad commentary on city and park planning that modern schoolyards and playgrounds are more likely to be surfaced in unyielding, sterile asphalt than in life-producing earth. City children would be happier and healthier if they could climb apple trees instead of jungle gyms and learn about bees by being stung. How can they possibly understand or appreciate this glorious universe when they can't even blow dandelion seeds into the wind, much less wonder over the beauty of a columbine?

But we are concerned with growing wildflowers—for whatever reason. And the one cardinal rule cannot be ignored with impunity: match the plant to the site. To grow wildflowers that are truly perennial you must give them the conditions they have come to need through many generations of natural selection.

Many will live long after the planter is gone. Those which are short-lived will set seed which in turn will germinate and mature into flowering plants if moisture, sun, climate, and soil are to their liking. In Chapter 2 is much detail on manipulation of available sites. We will not repeat it here except to stress that most difficulty in raising wildflowers in cultivation is the gardener's failure to recognize that many species have narrow limits of adaptibility.

For convenience the plants of this chapter have been divided into three sections: those which prefer at least some shade, those which must have considerable sun, and those which demand a moist home. Within each division, alphabetically by Latin names, are those plants recommended for that type of garden. Some may be interchanged, and I have tried to indicate in any individual description what such possibilities may be.

You ought to be warned not to be too kind to these wildlings. If they are planted in the right place with the correct environment, most will not benefit from fertilizing. With such encouragement, a graceful plant used to a thin diet may become a fat, blowzy caricature. Like the obese human it may well die long before its time. Most of these plants survived well without any help from man. It was only when *Homo sapiens* upset the natural environment and obliterated their habitats that the plants ran into trouble.

Within any one type of garden there are other factors which may be critical for a particular plant, such as soil makeup and acidity, drainage, or extremes of temperature or wind exposure. I have tried to note which of these are important for any one plant. If no such information is supplied about a plant, you may assume it will grow under normal conditions for its section. I realize it is arbitrary to divide all the perennials into only three main groups, but I have gardened long enough to learn that variations of sun, shade, and moisture make the main differences between gardens and what they can support.

I can only guess how hardy many of these perennials may be. They have not yet had enough trial in gardens all over the country. If you live where there are extremes of temperature or moisture, check again in Chapter 2 on how to overcome them.

Many of these wildflowers are available as plants from one of the houses specializing in native material. Do try to raise some from seeds yourself. Almost always plants so grown are healthier than those forced to undergo a long journey. Nor will your own seedlings have to acclimatize themselves to a new home. What's even more fun, when you raise wildflowers from seed, there is always a good chance of a sport appearing.

Unless otherwise described, these perennials need a full year of growing after germination of seed before they begin producing blossoms. Many develop into fine clumps with many sprouts after a few years. Removal of old heads before seed is formed often lengthens the flowering period and sometimes adds years to the span of a short-lived species.

THE SHADY GARDEN

To most easterners at least, "wildflower" means one of the lovelies described in this section, treasures of the retreating woodlands. Except for those which demand a very acid soil, they are also among the most rewarding to bring into ordinary home grounds. Actually it is quite easy to domesticate a few of them, for every property has at least a little patch of shade where you can tuck a favorite or two; many tend to take care of themselves.

My sandy bank where the asclepias and evening primroses keep company is equally a wildflower garden, but many neater gardeners do not care for the somewhat unkempt air of such a planting. Others do not want the constant upkeep associated with a formal border. Well mulched in humusy soil, the plants of the woodland do not need the constant attention of these sunny gardens. Much of the glory of a shady nook occurs in spring; summer's shade discourages rampant sun-loving weeds in such a spot. A few ferns to fill in the gaps left by those natives which wither away by early summer make the shady garden a delightful treat for the eye even in August.

Chapter 2 has suggestions on gardening in the shade, but it is worth stressing again that soil rich in humus is a must for most of these plants. Unless otherwise noted, most require neutral to moderately acid soil. Peat moss in generous quantities is the easiest and cheapest way to get a soil of the right consistency. Wood chips and composted or even dried and chopped leaves make the best mulches. They keep down weeds and unwanted volunteer plants and allow entrance of rainwater; but more importantly they hasten development of a porous duff like that of a real forest floor. This aids growth of helpful bacteria, adds nourishment to the soil, and keeps the roots of the plants cool in summer and insulated from the worst of winter's cold.

Let the leaves of autumn lie naturally on this garden so that each year a bit more humus is added to the top layer, and replace the original mulch as needed each spring. Most of these plants do not have deep roots, so that if the top foot or so of the soil is in proper tilth, you should be able to estab-

Fast-growing gray birch (*Betula populifolia*) may be short-lived but is ideal for new gardens.

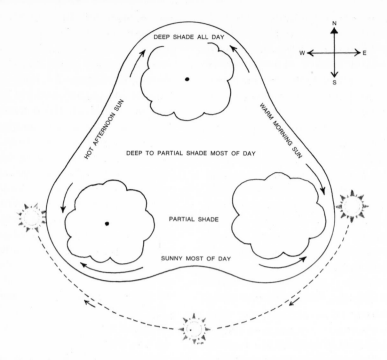

DEEP SHADE ALL DAY

DEEP TO PARTIAL SHADE MOST OF DAY

PARTIAL SHADE

SUNNY MOST OF DAY

HOT AFTERNOON SUN

WARM MORNING SUN

Fig. 12: Only three trees planted in a triangle create a pocket woodland with several varying shade zones.

lish good colonies of woodland plants. If satisfied, they will increase themselves either through seeding or stoloniferous roots. When this happens, you know you have been successful.

As pointed out too in Chapter 2, shade is where you find it. Every tree and bush, every building, even every large boulder, has a shady side. If, however, you are establishing a woodland garden from scratch or utilizing one or two trees already in place, the sun chart (Fig. 12) shows an ingenious way to provide the maximum spectrum of exposure so you can grow a number of some-

what different kinds of shady plants.

The chart illustrates only sun and shade exposure on flat land. If your topography is sloping, you should remember that it is always drier on the high side. Only a few plants can compete with the tree near the trunk, where it will be quite dry both from the tree's feeder roots and the umbrella effect of thick foliage during a rain.

Use American trees if you can for the shady skeleton of such a garden. Maples or other trees with voracious surface roots are a poor choice. I have made several such gardens with dogwoods, for their

natural horizontal branch growth casts a great deal of summer shade once the trees have been growing a few years. There is no reason why you can't mix your trees so as to have a dogwood for spring bloom, an oxydendrum or franklinia for summer blossoms, or a sweetgum for autumn color. Keep in mind the individual tree's requirements and growth habits too. For example, an oxydendrum has a narrow growth pattern, and a dogwood can prosper in some shade so is a good choice for the specimen on the north side of the garden. So is an evergreen, which also acts as a background to show off the beauty of the flowering trees.

Of course the woodland can be a great deal larger and contain many more trees if you have space and time. But no garden I have ever made has brought me pleasure and satisfaction to compare with these triangular pocket woodlands.

Before we get down to specifics it is also worth noting that there are many kinds of shade. Few green plants will grow in the deep, all-day dark of an evergreen grove. Many early spring-flowering plants, however, will do well under deciduous trees since they do their serious growing before the trees leaf out. If your trees have the lower branches trimmed out so that light gets in or if they are giants which form a canopy high overhead, there is lots of light even though little direct sun. This is just what later-blooming shady plants want.

92

Partial shade suits a great many species, but there is a real temperature difference between morning and afternoon sun. So plants which normally live north of your area are better on the easterly sides of a tree, while those from farther south are more apt to prosper on the western side where the four p.m. temperature in July is fierce even in light shade.

One more phenomenon bears mention. The farther north in the northern hemisphere you live, the more the sun is apt to be in the southern half of the sky. Thus the southern side of a shady garden far north gets considerably more sun at midday than it does in southerly states where the summer noontime sun is nearly directly overhead. Here at Philadelphia the southern

edge of a shady garden gets lots of midday sun in spring and fall, even when the leaves are out, but is partially shaded at noon in midsummer because the sun is higher in the sky. This quirk made life very hard for some summer-flowering things in my shady garden until I caught on and moved them outward.

ACTAEA ALBA (A. pachypoda, doll's-eyes, white baneberry): summer stalks of odd white berries, each with a purply dot at the tip, are more decorative than the small white spring flowers. A. rubra (red baneberry) has less showy red fruits. Both take deep summer shade.

AQUILEGIA CANADENSIS (eastern

wild columbine): this red-and-yellow species is listed first only because of my background. There are at least a dozen fine natives from Alaska to Texas. All lend an airy note to the garden and are beloved by hummingbirds. None transplants well except as small seedlings but all are easily started from seed.

Many gardeners complain because the dainty foliage of columbine discolors or is badly disfigured by leaf miners. From my observations such problems are much worse where the plants get either too much or too little sun. They thrive best where there is good sun in the morning but shade in the hotter part of the day.

A. canadensis is an early bloomer, often starting in April, wants only light shade in well-

White flowers are particularly showy in the shadowed woodland planting.

Aquilegia longissima typifies the long-spurred form of many American columbines.

drained soil, and will take full sun in northern gardens. It is very hardy, flourishes in rock gardens, seldom gets taller than 30 inches.

A. caerulea (Rocky Mountain columbine) has slightly fatter, long-spurred flowers in blue and white, may go to 3 feet. It also has varieties in pure white, yellow, and red shades, has been much used in hybridizing. Give it afternoon shade. *A. chrysantha* is a fine yellow, often 4 feet tall. *A. longissima* is from Texas and New Mexico, but proved hardy in my garden. It has very long-spurred yellow flowers, blooms later and longer than the others, sometimes even into August. It does not seem to mind full sun in the north.

A. jonesi is a curiosity from Montana and Wyoming only a few inches high with small blue flowers in early spring. Rock gardeners dote upon it, but find it hard to domesticate. Walter A. Kolaga in *All About Rock Gardens and Plants* suggests "a very deep gravelly root run, with an acid peaty soil, in sun or part shade . . . ample moisture in spring but thoroughly dry in summer." He terms *A. saximontana,* an equally diminutive blue-and-yellow species from Utah, much easier and recommends "gritty, well-drained lime soil in full sun or very light shade."

ASARUM CANADENSE (wild ginger): this whole family makes super-

lative ground covers in humusy soil and nearly full shade. The flowers of all species are curious purply-brown things that hug the ground in early spring; if you don't look carefully, you'll never notice them, but the big heart-shaped leaves are the main attraction. The eastern species is deciduous and spreads quickly by underground roots if the soil is damp and rich enough.

Two southern species are more or less evergreen in the north and quite hardy since they come from the mountains. Their smaller leaves are shiny, often mottled with whitish markings. Most are heart-shaped, but I have one with almost arrow-like leaves. One way you can tell *A. shuttleworthi* from *A. virginicum* is by its flowers, queer purply jugs which are considerably larger. To encourage their remaining green all winter in the north, protect from both sun and wind. Both are increasing well in my garden.

ASTER CORDIFOLIUS (blue wood or heart-leaved aster): since late-summer flowers are scarce in the woodland, this one earns a place even though it is hardly a spectacular species. It yields sprays of many pale-blue flowers on 2-to-4-foot stems in August and September and wants light shade. Watch that you don't put it where there are small choice things, since it is a root spreader. The big basal leaves are decorative even before bloom starts.

CHIMAPHILA MACULATA (striped

or mottled pipsissawa, spotted wintergreen, prince's-pine): often a feature of a Christmas terrarium, this rarity from the cool, dry eastern woods has dainty white, waxen flowers in July, about 10 inches high. They have a slight fragrance. It never produces enough of its evergreen white-veined leaves to qualify as a ground cover, but it is a lovely addition to a shady, quite acid garden. I have successfully planted terrarium specimens which had rooted by early summer. Use lots of peat moss. *C. umbellata cisatlantica* lacks the leaf mottling so is not nearly as pretty. Either is much easier than the related *Pyrola elliptica* (thin-leaf pyrolla), which I don't recommend for any garden except one naturally very acid.

CHRYSOGONUM VIRGINIANUM (golden-star): a big patch of this happy yellow daisy may yield some flowers from April to October. They average about 2 inches across, may reach a foot above the hairy basal leaves. It is found in moist humusy soil from Pennsylvania south. We find it blooms better and longer with some morning sun, then high shade the rest of the day. North of here I would give it more sun and the protection of a large rock to the north.

CIMICIFUGA AMERICANA (bugbane, fairy-candles): to give a lift to the partly shaded garden in late summer this species displays spikes of little white flowers from 3 to 5 feet tall. *C. racemosa* (black cohosh, black snakeroot) blooms earlier, can reach 8 feet, has ill-scented blossoms, but may be a bit hardier. Both want deep rich soil on the acid side and must have adequate moisture during the summer. The compound leaves are attractive if, like mine, yours refuses to flower.

CORNUS CANADENSIS (bunchberry): where the summer is not too hot and soil is very acid, moist, and full of humus, this tiny cousin of the dogwood tree is an exquisite ground cover for shade. The small white dogwood-like blooms of spring are followed by a cluster of red berries, both set off to perfection by a single whorl of clean leaves just below. Only a few inches high, it spreads by creeping stems where it is contented. Even in full shade it is hard to achieve this south of New York except in mountainous regions.

CYPRIPEDIUM (slipper orchids): many crimes have been perpetrated on the orchid family in the name of gardening. Whatever you do, don't try to transplant any from the woods. Don't ever pick any either. Should you be lucky enough to discover a group in some secluded hideaway, enjoy their beauty, then tiptoe away and leave them, hoping no one more rapacious will follow.

Striped pipsissawa is a darling in bloom as well as pretty for terrariums.

95

None of the orchids is easy to cultivate no matter what anyone tells you. But people and even dealers keep ripping them from their natural haunts to try. The American terrestrial orchids were never really plentiful. Their wants are so specialized, their enemies so many, and their reproduction so chancy that the minute the first Pilgrim picked one, the family started downhill.

I shall not even list most of them, for they are denizens of cool, peaty bogs, and trying to accommodate them in the home garden is usually their death sentence. I list *Spiranthes* and *habenaria* in the moist-plant section, but only with crossed fingers and a prayer you won't try them unless you're really serious. For best results buy plants when they are dormant either in fall or earliest spring. Sprinkle slug bait nearby as a preventive measure.

Of them all the slipper orchids with their showy pouch-flowers and fine green foliage are probably the easiest—as long as their wants are met and mice, slugs, or rot don't carry them off.

Start out with the yellow slipper orchid, which often will make itself at home in gardens. It may be cataloged either as a variety of *C. calceolus* or as a separate species. Many authorities consider there are two different American types; having seen them growing together, I agree with this latter and so treat them here.

C. pubescens bears large yellow pouches on stems as high as 2 feet in late spring and wants moist, neutral to slightly acid soil with lots of humus and light shade all day. *C. parviflorum* is much similar, but the flowers are smaller and fragrant, stems are seldom over a foot high, and it is much harder to cultivate since it prefers cool weather and damper situations. Many dealers do not differentiate, so if you live south of New York City, order from a southern house which is most likely to have *C. pubescens.*

Open such an order immediately and plant the orchids temporarily in pots if need be, for they are very subject to rot. If satisfied, they will slowly increase into a breathtaking group by root growth.

Though very rare in the wild any more and hard to locate commercially, the midwestern *C. candidum* (white lady-slipper, silver slipper orchid) often does well in certain gardens. It must have lime soil, will take some sun, and grows about a foot high. *C. reginae* (showy lady-slipper) has pink and white pouches about 18 inches high, wants cool moist neutral to slightly acid soil and light shade all day. It must never suffer for lack of water.

C. acaule (pink moccasin flower), though offered by many sources, is not for most gardens. Unless you have rich, humusy soil that is strongly acid, don't aid and abet in its further destruction by ordering any. *C. arietum* (ram's head lady-slipper) from the cold northern acid swamps should not even be attempted by anyone living in a mild climate, and isn't very decorative anyway.

Though out of alphabetical order, *Orchis spectabilis* (showy orchis) horticulturally belongs here too. I have never dared try it, but some experts tell me it will take about the same conditions as the yellow slipper orchid. Richer, moister, more alkaline soil is suggested by others. It produces several small white and purple flowers on a thick stalk less than a foot high in early May hereabouts, and has lovely dark green basal leaves.

DELPHINIUM TRICORNE (wild larkspur): in light shade during May this dark-blue easterner is quite showy although there are only a few flowers on its 12-inch spike. Its

Delphinium tricorne brings deep blue to the early spring woods.

tuberous root likes well-drained soil. Since the laciniated leaves disappear soon after blooming, mark well to avoid disturbance. It contrasts well with white crested iris. Of the interesting western species, I have tried only two red-flowered Californians, *D. cardinale* and *D. nudicaule,* and apparently have failed with both. Germination was good, but the plants died soon after transplanting to a well-drained, sunny slope. I marked the spot in case they have the disappearing habit of their eastern cousin; another spring will tell.

DICENTRA EXIMIA (fringed or plumy bleedingheart): if you grow only one wildflower in your shady garden, make it this one. Its foot-high racemes of dainty, pinkish-lavender, heart-shaped flowers in my garden begin blooming with the daffodils of early spring and continue until hard frost around Halloween. Delicate foliage is bluish-green.

The secret is to give the plants humus-rich soil and exactly the right amount of sun. Too much hot sunshine, and they sulk during the summer; too little, and they seldom bloom after the spring burst. In a copse of trees with the branches trimmed high, plant this dicentra on the eastern side, and it should do beautifully. I have already mentioned the plant here due north of the pedestal of my birdbath. Brought as a start from the old garden, it had no other shade avail-

From April to October *Dicentra eximia* produces her pink hearts in the half-shady garden.

able. The cylinder is about 6 inches across, while the bath itself offers additional protection only at midday. It is blooming well and increasing by basal growth. As soon as the little dogwoods nearby cast more shade, I expect it to begin to seed itself into a great mass of beauty as its antecedents did in another similar garden. One friend tells me it does not do well in her alkaline soil.

D. formosa from the West Coast is somewhat similar, but has the added distinction of a white form,

Sweetheart, which is widely available. Much-advertised Bountiful is said to be a hybrid between *D. eximia* and *D. oregana,* has all-season flowers in bright fuchsia-red. This latter is suggested for full sun, but I suspect it will bloom more freely during the summer with some shade, at least in warmer climates.

D. cucullaria (Dutchman's-breeches) and *D. canadensis* (squirrel-corn) have charming, basically white flowers in early spring, want rich, well-drained soil on slopes in light shade. Both have tuberous roots attractive to mice, and both go dormant soon after flowering. The latter prefers neutral soil.

DODECATHEON MEADIA (shooting-star): a very showy spring decoration for the shady rock garden, this species has a small foot-high umbel of pink to white hanging flowers with petals so reflexed they appear like tiny rockets. Its sister, *D. amethystinum* (jeweled shooting-star), is much smaller and blooms earlier, with deep purply-pink flowers. Though it takes several years before they are old enough to bloom, both are easily raised from seed. They prefer neutral soil. Mark well since the basal foliage disappears during the summer. There are several other species, mostly from the west, with flowers from wine-red to white. Any you can obtain are gems for the garden.

DRYAS OCTOPETALA (alpine avens): this is one of the few true alpines included in this book. Most of them are impossible for gardens except in the far north or in mountainous regions without summer heat waves. This one makes an evergreen mat with white flowers any time from May to September, and here at Philadelphia I have been able to keep a plant happy enough so that it is increasing, although yet to flower. Because it likes limestone soil, I put it near the foundation on the north side of the house. There prevailing wind will

help keep it cool, and shade from a nearby evergreen prevents sunburn any time. Moreover there are rocks to give it a cool root run, and I shoot the hose that way whenever I'm near. All of which trouble is why I don't recommend alpines for ordinary gardeners.

EPIGAEA REPENS (trailing arbutus): I sometimes wonder at all the fuss made about this state flower of Massachusetts. Yes, the little pinky-white flowers are deliciously fragrant. Here it blooms in early April, and no doubt anything so ethereal would be like a touch of Heaven after a New England winter. But even in suitable gardens, increase is slow, and the evergreen foliage looks ratty much of the time. Among wildflower enthusiasts it is a kind of status symbol, and I suppose some of my lack of enthusiasm could be sour grapes because I have not yet any spot where it will live.

Nor do I intend to plant another piece until I have very acid soil that tests at least pH 4.5 over a whole season first. I'm not compounding my sins until that some day comes. I pray you do not either, for this little plant which once grew plentifully in the eastern woodlands from Canada to Florida has had a hard enough time. In my mother's time it was ripped rapaciously every spring from its hilly homes and sold to make ephemeral bouquets to decorate the clothes of nostalgic city-dwellers. The few stands left

are likely to be equally desecrated by thoughtless dealers in wild plants, and all for naught in most gardens.

Luckily, it roots quite quickly from cuttings so that public-spirited dealers can raise it themselves, and these plants are the only ones worth using. At that they are better kept growing a year or two in a big terrarium before you set them out in shaded ground that must be strongly acid and never subject to any limy reaction from foundations, city water, or higher ground.

EUPATORIUM RUGOSUM (*E. urticaefolium,* white snakeroot): as autumn threatens, the generous heads of these tiny white flowers light up shady spots all along the eastern half of the country. I have used this 2-to-3-foot species for years to face down the trunks of dogwood trees in woodland gardens. They will bloom in spite of heavy shade and are one of the few flowers which can compete successfully that close to the tree. This species is the prettiest of several similar ones, makes fine contrast with bright fall foliage, and is lovely as a filler in bouquets of stiff zinnias. It will sow much seed, but it is easily weeded out in the spring before the plants get good roots; you can make this job easier by picking off the old flower heads beforehand.

GALAX APHYLLA: where the soil is acid and humusy in light or full shade, this southerner will provide a beautiful ground cover well into the northern states. Its toothed, round leaves are evergreen, show tints of bronze much of the year, and are picked extensively for use by florists. Galax spreads by creeping roots and makes a thick mat of foliage never more than a few inches high. Spikes of tiny white flowers often reach 18 inches, usually in May. Make sure the location is well-drained and mulch well with wood chips to encourage increase.

GAULTHERIA PROCUMBENS (checkerberry, teaberry, wintergreen): another fine evergreen cover for quite acid soil and considerable shade. This one bears little white urn-shaped summer flowers and red berries. Use lots of peat moss when planting, then press side branches down, and they will layer to make a good patch about 5 inches high. An excellent companion for azaleas and other heaths. There are several western species, the most famous of which is *G. shallon* (salal). It may reach 2 feet, has purply-black berries, and is found from Alaska to California.

GERANIUM MACULATUM (wild or wood geranium): in light shade the pinky-lavender flowers above the finely-cut palmate leaves are a good choice for April-May color almost anywhere. It prefers humusy soil, transplants easily, and seeds itself. Large colonies are especially attractive. There is much variation in

color and flower size in the wild, and there is a rare white form.

GILLENIA TRIFOLIATA (Bowman's-root, Indian physic): while these white or pink-tinged flowers are nothing spectacular, they come at a time in late May when most gardens need a lift at the end of the spring show. Almost any good soil is suitable, and the shade may be partial. Foliage is bushy, may reach 4 feet in time, remains good until fall, when it colors up bronze.

GOODYERA PUBESCENS (downy rattlesnake-plantain): despite its name, this is really an orchid and easier than most of its family because it prefers the shade of dry woods. Pines or oaks are ideal since they help maintain the acid soil it must have. Narrow cylinders of tiny white blooms on stalks a foot high occur in summer but are never prolific. The nickname arises from the grayish-green basal leaves which have prominent white veins. Because of their attractiveness, it is often an ingredient of winter terrariums. If such plants are carefully removed in late spring and planted in pots of nearly pure peat, they will often be ready to transplant by late summer. Until well established, however, give them light, frequent waterings in hot weather, and mulch well with pine needles if you can.

HEPATICA ACUTILOBA (sharp-leaved liverleaf): one of the pleas-

ures of an eastern childhood used to be the finding of the first hepatica of spring, which meant the winter had broken. The three-lobed leaves are evergreen, and the buds furry as if to protect themselves from the cold. When they open, the many small flowers may be white, pink, blue, or lilac. This species is the better choice for many gardens because it prefers neutral soil on a well-drained slope beneath deciduous trees. *H. americana* has round rather than pointed leaf lobes; it must have acid soil.

HEUCHERA AMERICANA (alum-root): perfect for rocky, dry spots in shade or part sun, the evergreen leaves of this eastern counterpart of the western coralbell are its main attraction. Each plant makes a big rosette of lobed leaves which turn bronzy in winter. Tiny greenish-white or purply flowers on thin 2-foot stems are a bonus in June. Use lots of peat when planting since it prefers acid soil, but keep well-drained.

JEFFERSONIA DIPHYLLA (twinleaf): while the small white spring flowers which resemble a bloodroot's last only a day, this plant is recommended for anyone with a semi-shaded garden. Its oddly divided leaves look like green butterflies, and the juglike seed pod which is held above them never fails to cause comment. It likes rich moist soil, seems equally happy in neutral or slightly acid soil.

99

LINNAEA BOREALIS var. AMERI-CANA (twinflower): all around the northerly latitudes we find this little evergreen trailer named after the great Swedish botanist. Unfortunately it is not suitable for any but cool climates where it wants very acid, humusy, moist soil. The pairs of tiny fragrant pink bells are borne on the branch tips a few inches high and produce yellow fruits. Included here more as a sentimental salute to Linnaeus than as a suggestion for gardens except in cool mountains.

MAIANTHEMUM CANADENSE (false lily-of-the-valley, heartleaf-lily): in damp, very acid soil and plenty of shade this is a pretty spring addition with little spires of white flowers no higher than 6 inches above a pair of shiny green leaves. The long-lasting blossoms are followed by reddish berries. Where satisfied, spreads thickly enough to be considered a ground cover.

MITCHELLA REPENS (twinberry, squawberry, partridgeberry): Christmas without a partridgeberry bowl is poor indeed, and luckily this little evergreen creeper increases easily, so we need not fear for its being overpicked to decorate our homes. The tiny pinkish-white bells are inconspicuous, but the bright-red berries are extremely long-lasting, hence their use in terrariums. Nearly every cutting will root, and established plants strike roots at almost every node, so it is

Few spring perennials can equal the adaptibility and beauty of *Phlox divaricata.*

easy to have big mats of it as a ground cover in shaded spots where the moderately acid soil has plenty of humus and does not dry out. By all means remove cuttings in your berry bowl carefully during the spring, plant in peat moss in flats, and keep well-watered until you think they can be safely transplanted to the garden. Mulch well the first winter with wood chips to prevent heaving.

MITELLA DIPHYLLA (miterwort, bishop's-cap): foot-high stalks of tiny white spring flowers and toothed, heart-shaped basal foliage

are the distinguishing features. It is readily grown in rich neutral soil and full shade but not nearly as decorative as it cousin, tiarella.

PANAX QUINQUEFOLIUM (American ginseng): although much grown in the South for the sale of its roots in Chinese markets or occult shops, this rather coarse plant has some garden merit. Its palmately compound leaves beneath umbels of tiny white flowers 18 inches high in June and July add a cool note to the shady garden at a time when it needs it most. Red berries follow. Dwarf ginseng *(P. trifolium)* is simi-

100

lar but only a few inches high and blooms in early spring. Both like moisture, but are very difficult to transplant; try to obtain seed.

PHLOX DIVARICATA (wild, woodland, or May phlox): even where there is only slight shade, this beauty will thrive if there is adequate moisture and humusy soil. Ours begin in April, and plants in deepest shade will bloom almost a full month later than those in half sun to prolong its display. Mostly in shades of blue to lavender, it also has a fine white form. Since all increase well by side shoots, you can establish great swathes under

Phlox stolonifera is ideal ground cover for dry, shaded spots.

trees, especially effective on slopes. The small flat heads of bloom are a foot or two high and quite fragrant. I don't see how anyone could have too much of it, and the foliage is evergreen too.

As a ground cover in dry woods where the soil has plenty of humus, *P. stolonifera* is another wonder, but it should not be put near too choice things since it is a rapid spreader. It opens here in early May and lasts a long time with bright pink to red-purple flowers 6 inches high. There are two good named forms: Blue Ridge has quite startlingly blue flowers, Rosalie's are deep rose. All have round basal leaves. *P. ovata* (mountain phlox) is much similar but has taller flowers.

PODOPHYLLUM PELTATUM (Mayapple, mandrake): although its foothigh, umbrella-like leaves, white spring flowers, and yellow fall fruits are all decorative, don't put this in a choice spot. It spreads too rapidly by tuberous roots in shady spots with moist humusy soil.

POLEMONIUM REPTANS (Jacob's-ladder): small clusters of blue-violet bells a foot high in spring are delightful in partial shade, but I treasure this even more for its foliage. It is alternately pinnate almost like a fern and stays clean and green all summer, making lush clumps where moisture is adequate. There are a number of western species but I am content with my

local native except for wanting *P. mellitum,* a white-flowered Rocky Mountain inhabitant. I am told *P. carneum,* a pinkish-purple West Coast species 12 to 24 inches high, is a delight. Never be misled with *P. caeruleum,* a tall-flowered form from Europe which is ugly.

POLYGALA PAUCIFOLIA (gaywings, fringed polygala): if you have a shady cool spot with rich humusy acid soil, this is a rarity that is darling as a ground cover beneath acid-loving shrubs. Only a few inches high, it produces magenta flowers a bit like orchids and spreads by underground runners. There is a rare white form. Polygala is difficult unless its wants are completely satisfied.

SANGUINARIA CANADENSIS (bloodroot): asking no more than to be left alone to proliferate, the bloodroots are gay, early-spring flowers with white petals and prominent yellow stamens. The gray-green leaves enfold the flowers in a way that reminds me of a pretty girl with her skirts blown high by a capricious wind. It is fine for the edge of a shady garden where early sun makes the flowers glow. Later tree shade will protect the leaves and keep the creeping rootstock cool. Indians are supposed to have used its red juice for a dye. Make sure soil is rich but well-drained and place plants in varying exposures to spread bloom over a month or more.

101

Some flowers have a pinkish tinge, but the most incredible treasure in my garden right now is a white double bloodroot, var. *multiplex* or *flore plena*. It has to be seen to be believed.

SEDUM TERNATUM (threeleaf stonecrop): most members of this family are rampant growers best kept out of the garden, but this is a gem only a few inches high with small white flowers in May on a branched stalk. After watching it for some years at Bowman's Hill I can report it is not at all aggressive and a lovely thing for any well-drained, lightly shaded spot but especially good for rocky slopes.

SHORTIA GALACIFOLIA (Oconee-bells): since it is widely offered by many different nurseries, shortia must be far easier to cultivate than to grow in the wild, given the right combination of well-drained, humusy, moist, acid soil and enough shade to keep it cool. It originally grew in a very limited area in the North Carolina mountains, and was so rare that botanists disbelieved its first report until a subsequent discovery many years later confirmed its existence. The leaves are evergreen, much like galax but smaller, with white or pink open bells an inch wide and a few inches high in very early spring. It is hardy well into New England.

STYLOPHORUM DIPHYLLUM (cel-andine-poppy): if you have a

woodsy slope where the spring sun is later shaded by trees, these gay yellow foot-high poppies are a good choice. Hairy seed pods follow, and the whole plant matures quickly after spring flowering. Better started from seed. This is not the weedy celandine from Europe.

THALICTRUM DIOCIUM (early meadow-rue): full to partial shade and dry but humusy soil will suit this, worth growing for its delicate foliage alone. The leaves, somewhat like a columbine, stay green and decorative well into the fall. May to June flowers are panicles of fluffy purply stamens about 2 feet tall.

TIARELLA CORDIFOLIA (foam-flower): no more glorious ground cover for shady spots exists, and it has lacy cylinders of tiny white stars about 8 inches high in April too. As fall nears, the heart-shaped leaves, which are sharply lobed, take on brilliant tints. In a single season one plant will increase to perhaps three offsets so that by diligent spring division you can soon cover a considerable area with a fine green carpet. Unfortunately it is not evergreen, but you can't have everything. To make good growth it should have soil with plenty of humus and not too dry, especially in more southerly states. I have a patch in half-shade, but it is watered well in drought. The farther south one gardens, the more shade it requires.

VIOLA (violets): for all their shy innocent appearance, violets have an alarming sex life. When I was quite young, I moved some clumps of the lovely marsh violet (*V. cucullata*) into my mother's garden. In a few years they were all gone, replaced by a huge-flowered dark-purple hybrid of their own making. Thus discouraged, I am weak on the family. There are about 100 species native to the United States, 30 or more of them in Pennsylvania alone. Differences are often minute, hard to see for anyone but a botanist, and when they begin to hybridize, quite impossible.

If you have a local favorite, enjoy it, but don't be surprised if it seems to change over the years! One precaution is to keep similar sorts separated as much as possible, which may cut down on the hybridizing.

Since I disapprove of gardeners robbing the wild for plants, I do not wish to encourage desecration even of a species as common as most violets. So the few described below are restricted to those I have been able to locate in the trade. Several have flower or leaf characteristics which make them somewhat different, thus perhaps more decorative.

Except where noted, violets want cool humusy soil, moderately acid to neutral, and at least some shade. Being a hardy tribe, most are winter-proof in all but the coldest boundary states and worth trying even there. Only a few are markedly

Viola pubescens illustrates growth habit of a "stemmed" violet.

fragrant. Many have contrasting eyes or veining, particularly on the lower petals. Nicknames often betray leaf characteristics.

Many produce late-season, cleistogamous flowers near the roots or hidden under the leaves. These have no petals but produce many fertile seeds and tend to spread widely. Many types also have creeping rootstocks. A species with either of these habits may soon overrun its boundary, so watch new arrivals until you're sure.

In almost any locality there are violets with flowers basically yellow, white, or some shade of blue-purple, but this is not the best way to divide them for garden use, although it is certainly important. Growth habits govern the positioning of a plant within a garden, so I have sectioned them into two groups: "stemmed" with flowers on a leafy stem that may reach well over a foot and "stemless" with the blooms atop a scape arising directly from the root and seldom more than a few inches high. The latter make fine foreground plants.

The most common violet is one to use only as a ground cover under shrubs or in waste areas because it is too rampant. Now correctly named *V. sororia*, it is still *V. papilionacea* in most catalogs. It has large purple flowers and heart-shaped leaves and is a fierce spreader. The grayish Confederate violet is probably a variety of this and equally invasive.

Of kinds for gardens let us consider the "stemless" blues first. My old bugaboo, *V. cucullata*, has blue to white flowers with a darker throat, is hardy into Quebec but loses its delicacy unless kept in a half-shaded, mucky place. *V. palmata* has big pale-blue flowers and palmate foliage 4 to 12 inches high, takes dry shade. *V. pedata* (bird's foot) takes its name from the shape of the finely cut leaves. It has flat, very showy lilac flowers; it will take much sun but demands sterile acid soil. Its variety *bicolor* sports blooms with the top petals dark violet, the bottom pale lilac. *V. sagittata* (arrow-leaf) has long leaves and bright violet-purple flowers, likes sandy, moist places. *V. adunca* is scarcely 4 inches high, with violet to red-purple flowers, and is found from Alaska to California. *V. pedatifida* (larkspur) has fan-shaped leaves and big violet-purple flowers, likes a well-drained spot with some sun, and is native from Ohio to Arizona.

White-flowered stemless types include *V. blanda* (sweet white), which is very early, and has fragrant, reflexed flowers. It seldom goes over 5 inches but spreads quickly and grows up into Canada. *V. primulifolia* (primrose-leaf) has

purple lines on its lower petals, is "pungently fragrant," and wants a moist very acid soil in some sun.

V. rotundifolia (round-leaf) is one of the few common stemless yellows. It is extremely early with small, short yellow flowers and does much better in the acid shade of cool states, where its later leaves make good ground covers.

Moving to the stemmed types, let's remember they tend to make somewhat sprawling plants. The flowers are borne in the axils of the leaves. Among the violet-hued the most outstanding is the 8-inch *V. rostrata* (longspur), which is lilac with darker spots, has a spur a half inch long and heart-shaped leaves. It prefers cool rocky woods, being hardy to Quebec.

V. rugulosa, found from Alaska to Colorado, has large leaves and white flowers tinted pink or violet, may reach 2 feet, and spreads by underground runners, so is often used as a ground cover. Not quite so tall is the very hardy *V. canadensis* (Canada violet), whose white flowers have a purply back and a yellow eye; it prefers a cool moist shaded home.

Yellow stemmed species include the beloved *V. pubescens* (downy yellow) and *V. eriocarpa* (smooth yellow). Both are very hardy, like rich woodland, and stay around a foot tall. From the West there is *V. vallicola*, which has a purple tinge to its upper petals. *V. hastata* (halberd or triangle-leaf) is a quite rare species about 10 inches high

which likes dry woods and may not be as hardy as many of the others.

FOR SUNNY SITES

By my definition a sunny garden gets either full sun or else is shaded only for an hour or so at one end of the day or the other. A sun-loving plant given too much shade becomes either a floppy mess from trying to reach for the sun or else refuses to flower at all. Such a garden is not necessarily inordinately dry. Good humusy soil and adequate rainfall may be too much for many western plants, however. Remember that a southern plant which likes some shade may be able to take full sun farther north, and that plants which grow in sun in northern latitudes may need light shade to survive where it is much hotter. Most of these plants do very well in the sunny border; check descriptions to prevent putting rampant spreaders in choice spots.

AMSONIA TABERNAEMONTANA (willow amsonia): while it will grow in part shade, this eastern amsonia is far more flowerful in full sun. It begins to bloom with the tulips and lasts quite long. Flowers are pale-blue stars in clusters that remind me of small lilacs. By fall the bushy foliage may be as high as 3 feet, and turning a bright

Amsonia tabernaemontana makes a lovely companion for late tulips.

Pearly everlasting provides a late-season white note in dry places.

yellow. It is very easily raised from funny cylindrical seeds and makes good clumps in time. Remove seed heads during the summer if you don't want it to self-sow. I have never seen it bothered by insects or disease. *A. ciliata,* a southerly species, has slightly darker flowers in smaller clusters and wider leaves; it is not as good a choice.

ANAPHALIS MARGARITACEA (pearly everlasting): perfect drainage is the secret of growing this easterner. Its low tufts of woolly foliage are very prone to rot the first winter. During their second summer they suddenly send up shoots as much as 24 inches high and in September and October bear clusters of tiny white double daisies atop silvery leaves. They have a curry-like smell and dry well for winter bouquets. The tiny seeds can be shaken out in late fall, but germination is very poor, so sow lots to get even a few plants. Once established, they usually last for years, however. Don't be led astray by noticing anaphalis growing on road cuts where there is seepage. The site will always be precipitous cliffs with rocky, thin soil where there is no chance of standing water.

ANTENNARIA PLANTAGINIFOLIA (pussy-toes): increasing well, this is a good ground cover for autumn-flowering croscuses, which like a dry summer roasting. The clean little silver-and-green leaves are scarcely an inch high, but in spring the furry pinkish-white flowers (which at one stage are uncannily similar to a tiny cat's paw) may reach from 6 to 15 inches. This one thrives in dry heat and will keep weeds out of the poorest, thinnest soil you have. It is especially nice to hold slopes in the rock garden, but should not be allowed to wander out of bounds. This is the easiest to find and very hardy, but there are other species too.

ARCTOSTAPHYLLOS UVA-URSI (bearberry): if it has the very acid soil it demands, bearberry is an outstanding ground cover for sunny dry slopes in sandy soil. It is a very hardy, woody, creeping plant with shiny evergreen leaves, tiny pinky-white spring bells, and per-

106

sistent red berries. Once successfully established, it can be layered to increase into huge mats only a few inches high. Foliage turns bronzy as frost comes. Winter cold, summer heat, wind, and even salt spray bother it not at all if the soil is right. It will even take a little shade. There are many tenderer members of this family native to the West Coast, where they are called manzanitas and are useful as anti-erosion agents.

ARNICA: several good rock-garden species with yellow flowers, mostly from Alaska and the Northwest, are available, but I have not grown any of them. Reputedly they prefer acid soil.

ASTER: there are more than 200 American varieties of aster, but very few are acceptable for garden use. Several are valuable for wet or shady places and are listed under those divisions. You may have a local aster you love. By all means let it in your garden, or better still in a half-wild section of your property or among shrubbery. I do this with *A. ericoides* (white heath or wreath aster) simply because it is so gay in fall, but I have to restrain it by weeding since it has the spreading habit of so many of its tribe. It provides fingers of many tiny white asters on bushy plants which average around 30 inches high and thrives on dryness. I like it for cutting too.

One real exception to the above

hedging is *A. linariifolius* (stiff-leaved or bristly aster). Its tiny stiff leaves do make the branches look bristly. Violet rays surround the typical yellow eye of the aster family, the inch-wide flowers appearing from early August until mid-fall. This neat plant remains about

12 to 15 inches high, never needs staking, and is ideal for rock gardens or dry border use. It does not spread by creeping roots, but is easily propagated in the spring by root division and looks best if planted in quantity. Many houses can supply it.

Low bushes of *Aster linariifolius* are studded with small lavender flowers.

Although you would not know it from all the words about "English" asters in many catalogs, the famous Michaelmas daisies are actually hybrids and selections of our native asters. Experts differ on which ones are more important in the blood lines, but we don't have to care, merely nodding thank you to the patient European plantsmen whose work made them available.

There are tall and dwarf types, most with the yellow eye but with rays varying from white through many pinks and blues to dark purple. These are quite the best asters for gardens and provide fine color in the late summer and fall. You can avoid some staking of the taller kinds by nipping the shoots in early summer, but they tend to be spreading plants, most effective used in masses. Every few years they need dividing just like chrysanthemums; discard the woody centers and transplant thrifty new starts from the outside growth.

Some of the dwarf types come into blossom quite early and are very good for filling in spots in front of empty places left by maturing early bulb foliage. West Coast species as well as eastern forms have contributed to this line of wonderful garden flowers.

BAPTISIA AUSTRALIS (wild blue indigo, false indigo): easily raised from seed, baptisia should be trans-

Dark-blue flowers of *Baptisia australis* betray their pea-family relationship.

planted to its permanent home no later than the spring after sowing before its roots get too long. Because the roots are so far-reaching, this plant could well be used for erosion control, but it is far too lovely just for such mundane usage. In late May or June (about the time the Siberian iris bloom), great racemes of showy, dark-blue, pealike flowers are produced in profusion after the plants are old enough; don't expect much bloom until the third year after sowing. Flowers are followed by swollen pods which blacken after frost and are much prized for dried arrangements either plain or gilded. The ripe seeds inside rattle noisily, and my children played Indian dancer with them as well as gathering the green pods for doll food.

An established plant is very long-lived and puts forth many foliage shoots, covering two or three square feet with its clean silvery-blue foliage. I once used a row of them as a deciduous hedge since they grew a good 4 feet high and too thick to see through. You'll get good service from it as an all-season garden plant, but give it enough room to make a good clumping.

B. leucantha is similar but may reach 6 feet and has white flowers. So does *B. bracteata,* but it seldom tops 2 feet and has drooping racemes. *B. tinctoria* is inferior in comparison, having yellow flowers so small as to be hardly noticeable; it is valuable only for very dry sites with acid soil. There are some interesting baptisia hybrids with

cream, gold, bronze, and chocolate flowers.

BOLTONIA LATISQUAMA: though supposedly a plant of moist conditions in the Midwest, boltonia in my garden has proved capable of growing anywhere. It has bluish-tinted foliage and bears myriads of small pink- or lavender-rayed flowers with yellow disks in late summer on stems often 5 or 6 feet tall. They are useful for picking at a time when the supply of flowers is getting scarce. It will self-sow freely, but plants in shade tend to fall over. In full sun give it a low spot where extra water collects for best bloom. *B. asteroides* from the East can reach 8 feet, has slightly smaller flowers.

CALLIRHOE INVOLUCRATA (wine cup, poppy-mallow): if you can live with the harsh red-purple color, callirhoe is a conversation piece for any very dry garden. The large flowers are produced intermittently during the summer on plants which tend to sprawl. Sow the seed where it is to grow, since its taproot may be hard to transplant. Drainage must be absolute or it will rot. Many catalogs rhapsodize about it, but the best I can say is that it will survive terrible drought.

CAMPANULA DIVARICATA (North Carolina harebell): unless used in quantity, these tiny blue bells on open, arching panicles will be overlooked, but they are incredibly

Individual bells of *Campanula divaricata* are no larger than pencil erasers.

109

Brown seed pods of cassia resemble string beans.

dainty. Try to give them a background to show them off. They will take sun or part shade, but tend to get floppy in the latter. Flowering begins in mid-July, lasts all summer.

C. rotundifolia (Scotch bluebell, harebell): this narrow-leaved bluebell makes itself at home in northern latitudes all around the world. Violet-blue bells nearly an inch long hang on wiry stalks from 6 to 18 inches high during the summer. It prefers rocky or sandy slopes, and here its rapid spread by underground roots is slowed a bit. This is not a plant for the choicest part of your garden but will give a good account of itself in thin soils where better plants do not thrive. Since it comes from cool climates, give it some afternoon shade and extra moisture to the south.

110

CASSIA MARILANDICA (wild senna): a shrubby perennial that may reach 5 feet with pale-green, compound leaves and clusters of yellow flowers in summer. It will take light shade and moisture but is most valuable because it will grow in dry sites on the acid side. Seeds are like thin string beans. Not hardy far north.

CHRYSOPSIS (golden-aster): the nickname is a perfect description of these flowers which like dry, hot, sandy soils in full sun and provide a bright note in the summer garden. Seed of three species is available. *C. falcata* of the Northeast seldom tops 12 inches; *C. mariana* from more southerly states reaches 24 inches; *C. amplifolia* from the West stays around 20.

COREOPSIS: few perennials endure more neglect or give flowers over a longer span. *C. lanceolata* (smooth-leaved coreopsis) has been in gardens for generations, bears yellow blossoms ideal for cutting on long wiry stems about 20 inches high. There are several double forms in the trade, and they will grow anywhere without making a nuisance of themselves. *C. verticillata* (thread-leaved coreopsis) spreads too quickly by creeping roots for most gardens, but I have had a welcome piece for years in the hot sterile clay of various driveways. It has thin palmate leaves and small yellow flowers and seldom tops 15 inches, making bushy, weed-

free growth which I have always been able to keep under control. For annual species see Chapter 11.

ECHINACEA (coneflower): imagine black-eyed-Susans with white, pink, or purple rays around the central disk, and you have coneflowers. They come from the Midwest, take dry summer heat well, and grow 3 to 4 feet tall. *E. angustifolia* is a slightly lower plant than *E. purpurea.* Seed of both is available. Some of the mail-order houses offer plants under fancy names, sometimes under the mistaken listing of rudbeckia.

EPILOBIUM ANGUSTIFOLIUM (fireweed, blooming Sally): if this were

Rare white form of epilobium shows flower habit; bloom begins at bottom of stalk which gradually elongates over period of months.

just a little less rambunctious, we would treasure it in our gardens, since it has a bloom period of nearly three full months. If you have a waste spot where its magenta will not clash with anything else, it will do yeoman service. Plants can reach 6 feet, and bloom begins at the bottom of the bud stalk, which gradually lengthens. It spreads by roots as well as seed and is a common sight as the first plant to take over burned-out forest areas, especially in the Far North. I have a piece of the pure-white form, which is a real beauty if you can locate it. I have it growing with bayberries in a dry spot where it can do no harm to other plants.

Eupatorium coelestinum spreads rapidly in wettish spots.

EUPATORIUM COELESTINUM (mistflower, hardy ageratum): most of the members of this family (Joe-Pye-weed is a good example) are far too weedy for gardens. Mistflower, however, is easily kept under control if not given too much water and provides wonderful blue spots for late summer. It will take some light shade and spreads by creeping roots. While it can be rampant and 4 feet tall under moist conditions, in the drier garden it stays around 3 feet. The heads do resemble ageratum and cut well.

GAILLARDIA ARISTATA (blanketflower): native from Minnesota to New Mexico, perennial gaillardias will take the driest, most sterile

soil without complaint, and also do well in garden loam. Bright yellow and red composite flowers on long stems good for picking are borne all summer if seed heads are removed faithfully. Older named garden varieties, of which there are many in all sorts of combinations of the two basic colors, make 30-inch plants with a somewhat floppy habit. Newer dwarf types around a foot high are probably neater. Often gaillardias flower the first year from seed and can be counted on to self-sow.

HELENIUM AUTUMNALE (sneezeweed): although likely to be found wild in damp places, helenium does fine in the sunny garden. Just give it a depression which is easy to fill with water. On plants from 3 to 6 feet tall you will have a gay display of composite flowers in the yellow to red spectrum in August and September. I have a plant of the form Bruno whose flowers start out bronzy-red, and age to all sorts of lighter orange shades. It is really dazzling. Easy from seed, this helenium is hardy even into Canada. In the catalogs there are also some dwarf types which are said to stay around 2 feet as well as several species from the West.

HELIOPSIS (summer-sun, sunglory): use this bright daisy instead of regular sunflowers (Helianthus). The latter, although fine upstanding Americans, are simply too big or too spreading for gar-

111

Heliopsis provides bright-yellow daisies in profusion.

HESPERALOE PARVIFLORA: probably not hardy much north of Philadelphia, this is a plant for dry, desert-like conditions. I put mine on the south side of the house under an overhang where water seldom penetrates. It is hot and dry there to help it get through our winters. Basal foliage is similar to the yucca but much smaller and thinner. Flower stems of nodding pink flowers can be as tall as 4 feet. I have seen a red-flowered form which was successfully wintered nearby.

HEUCHERA SANGUINEA (alumroot, coralbells): although their tiny red, pink, or white bells may be carried on 24-inch stems, heucheras are perfect for the foreground of the sunny garden. Mounds of evergreen foliage remain attractive all year long, and the flowers are so dainty no one minds them wherever they are placed. Good drainage is important, however, for these westerners are usually found on cliffs. They are especially effective in rock gardens and will take a little shade. Named horticultural varieties are easily found and hardy everywhere.

H. americana, the eastern counterpart, is described in the shady-plant section, but it will take considerable sun in cool climates. The southern cousin, *H. villosa,* however, belongs here since it will grow in nearly full sun or partial shade. I do not know how far north *H. villosa* survives, but it is worth a bit of

dens. Culture is the same: full sun and any ordinary soil. But the heliopsis has prettier leaves and good cutting qualities and seldom tops 5 feet, so is much more easily placed. Flowers are as much as 4 inches across in some varieties, bright-yellow, and often double. Seed sown in early April began blooming in August of the first year. Since they branch, there is continuous bloom until frost. Rich soil means taller plants. Do not let them want for water in blazing weather.

112

Beautiful leaves of *Heuchera villosa* set off delicate white summer flowers.

protection at its back (like a big rock on a southerly slope) to introduce it to your garden. The other heucheras have round-lobed leaves like geraniums, but *villosa* has sharply pointed lobes somewhat like a maple which show bronzy tints even in summer; it makes a superb ground cover. The tiny white flowers in airy narrow panicles about 15 inches high are neither as big nor as colorful as the western species, but they last an incredibly long time. In my garden they have appeared in June and some have remained at frost. In the South *villosa* may need more shade, but it has been wonderful here in only light shadow part of the day.

LUPINUS PERENNIS (eastern lupine): All lupines are flops for me, although I have the acid soil they want, but this one I shall keep on trying to introduce. Eventually I may find the right dry sandy spot that has whatever odd nutrient it demands. One trick is to nick the seed and roll it in nitrogen-fixing inoculent before sowing.

Eastern lupine has palmate leaves and racemes of blue pea blossoms up to 2 feet tall in May or June. It used to be common along roadsides and railroads where the soil was sterile, but overpicking and highway improvement have nearly removed it from the scene. Once successfully introduced, this lupine will live for years and self-sow too, but the initial attempt on land

Long-lasting *Melampodium leucanthum* blooms the first year from seed.

which has never supported them can be frustrating. Our west has numerous other lupines, the most exciting of which are the tree forms of California *(L. arboreus),* which make 8-foot shrubs with mostly yellow or white flowers; I doubt they are frost-hardy.

MELAMPODIUM LEUCANTHUM (blackfoot, desert-daisy): only a single seed of this westerner germinated for me, but I am delighted with the resulting plant and hope it will self-sow. Sown outside in late March, it began blooming August 4 of the same year. It is a gem for sunny rock gardens. The inch-wide

flowers have white rays, and yellow disks, and each lasts a very long time. Foliage is small and scarcely 6 inches high.

MONARDA (bee-balm, wild bergamot): this member of the mint family will grow almost anywhere under almost any conditions. Many nurseries offer pink, lavender, red, and even white forms. It is a rampant root spreader in wettish situations and should be planted only where it can be kept in bounds. One reason for having it is its attraction for hummingbirds and butterflies. *M. didyma* (Oswego-tea) is usually red, raising round heads of lipped flow-

113

ers 4 feet in midsummer where it gets plenty of moisture but a bit lower in drier situations. *M. fistulosa* prefers drier territory and has flowers in the pink-to-lavender range. Both types will grow in considerable shade, where they are often taller and tend to flop.

OENOTHERA FRUTICOSA (sundrops): among the many evening primroses this is the only one worthwhile for most gardeners. It opens groups of bright-yellow cups about 2 feet high during the daylight hours of June and July and asks for nothing except plenty of sun and a well-drained site. Red stems make a planting even more colorful. There is increase by offsets but not on a scale you can't control. Some houses offer the improved variety *youngi*.

In the right spot *O. missouriensis* (Ozark sundrop) might be useful. It is a sprawling plant about a foot high with yellow midsummer flowers and good for rock gardens. There

Bright-yellow opuntia flowers are followed by red fruits.

are other white- and rose-flowered species, but most are either weedy or not decorative enough for the space they need; many open their flowers only at dusk.

OPUNTIA COMPRESSA (pricklypear): while there are nearly 300 species of this desert dweller in the New World, this one is the eastern type and widely adaptable. Some opuntias are even hardy into Canada. Like many others it bears showy bright-yellow flowers in midsummer. Inch-long fruits, which eventually turn red, follow. They too are decorative, although insipid to the tastebuds. Give it the driest, sunniest spot, preferably on a slope, and keep its soil thin and poor. The typical cactus leaf has only a few bristles and puts forth several joints as it ages, rarely getting higher than a foot. You can increase plants by breaking off a joint and pressing it slightly into the ground in early

spring. Prop it with stones until it roots if it is too heavy to stand by itself, but never bury it far into the ground lest it rot. In the West there are many other species, some with pink or red flowers, but winter wet is always a problem in states with adequate rainfall.

PENSTEMON HIRSUTUS (eastern penstemon, beard-tongue): flushed with the success of my planting of this local native, I shall try some of the more beautiful westerners again, but I can truthfully only recommend this white-and-violet species as being dependably perennial in the East. It does very well in dry poor soil, making big patches. The flowers are borne so profusely that an area in May is a veritable fountain of bloom about 18 inches high. Unless you want it to spread, remove old flowers before seed forms.

Of the more than 200 species from the West, I can only report

Closeup of oenothera flower head.

114

that I have never been able to get seedlings through their first winter. I think this is not so much because they are not hardy here as an excess of winter moisture. They are such beauties, mostly in shades of blue, pink, or red, that they are worth extra effort. The secret I'm sure is perfect drainage, although there are some which are tender. Now that I have a sunny slope with sandy soil, I am going to give it another go. This time I shall use seed of the Viehmeyer Hybrids developed in Nebraska, which certainly ought to be hardy here.

PHLOX: no matter what the fancy catalogs may imply, all the phlox the world's gardens wear are Americans. The one exception, a little-known Siberian species, also occurs in Alaska. The ones in your garden right now, for all their pretty names and whatever the country of their hybridizer, are only crosses or selections of phlox whose antecedents came from somewhere between the Atlantic and the Pacific. I never yet saw a phlox I didn't like, but only a small percentage of the species (and their hybrids) are in cultivation and commerce.

Some of my favorites are in the shady-plant section, but four types are among the most valuable assets of the sunny garden. Foremost among them are the justly popular summer phlox. *P. paniculata,* which grows wild from Pennsylvania west

Phlox paniculata is a superb summer garden plant.

115

and south, is the main parent of them all, and some natural forms are quite as beautiful as any of the named hybrids. Trusses are larger and color selection wider among the hybrids, however, and they are the easiest to obtain. You can have them in pure white and every shade of pink as well as in some hues that border on lavender and lilac. Many have contrasting eyes. Heights range from 2 to nearly 4 feet, depending on variety.

It will take two or three years before the plant you buy grows out into a decent clump, but then you will have months of summer color to look forward to if you remove old flower heads before they go to seed. Every four or five years thereafter it will keep your plants thrifty if you chop them apart, discard the older central sections, and replant the younger ones.

Sometimes phlox gets mildew in late summer. This can be from excess moisture, so hose them only during sunlit hours. It is unsightly but doesn't seem to bother the plants. They also like air circulation, so don't plant too closely. Other than that all they want is rich, deep garden loam, full sun, and adequate summer moisture. The only mistake you can make is to plant too many different hues together. For greatest effect group them with at least three plants of a single shade together.

The same advice is offered when dealing with *P. subulata* (creeping phlox, moss or mountain phlox or pinks). Too often one sees rock gardens where the owner achieves a crazy-quilt effect with moss pinks of a dozen different shades all mixed together. Healthy plants bloom so prolifically in spring that a clump is a solid mass of color; without some space between different hues, it becomes just too much of a good thing. Try instead to use swathes of a single shade in separate places. Color range is the same as for their taller cousins, but the ground-hugging, needle-like foliage remains evergreen. It makes a fine carpet for all sorts of little bulbs but is particularly recommended for autumn-blooming kinds. This phlox will increase well, forming huge mats if given a well-drained sunny position.

Downy phlox (*P. pilosa*) will take open shade but does just as well in full sun and is recommended for dry sites. It is somewhat of a sprawler with small clusters of flowers in pink, rose, or white, sometimes with contrasting eye, on 18-inch stems in late spring. The leaves of this variety are very narrow. It does not creep but is easily increased by dividing.

Some catalogs list *P. suffruticosa* or even *P. glaberrima*. What they are offering are really early forms of *P. carolina,* and they are superb additions to your phlox collection because they fill the gap between the end of the spring-blooming kinds and the start of summer phlox. The most famous form is Miss Lingard, a pure white which began blossoming here June 9 this year. There are also color selections, and if seed heads are removed quickly, this type often gives some repeat summer bloom. Generally these phlox are not quite as high as *P. paniculata* and will take a little light shade.

PHYSOSTEGIA VIRGINIANA (obedient-plant, false dragonhead): found in the wild in moist situations, this makes an excellent garden plant under ordinary conditions. Indeed, in wet meadows, physostegia spreads like wildfire by

Spikes of white physostegia contrast well with the many round daisies of summer.

116

creeping roots. Even in the garden the type, which has long racemes of pinkish-lavender lipped flowers from 24 to 36 inches high, must be watched lest it get out of bounds. But it brings fine color to late August and is easily raised from seed or from a small rooted piece. There is a dwarfer selection named Vivid which I found not as bright a color as the type.

The start of the family is the pure-white form, which I treasured for years in a fairly dry garden. There its spread was never uncontrollable, and the cool white flowers around

Saxifraga virginiensis is a tiny gem for rock ledges.

24 inches high made a welcome note in hot weather. Mine blooms weeks earlier than the type and will put out a second crop of flowers if seed heads are removed early.

Arrangers ought to like this native. It gets its nickname from the adjustability of the flowers, which can be pushed in any direction along the square stem.

ROMNEYA COULTERI (canyon or Matilija poppy): many westerners proclaim this the most beautiful of our wildflowers. On stalks 5 to 8 feet high it produces fragrant silky white flowers often 5 inches in diameter and centered with a golden mass of stamens around the prominent stigma. They color the canyons of California as high as 3,000 feet in May and June. I am told that in dry, well-drained spots they can be successfully wintered at least as far north as Philadelphia. The catch for easterners is even to get a plant with which to experiment.

Like all poppies, this one transplants with difficulty, but I ordered one from California anyway. Extra postage to hasten delivery did no good, and the plant arrived badly rotted. The remains were planted in my dry garden, and a small shoot of bluish foliage gives me hope I may one day have something. Two batches of seed did nothing. One was started in time-honored fashion in March but kept fairly dry; the other was planted in sandy soil,

heaped with pine needles which were set afire, then watered. (All this latter per explicit directions from a California grower.) I plan to try again with seed from a different house in the East which recommends starting it *in situ* after the soil warms up in the spring.

RUDBECKIA (coneflower, black-eyed-Susan): everyone knows these bright ray flowers of summer, and chances are you may have a volunteer, since they self-sow prolifically. If you want to keep them going in an odd corner or part of a field, don't pick all the flowers, for most of the dark-eyed ones are either annual or biennial and must renew themselves. You can increase a planting by sowing a few seed heads in the fall after they are ripe.

There are several rudbeckias which are more truly perennial. Golden Glow (the horticultural form of *R. laciniata*) used to be in every garden but has apparently gone out of style, which is a shame because it was nearly indestructible and wonderful for summer cutting. About the only way you can get a piece is from an old gardener who still treasures it in a spot by the garage. One of my favorite seed houses offers Golden Ball, which sounds similar with double flowers on 7-foot plants. The single form has green disks, but I don't know of any source.

Burpee has recently introduced a coneflower which they named Irish Eyes in honor of its green center.

blatouch

vráskavec
chipa
kandik-p

clarkia
střevčník
kapra

OPPOSITE:
TOP (l. to r.):
Thymophylla tenuiloba, Actaea berries,
Caltha palustris
MIDDLE (l. to r.):
Sanguinarea canadensis, Dodecatheon meadia, Centaurea americana, Physostegia virginiana, white erythronium
BOTTOM (l. to r.):
Clarkia mixture, *Cypripedium pubescens,* spring fiddleheads

It is only 30 inches tall with leaves not at all like those of *laciniata.* They consider Irish Eyes perennial and list it with their Gloriosa Daisies. These latter are rudbeckias which went to finishing school. I have seen Gloriosas from 2 to 5 feet tall, the ray flowers variously marked with yellow and mahogany, single and double. In any one planting of these from seed some will act as annuals, some as biennials, while a few persist for years.

RUELLIA CILIOSA (wild petunia): not often seen, the ruellias are more for southern gardens, but this one deserves being tried at least as far north as southern coastal New England. Late in summer it bears 2-inch lavender-blue flowers much like a petunia. It is a somewhat prostrate plant that seldom exceeds 2 feet, and while in the South it grows in light shade,

here in Pennsylvania it does well in nearly full sun. Everywhere it thrives on dryness.

SAXIFRAGA VIRGINIENSIS (early saxifrage): as you garden farther south, this inhabitant of rock ledges will do better with some shade, but from Philadelphia north it wants more sun than shadow to bloom well. Clusters of tiny white stars are borne on stems that vary from a few inches to nearly a foot in early spring. The rest of the time the foliage rosettes are pretty decorations for rocky places. Saxifrage demands sharp drainage but wants a cool moist root run, so makes itself most at home in slope gardens with large rocks. It will self-sow into delightful colonies, but slugs gobble it up in the garden. The rarer *S. leucanthemifolia* is often cataloged as *S. michauxi.* Its leaves are larger, and the flower heads may be from 6 to 18 inches high. It is for rock gardens with some shade. There are also many hard-to-locate forms from the western mountains which rock gardeners treasure.

SCUTELLARIA (skullcap): garden flowers are scarcer in late June and early July, which makes the blue skullcaps more important, and their display can be lengthened by removing the spent heads. The seed capsules, however, are quite different-looking and sometimes used in dried arrangements. Best of the lot is *S. serrata* (showy skullcap), which has open spikes of violet-

blue lipped flowers, but seed is hard to locate. Several firms carry *S. integrifolia,* a similar but more northern species; it has a rare pink form too. *S. resinosa* is a dwarf western form seldom topping 10 inches.

SILENE (Indian pink, catch-fly, campion): three quite dissimilar plants among the native species are all good garden subjects. *S. virginica* (fire-pink) has red stars as bright as any flower on earth, rising on weak stems a foot or two high in sparse clusters during May and June with some repeat bloom. It will

Silene caroliniana makes mounds of gay pinkish flowers.

take light shade. Though usually recommended for dry slopes, it is sometimes found in rich bottomland too. *S. stellata* (starry campion) has smaller fringed white flowers on stems as high as 3 feet and blooms later; it really prefers half-shade here.

S. caroliniana var. *pensylvanica* is the darling of them all but sources are hard to find. In May it

119

produces a profusion of dianthus-like flowers which literally cover the basal foliage. Colors range from nearly white to dark pink. Since it is only a few inches high and must have dry, well-drained soil, it is ideal for a rock garden. Some catalogs list the species *wherryi,* a practically similar midwestern form.

SISYRINCHIUM (blue-eyed-grass, satin-flower, rush-lily): ever since a plant of this tiny iris volunteered itself and then established a colony on my driest sunny slope, I have been treasuring it in gardens. As a child I can remember considering it a rare treat to find its tiny blue stars in damp meadows, which should give you an idea of its adaptability.

Easiest to find in the catalogs is *S. angustifolium,* but it really doesn't matter which of the blue-flowered sorts you have. All make a big tuft of grassy foliage which from mid-May until midsummer is dotted with small blue flowers, each centered with gold and seldom a foot high. Gather some of the little round seed heads after they ripen to start another patch almost anywhere. If you have only seen the plant struggling amid grass, you cannot conceive what a lovely thing this can be when given a bit of encouragement. Excess seedlings are easily weeded out if you get too many.

I have a lush colony of *S. albidum,* the white form, started from seed this year. I cannot wait to see whether it will actually come true to color. In a dry, protected part of the garden there are seedlings of *S. californicum,* which has all-yellow blooms but is not as hardy. What I really want now is a start of *S. inflatum* (grass widows, purple-eyed-grass), which has the largest flowers of all in a bright pinkish-purple. It grows in the low hills of the Rockies and should be hardy enough, but no one offers seed.

Sisyrinchiums will never be accused of flamboyancy, but they are darlings who ask only a few inches of their own to put on a lovely display. I had some in a rock garden once which spread downhill by themselves to make a dainty waterfall of foliage sprinkled in season with blue stars.

STOKESIA LAEVIS (Stoke's-aster): why this native isn't seen in more gardens I cannot understand, for it is a real contender in my contest of species with the longest flowering season. A test plant which was kept from forming seed began blooming in May, and kept on sporadically until late September. The blossoms vaguely resemble an annual aster and can range from 2 to 5 inches in diameter. Colors range from pale blue to lavender, and I covet the pure-white form.

Stokesia comes readily from seed. Many houses offer seedlings, but bloom is much better on older plants. Some doubt exists as to how hardy stokesia is; it has been recorded as far north as Rochester, N.Y. It is one perennial really worth

Stokesia laevis yields months of blossom.

120

Talinum teretifolium's vibrant color calls attention to the small flowers.

extra protection if needed. In a warm sunny dry location it should give a good account of itself in all but the worst climates.

TALINUM TERETIFOLIUM (fame-flower, sunbright): although I dislike magenta, this eastern flower has won its way into my garden. It puts up wiry stems 6 to 12 inches high in midsummer with nickel-sized, bright-rosy-pink stars prominently centered with yellow stamens above tufts of light-green succulent leaves. What it wants is the hottest, driest part of your garden, and there it will sow itself into fine patches with most plants blooming the first year. For best effect plant it as close together as possible so you have swathes. Oddly, the flowers open only a few hours at midday, but the foliage is pretty of itself, much

more so than that of its cousin, portulaca.

You may also be able to find seed of several others. *T. menziesi* from the southern states is similar but a little larger in every way than *T. teretifolium. T. calycinum* from the Midwest gets only about 4 inches high. *T. paniculatum* (jewels of Opar), another southerner, grows as high as 2 feet and has lighter pink flowers. Its seed heads are ruby-colored, which accounts for the nickname, but the legendary country ought to be spelled Ophir!

THERMOPSIS CAROLINIANA (bush-pea, Aaron's-rod, golden-pea): those who can't grow lupines depend on this stately southerner to give somewhat the same effect. The long racemes of yellow pea-flowers are produced in June on stems from 3 to 5 feet tall, perfect for the back of the sunny border. With age the plants make good clumps, each with many flowering stems. It wants full sun, can take considerable dryness, and is hardy in the north.

VERBENA BIPINNATIFIDA (fern verbena): I wouldn't give you two cents for several of our native verbenas, and a number of other pretty ones found wild in the South are garden escapees of South American species. This pinkish-lavender beauty is another question. Coming from South Dakota, it can be depended upon as hardy nearly everywhere and blooms the first year

Tall spires of pure yellow are the contribution of *Thermopsis caroliniana.*

from seed. I did not find germination very good, but my three plants soon began to fill in the space I had allotted. Each branch roots where it touches the ground, so that in a single season a seedling covers at least a square foot with generous bloom. Since it is only a few inches high, it makes a good ground cover for a dry sunny corner.

VERONICASTRUM VIRGINICUM (Culver's-root): often cataloged as a veronica, to which it is closely related, this easterner belongs in the back of the border and will take some shade as well as almost any kind of soil. In wet situations it makes great thickets, but in the dry garden its stoloniferous roots spread less thickly, although I suggest keeping it away from really choice things. During the summer it produces spikes of tiny white flowers 4 to 5 feet high and contrasts well with the many daisylike summer flowers.

YUCCA (soapweed, bear-grass, Adam's-needle, Spanish-dagger or bayonet): you can't kill a yucca once it gets a good hold in a dry sunny spot. I think of this every time I take the train into Philadelphia; there is a bedraggled spot between the tracks and an abandoned warehouse where several yucca plants are sturdily flowering, although it's probably been a generation since anyone said a kind word to them.

We think of yucca as a desert plant, and it does want dry sandy soil, but actually most of those in commerce are native to the southeastern states rather than to the West. Use them for bold effects. The sharp foliage accounts for some of the popular names. Threads often hang from the rosettes of leaves which can be several feet tall. Flower stalks may reach from 3 to 12 feet, depending on the species,

and there are non-hardy western types which make trees.

For northern gardens the best choice is *Y. flaccida,* which comes from the southern Appalachians, has the smallest leaves, and bears creamy white bells on stalks to 6 feet. *Y. smalliana,* usually offered as *Y. filamentosa,* produces many white bells on stalks as high as 12 feet. Both bloom in July.

Y. glauca from the plains ranges to 6 feet and tends to be the earliest-blooming. *Y. gloriosa,* another southerner and outstanding, has greenish-white to reddish flowers on 6-to-8 foot stems and blooms from late August to frost in the north but often only in alternate years. *Y. aloifolia* can reach 25 feet, has white flowers which are often tipped purple, and is not recommended for the north. Like several others, it has a variegated form with striped leaves.

ZAUSCHNERIA CALIFORNICA (hummingbird-fuchsia): remarkably resistant to drought, this half-hardy Californian can set fire to the dry sandy garden in the fall with small bright-red flowers above grayish leaves. It makes a sprawling plant a foot or so high which should be nipped back in early summer to make a thriftier bush. In its native state it is not encouraged in gardens because it spreads by underground roots and looks unkempt much of the time. In less kind climates it is a challenge just to get it through the winter and makes a

remarkable flower for late summer. Give it the hottest, driest spot and don't do any artificial watering. I doubt it can be wintered outside north of Philadelphia; give it perfect drainage if you try.

ZINNIA: most of the gay annual zinnias in today's gardens have a Mexican background; after seeing one American species I must doff my hat to the hybridists who developed the modern giants. Zinnia Apache Snowflakes is offered as a hardy perennial. It is incredibly dwarf with almost threadlike leaves on stems less than a foot tall. My plants did not bloom the first year, but the white flowers are supposed to be less than an inch wide, and it is reputedly rock-hardy, being cataloged as *Z. crassula pumila* from Arizona. Bailey lists a perennial *Z. grandiflora* from Colorado and Arizona which sounds very similar. Interesting as a novelty for a sunny corner, but that's about it.

FOR MOIST SITES

Many of the more adaptable native perennials will grow vigorously in moist situations. As noted in the preceding section, some too rampant ones are tamed by being grown under drier conditions. These include several iris, heleniums, physostegias, monardas, many violets, and *Eupatorium coelestinum.* Several bulbs from the next chapter are also possibilities.

Those found in this division will

not do well at all unless given more moisture than is found in the average garden. Use them for low spots where water collects or along a brook or some other water source. Extra humus in the soil will help keep it more moist, but these plants require more than that. There is a difference between the "moist" conditions of good woodland soil and those sought by these plants. In this section the water table itself is never too far from the surface.

Odd hooded blue flowers of *Aconitum uncinatum* come in late summer.

Brooks and ponds create charming gardens.

ACONITUM UNCINATUM (climbing or summer aconite): hardly spectacular, aconite is nevertheless valuable for bringing summer color to partly shaded places where few things are then in bloom. It begins in late August with sparse groups of blue hooded flowers on stems 3 to 5 feet tall. Since they are weak, it is showiest if given something to clamber on. Mine are supported by a clethra bush in a depression where they get extra moisture and plenty of light but little direct sun on the northern side of a building.

ALETRIS FARINOSA (colic-root, star-grass): if you have a spot with very acid soil, dependable moisture, and sun, this is a good choice. Without those factors it will die out quickly. The basal foliage is clean-looking, and in June there are spikes 2 feet tall with many tiny white bells clustered along the top half. Long after flowering, the maturing seed capsules continue to be decorative. Hardy to Maine.

ASTER PUNICEUS (swamp aster): for wet places in sun or part shade this is a good choice, with light violet blooms on 3-to-5-foot plants in August or September. Valuable only where little will grow because of water and hardy in farthest north.

CALTHA PALUSTRIS (marsh-marigold): if you possibly can arrange a hollow which is wet in spring, try this darling. It produces masses of 18-inch-high bright-yellow buttercup-like flowers in early spring when such notes are scarce. While usually found along streams or swamps, it does quite well in spots which dry in summer when the plant goes dormant. I try to hit mine with the hose whenever I am down that way, since its home dries up in drought. Old-timers used to gather the succulent heart-shaped leaves in spring and boil as for spinach. With modern food selection this is inexcusable, for this outstanding native is in real trouble in the wild.

Out in the Rockies is the white *C. leptosepala.* It is a water-loving sub-alpine for which seed is available if you think you can make it happy.

CAREX FRASERI (Fraser sedge):

one of the very first natives to flower, this grasslike oddity has long evergreen leaves and showy white spikes as high as 18 inches. Try it only where you have rich humusy soil, plenty of summer shade, and moisture. There are other sedges, less decorative and seldom offered but probably hardier.

CHELONE (turtle-head): unless these summer-blossoming cousins of the penstemons have moisture, they just wither and die even if given extra shade. They do best with acid soil and some sun protection. Sparse heads of flowers aptly described by the nickname are produced on leafy stems which can be 3 feet tall under the right conditions. The two easiest to find are *C. glabra,* which is white, and the pink *C. lyoni.* Both hardy well north.

GENTIANA ANDREWSI (bottle or closed gentian): probably the easiest gentian, this wants moist, humusy soil and light shade. It transplants quite well when small but will not yield its curious bluish-purple autumn flowers unless it has adequate summer moisture. The ovoid flowers borne in terminal clusters never open. There is a rare white form offered which is much showier. *G. clausa* is very similar to *andrewsi.* Both are worth trying unless your soil is alkaline, but other native gentians are only for specialists. You can raise them from seed too, but it is like dust and must be handled very carefully.

HABENARIA (fringe orchid): not easy garden subjects, these rarities should not be attempted unless you are willing to cater to their special wants; even then it is chancy. Never dig any in the wild. Two types are widely offered. *H. ciliaris* (orange or yellow fringe orchid) has a stalk as high as 30 inches but usually lower with many little summer flowers having a deeply fringed lower lip. It does not seem as picky about the acidity of the soil but must be fairly moist; partial to full shade is also mandatory. In the wild it is found in peaty bogs and wet sandy soils as well as clay. *H. psycodes* (small purple fringed orchid) is often found farther north into Canada and seems to prefer a cool climate as well as lots of shade and moisture. Either would be fine near a spring or brook, but I don't see how they can do well in an ordinary garden.

HIBISCUS PALUSTRIS (swamp rose-mallow): if you are willing to do a little extra summer work with the hose, you can easily make a home for this showy swamp denizen in the garden's low spot, but it is not for small nooks. Red-eyed pink flowers, which closely resemble hollyhocks, decorate stalks 3 to 8 feet high during most of the summer. Give it rich soil in sun and allow space for it to grow into big clumps. Hardy in the wild into Massachusetts and Michigan, it is slow to come up in spring, so don't despair if it seems laggard. White and purple forms are not unusual, and many garden hybrids have been developed. *H. moscheutos,* usually creamy-white with a red or purple eye, has a more southerly range.

HOUSTONIA CAERULEA (bluets, Quaker-ladies, angel-eyes): if your soil is acid, you may be able to introduce these 4-inch dainties to a wet hollow. The yellow-eyed blue or white flowers are tiny but en masse give wet meadows an azure tint in April and May. They do not always take to civilization, but try some in either sun or part shade. If satisfied, the little tufts of foliage will spread quite quickly. I love them in the grass, but perfectionists probably wouldn't. *H. serpyllifolia* (creeping bluet) is about the same height but the stems are longer. *H. purpurea* (mountain houstonia) is sometimes offered. It has tiny purply flowers in July but on 20-inch stems, which sounds pretty absurd.

LOBELIA CARDINALIS (cardinal-flower): to come upon this plant in a half-shaded spot in the wild is to understand at least part of God's wisdom, for its fiery redness is accentuated by the shadow whereas in full sun it loses some of its brilliance. Before man took over, it was quite common beside streams and boggy places all along the coast from Canada to Florida. Luckily it adapts quite well to cultivation in damp places.

Chelone's lipped flowers give it the nickname "turtlehead."

125

In case you have never seen it, cardinal-flower produces a long narrow head of showy red flowers on stems 2 to 4 feet tall in late summer. Butterflies and hummingbirds find it irresistible. So will you if you can possibly support it.

Give it half sun in deep, rich soil with lots of humus and never let it want for water. It seems to prefer an acid reaction. Naturalists point out that it is not found in the water but rather at the edge where high water deposits the seeds. A woodchip mulch will help prevent heaving of the shallow roots the first winter. If you allow it to form seed, it may self-sow generously, but the mother plant is then short-lived. Dr. Wherry suggests cutting the stalks back before seed forms so they will produce new basal shoots instead.

Closely allied is *L. siphilitica* (great blue lobelia). It prefers a wetter situation, but will take neutral soil, does not get quite so tall, and of course has blue florets. It wants at least half sun. White forms of both lobelias exist. All can be grown from the very fine seed sown either in earliest spring or late fall.

MARSHALLIA GRANDIFLORA (wild bachelor's-button): although I do not know a single conventional source of seed or plants, this fine native is included here in the hope someone will be inspired to offer it soon. It transplants well and is also easy from seed. In June the 12-inch stems rise from lush basal

Pink daisies of marshallia are unusual among damp-loving wildflowers.

foliage to display long-lasting, pinkish-lavender daisies. It wants at least half sun and deep rich moist soil, and will slowly make thrifty clumps.

MIMULUS RINGENS (Allegheny monkey-flower): these small flowers resemble snapdragons (to which they are related) but are borne singly in the upper leaf axils of the 2-to-4-foot stalks. Unless used in quantity and planted close together, mimulus are not very showy. Bloom is in June, and there is some repeat if spent flowers are removed. Pink, blue, and white forms exist.

It is hardy into Canada and wants half shade and plenty of moisture. In the wild it actually grows in water. Western species have red, pink, or yellow blossoms, most of which appear from pictures to be more bell-shaped than the eastern types. They too prefer moisture even though many are found in the mountains.

SPIRANTHES CERNUA (autumn or nodding ladies-tresses): only this one species of these tiny orchids is usually offered, but luckily it is the easiest to establish in the garden as well as one of the showiest. Rows of little white flowers are borne on stalks no higher than a foot above grasslike foliage in late summer or fall. I have seen it always in grassy ditches alongside the road and heard of it growing with fringed gentian in neutral soil but some authorities suggest moderate to strong acid soil. Try to find a low spot in at least half sun, use lots of peat to increase both acidity and humus content, and resort to the hose whenever the weather's dry. I don't guarantee anything, however.

THALICTRUM POLYGAMUM (tall meadow-rue): as long as it has moist soil, this meadow-rue enjoys either sun or part shade. During June and July its large panicles of fluffy white flowers on 4-to-8-foot stalks add a graceful note to the wet garden. Mine thrives in a low spot where it receives extra water

Dainty white flowers of *Thalictrum polyganum* cut well too.

with an occasional great head of water. It will grow in any half-shaded spot.

VERATRUM VIRIDE (false or white hellebore): if you have a really swampy spot, this has a much more decorative flower than skunk cabbage. Great green leaves support a 3-to-5-foot stalk on which an impressive compound head of greenish-white flowers is borne in June. The leaves wither soon afterward. Incidentally, skunk cabbage itself (*Symplocarpus foetidus*) covers its ill-smelling, very early spring "flowers" with lush green foliage that has merit as summer decoration for wet places. In addition, it is very long-lived once it has become established.

only when it rains, but I do give it a good wetting whenever drought threatens.

TRADESCANTIA VIRGINIANA (spiderwort): never let this one into the garden proper, for it spreads everywhere. There are forms with blue, white, or pink flowers. Individually they last only a day or two, but they are borne over a long period in spring and early summer about 15 inches above the lush, rather untidy foliage. I include this genus (there are other species) only because it has real merit as an anti-erosion agent in culverts or brooks

Early spring flowers of skunk cabbage are soon hidden by lush green foliage.

For lakes and streams

Houses which specialize in aquatic plants may be able to supply the following natives which have especially decorative effect for water gardens. Be forewarned that muskrats relish the roots of all. I don't know whether wire baskets would foil them or not. All but one of these bloom better if given plenty of sun.

NUPHAR ADVENA (spatterdock, yellow pond-lily, cow-lily): spreading too rapidly for the small pool, this genus is fine for the shallow waters of ponds. Heart-shaped leaves as long as a foot float below the summer yellow flowers which resemble a big buttercup. Hardy in Vermont.

NELUMBO PENTAPETALA (*N. lutea,* American lotus): plate-shaped leaves as much as 2 feet across and pale-yellow flowers as big as 8 inches in diameter are the distinguishing characteristics of this hardy aquatic. It will grow in both lakes and sluggish streams, and the leaves, flowers, and odd seed pods are borne high above the water so they will

never be overlooked. It needs water at least 2 feet deep and spreads rapidly by creeping rootstocks so is not for small pools. Bloom is best if it does not get too crowded. Hardy well into the northern states.

NYMPHAEA TETRAGONA (pygmy water-lily): this and other hardy American water-lilies have been much used in hybridizing for fancy pond decoratives. Tropical species have more spectacular flowers, but our natives lend northern vigor to breeding. If you have a small pool only a foot or so deep, this is an ideal choice, being hardy well into Canada and not spreading horizontally to clutter the water. It yields white flowers about 2 inches across all summer and has leaves not much larger. The blooms open in the afternoon, and each lasts several days.

Even lovelier because of its fragrance is *N. odorata* (fragrant pond-lily), which has big leaves and flowers as large as 5 inches across, each lasting several afternoons. There is also a pink form; both are hardy well north. These like quiet, shallow water and blossom from June to August.

N. tuberosa winters well into Can-

ada too, but is not as wise a choice for small pools because of its rapid spread. Flowers and leaves are larger than in the preceding species, the former opening in the mornings with little or no fragrance. The variety *richardsoni* has more petals and is often offered.

Your supplier will give you directions on how to plant water-lilies in your locality. Usually these small species can be accommodated in large flower pots. He will also have hints on the best techniques for wintering them.

SAURURUS CERNUUS (lizard-tail): the long white spikes of the lizard-tail during the summer add a pretty note to the edge of the large pond or stream. It is the only flower described here which prefers shade. It spreads too rapidly for small pools and may get as high as 3 feet, but the delightful vanilla perfume of the flowers is a real bonus for anyone who can give them a wet home. The same hedging about size and spread is true of *Sagittaria latifolia* (arrowhead, duck-potato), which can reach several feet and has midsummer white flowers and big arrow-shaped leaves. It belongs on the wet marge too.

BULBS
FROM THE APPALACHIANS TO THE ROCKIES 8

Strictly speaking, some of the natives in this chapter are not bulbs. All, however, have a thickened storage apparatus of some sort in the ground. It may be a true bulb like camassia, a creeping rhizome as in the case of many iris-family members, or a thickened tuber like mertensia or trillium.

While there are always exceptions, most such plants must have well-drained soil or the root/bulb will rot. Even with plants like turkey-beard, which is often designated a bog inhabitant, in the wild one finds it growing on a hummock or dry bank near the water. Its roots may go in search of moisture, but its fleshy tuber is quite dry.

Planting bulbous subjects on sloping terrain is one way to ensure they will never sit in water. So is deep preparation of the soil. Woods inhabitants like trillium want lots of humus in the soil, which conserves moisture, but they also demand good drainage and do better in cultivation in drier spots than you may find them growing in the wild. You can always water during drought, but you can't dry up low spots in wet seasons. Those with rhizomes should be transplanted before midsummer to form anchoring side roots before frost. Except for those which bloom in late summer, the rest are better moved in late fall when they are most dormant. If you do spring planting, make it very early; even then bloom may not occur that first year.

It is also mandatory that these plants be allowed to produce luxuriant foliage after blooming so they may store nutrients in the bulb or tuber for another year's flowering. This is true of all bulbs, incidentally. Don't clean away the foliage until it has turned brown and thus completed its job. I water my bulbs after flowering in dry seasons to keep the leaves growing as long as possible.

Face the fact that you cannot cut bulb foliage indiscriminately. Some things like trillium should never be picked, since it is impossible to do so without removing the leaves. If you do, the trillium tuber will either perish or lose so much vitality it will require several seasons to return to flowering size again.

ACORUS CALAMUS (sweet-flag): as if to prove my point about drainage, I have a volunteer sweet-flag spreading well near the corner of the house wall, far from the bog in which it is most often met. I don't know how it got there, but it has even produced some of its odd blossoms, a spadix covered with tiny yellow flowers in early summer. Under these drier conditions, the thin iris-like foliage is only about 24 inches high, but in wetter situations it may reach 5 feet. Plant the thick rhizome just on the surface like an iris. Acorus is fine for along a stream or pond side, but really not decorative enough for the garden.

ALLIUM (wild onion): the best of this family is the hardest to find,

129

but get, if you can, *A. stellatum* (autumn wild onion). It yields clusters of small pinkish-lilac flowers 3 to 18 inches high in fall, wants full sun, and is a darling for the rock garden. *A. tricoccum* (wood leek, ramsons, ramps) is for humusy soil in shade. Its pretty spring leaves are wide like a lily-of-the-valley and disappear completely before the small heads of white bells appear in early July. Like its autumn cousin it is best given a low ground cover to relieve the starkness of the flowers. *A. cernuum* (nodding onion), with white or pink nodding flowers, takes sun or part shade, but spreads too rapidly for the ordinary garden. There are other alliums from the Rockies I would love to try if I could find a source.

ANEMONE PATENS (pasqueflower, wild-crocus): no early spring rock garden should be without the gay 2-inch purply flowers of this denizen of the plains. Despairing of ever finding plants (although everyone offers the related European pasqueflower, *A. pulsatilla,* in assorted colors), I finally sowed seed outside in March. Germination a month later was good, and the little plants were transplanted to several dry sites where I expect good things to come. Among its attractions are the ability to withstand all extremes of weather, finely cut foliage which remains all summer, and fluffy decorative seed heads. Occasionally a white flower

Anemonella thalictroides slowly colonizes in light shade.

is found. Because of its fleshy root, never place this in a low, wet spot. State flower of South Dakota, it is the only native anemone good enough for the home garden.

ANEMONELLA THALICTROIDES (rue-anemone): if I had to pick a favorite wildflower, this is it. Framed by delicate green leaves, the little white flowers with prominent yellow stamens are borne about 4 inches high. In moderately acid woods soil it increases slowly into a delightful patch which sways with every breeze, seeming alive with white butterflies. Anemonella springs from clusters of tiny tubers, wants good drainage and only light shade. Flowers of the double pink variety are worth every cent of the terrible price. Blooms of this sterile form last at least three weeks in my spring garden.

ARISAEMA TRIPHYLLUM (Jack-in-the-pulpit): here is a plant decorative from early spring, when its first tropical-looking leaves unfold, until late fall, when prominent heads of red berries light up the frosted woods. It wants shade and rich moist humusy soil to produce its picturesque spring flowers. *A. pusillum* (swamp Jack) demands a more acid soil and a cool, wet site. *A. dracontium* (greendragon) is not as interesting a flower but a good selection for slightly drier sites where the soil is neutral. Never handle any of these bulbs with bare hands as they have an intensely irritating property.

Arisaema tripyllum hides its "jack" spadix within the hooded "pulpit" of its spathe.

130

Butterfly-weed's flower heads are usually flaming orange.

Seed pods of butterfly-weed betray its milkweed ancestry.

ASCLEPIAS TUBEROSA (butterfly-weed): easily started from seed, this is one of the brightest, most undemanding choices for the dry sunny garden. Flowers are borne during summer from 12 to 24 inches high in large flat heads; they may vary from pure yellow through all the orange shades to ruby red. Foliage stays clean and neat no matter how dry the summer. During their first winter after sowing, press tubers back into the soil carefully during periods of thaw since they tend to heave until a good root system is produced. Never try to transplant mature plants; instead

gather seed when the big pods are turning brown. Before sowing, remove the silky parachutes. This is really a milkweed and the only one worthy of a home in the garden. Butterflies come from all over to visit it.

BRODIAEA (California-hyacinths): all native to West Coast states, these bulbous beauties are well worth trying in the East, but give them thin, rocky, well-drained soil and a hot sunny location to get them through our winters. A sloping rock garden is perfect. Flowers range from pure white and yellow

through every shade of purple and blue, borne in clusters around a foot high. Often the leaves fade before the flower scape appears. Eastern bulb specialists seldom offer them except in mixture. Clyde Robin, one of the bigger western dealers, lists seed of eight different species in his last catalog. It takes two to four years for these to bloom, but germination from early spring sowing is tremendous, so give it a try.

CALLA PALUSTRIS (water arum, wild-calla): give this the cold, wet acid soil it demands and it will

131

reward you with remarkable early summer flowers. They are greenish on a blunt spadix backed by a white showy spathe and followed by red berries. It seldom reaches above 16 inches, has good heart-shaped leaves, spreads by a creeping stem, and is really a bog plant. In northern states you could try it on the sunny margin of a small stream, but here it needs some shade.

CALOCHORTUS (mariposa-lily, globe-tulip, cat's-ears, star-tulips, fairy-lantern, butterfly-tulip): such a multitude of nicknames usually means a flower is held in high

Some forms of calochortus have fascinating designs within the chalice.

esteem by the local inhabitants, and also reflects the multitude of forms. I am told that in the West, where they are native, these bulbs grow in profusion. Such descriptions break the heart of eastern gardeners who struggle mightily to keep even one happy. They are incredibly beautiful late-spring flowers, though somewhat leggy, often needing the support of a stake or surrounding plants to keep them upright.

It is not the cold that kills them here but the alternate freeze and thaw of our winters. I managed to keep some in my former garden over several seasons by giving them a hot dry spot on a sharp slope where water never lay and the soil was thin but clayey. It was shaded from the morning sun by an evergreen so that in winter the ground never got a chance to soften. In summer it baked hard. In my new garden I am putting them in sandier soil for good drainage.

Bulbs are hard to come by. Plant about 3 inches deep if you can locate some. Clyde Robin lists seed of 10 species with flowers ranging from white to yellow and all shades of lavender and purple. Different species differ widely in flower form. Many have interesting color blotches in the center or prominent hairs. In the wild they have varying habitats, but those we can obtain seem to do best with the spare treatment suggested here.

I have not found seed germination too good, but plant the whole block

of soil intact in the hope there will be additional plants the next year. This delayed germination often happens when growing bulbs from seed. Count on at least three years before expecting bloom. The famous sego-lily, state flower of Utah, belongs here. I just wish someone would give this American tribe the attention accorded the related tulipa of the Mediterranean.

CAMASSIA (Indian quamash or lilies): one of the most adaptable native bulbs and fairly easy to find in the trade. In the wild these lovely May-flowering beauties vary from pure white and pale blue to dark blue-purple. Selections in the bulb catalogs give some idea of this range, but the white ones are somewhat rare. My favorite is *C. leichtlini,* which produces spikes of pale-blue star flowers nearly 3 feet high. *C. cusicki* is much like it. I still mourn the white form of *C. leichtlini* I left behind when we moved; it had a greenish cast of the blooms and purplish anthers. The eastern species, *C. scilloides,* seldom reaches more than a foot and has smaller flower spikes. Mine are a vibrant midnight blue, which fights with nearly everything except pure white. *C. quamash (C. esculenta)* is very similar.

All camassias like rich moist soil and benefit from extra water during and just after flowering. As the leaves die down in early summer they prefer being left dry. In my garden there is good increase by

Eastern camassia is often an electric-blue shade.

offsets. If they are dug and separated every few years after the foliage matures, bloom will be fostered. Put bigger bulbs 4 to 5 inches deep and at least 10 inches apart. In warmer states camassia blooms last better if given afternoon shade. Western Indians went to war over possession of lands rich in quamash, which they used as food. Luckily we can eat potatoes and relish the flowers instead.

CHAMAELIRIUM LUTEUM (fairy-wand, devil's-bit, blazing-star): found from Massachusetts south in damp open woods and rich, moderately acid soil, fairy-wand is a fine garden subject. It will take considerable sun, providing its other wants are recognized. The pretty white flower spikes appear toward the end of May and last well. Rosettes of clean foliage stay presentable until late summer. Male plants have the showiest blossoms, but either is nice. I have successfully transplanted them even in bloom, taking a good ball of earth with the fleshy root.

CLAYTONIA VIRGINICA (spring-beauty): anyone lucky enough to come downwind upon a lush flowering colony of this adaptable easterner will be charmed by the sweet fragrance. It wants porous moist soil and at least some sun for good blossoming, and has a very long season. Often seed is ripe from the first buds to have bloomed while the last flowers on the stem are still opening. Semi-double forms are not unknown, and there is much color variation from nearly pure white to deep pink.

The little tubers increase well in friendly surroundings. Plant them only 2 to 4 inches deep, although they are often found much deeper in the wild. Since they wither almost immediately, never pick these tiny gems, for it is impossible to do so without removing the entire leaf stem. The whole plant scarcely

reaches 6 inches high, but it likes to grow in patches. After seed is mature, the thin fleshy leaves quickly disappear, and it does not then seem to care if its home goes quite dry. Thus it is a good choice for spots which are wet only in winter and spring. Leaves usually reappear in the fall.

C. caroliniana is very similar but flowers earlier and a bit less exuberantly. It has much broader leaves. I suspect the two hybridize, since intermediate forms are often found where they are growing close together.

CLINTONIA BOREALIS (yellow bead-lily, bluebeads): while the little groups of yellow bells and the blue berries which follow are quite pretty, this woodlander should not be attempted in cultivation unless you can give it a cool, moist, shaded spot with strongly acid soil. *C. umbellata* (white bead-lily, speckled clintonia) is more adaptable, needing only moderately acid, rich woods soil and shade. Its flowers are fragrant, its berries black. Both types seldom top 15 inches and bloom in May and June. The red-flowered *C. andrewsiana* of California's redwood country must be a real beauty.

CONVALLARIA MAJALIS (lily-of-the-valley): botanists differ as to whether our native example of an all-time favorite is a separate species. We shall not quibble but pause only to say that it makes a

133

wonderful ground cover for shady spots with rich soil, the leaves staying green all summer. Spring's very fragrant flowers are followed by red berries. I suppose the creeping rootstocks could be a pest under very formal garden conditions. My mother's solution was merely to rip up the excess every few years and find another tree to put them under. If big "pips" with a few roots are carefully taken up during an early winter thaw and potted, they can be gently forced in the house quite easily for indoor bloom. The much-touted pink and double forms are not nearly as graceful as the single white.

DISPORUM LANUGINOSUM (fairybells): while its one or two small yellow bells in late spring are not highly decorative, this plant is valuable because of its adaptability. It will grow in neutral or moderately acid soil and prefers wooded slopes. The flower stalk ranges from 12 to 24 inches high, and red berries follow.

ERYTHRONIUM (trout-lily, adder's-tongue, dogtooth-violet): our western states produce some of the best trout-lilies, but you will have to search carefully for houses which carry them. Generally they bear bigger, showier, more dependable flowers than our eastern species. Some have more than one bloom per stem. I have had good luck planting them in partial shade with average soil well mulched

with leaves. The spot, however, got frequent soakings because of a nearby ditch, but had sharp drainage so water seldom stood.

Among those recommended are *E. revolutum* (white), *E. tuolumnense* (yellow), *E. grandiflorum* (yellow), *E. hendersoni* (purple), and *E. californicum* (creamy-yellow).

Our eastern trout-lily *(E. americanum)* is often found wild in spots which are under water during early spring and quite wet until summer drought arrives. They make great patches of leaves mottled with brown but are chary of producing their small fawn-yellow flowers, probably because they are too busy sending out stoloniferous roots to make new bulbs. Give them a half-shaded spot with rich moist soil and plant the tubers only 3 inches deep, placing a stone under each one. Eventually they may reward you with some bloom; the foliage is pretty of itself but disappears as summer approaches. More striking and likely to be freer-blooming is *E. albidum* (white trout-lily) from the Midwest. It will take a drier site as will *E. mesachoreum* (narrow-leaved trout-lily), which is lavender and reputedly the best-flowering of the more easterly species.

FRITILLARIA: our American species, all native to the Pacific Coast, are very variable and little grown or understood in the East; bulbs are hard to locate, but some are available through seed from western sources. Heights even within the

same species range from 6 to 24 inches.

Quoting the late Carl Purdy, who did more than anyone to stimulate interest in our far western flora, these rules of thumb for culture are advanced.

The first group grows naturally in sunny open fields in heavy clay soil, and Purdy suggests a rich garden loam and slight shade to prolong bloom. These include *F. biflora* (dark chocolate brown), *F. liliacea* (white, veined green), *F.*

OPPOSITE:
TOP (l. to r.):
some famous sports: white mertensia, double pink anemonella, double *Trillium grandiflorum*, double bloodroot, pink mertensia
SECOND ROW (l. to r.):
Magnolia virginiana flower and fruit;
Kalmia latifolia winter foliage and flowers
THIRD ROW (l. to r.):
Smilacina racemosa, Amsonia tabernaemontana, annual gaillardia, *Tiarella cordifolia*
LAST ROW (l. to r.):
Chamaelirium luteum, Penstemonhirsutus, Phlox pilosa, Sisyrinchium angustifolium, pink clethra

pluriflora (rosy purple), and *F. purdyi* (white, tinged purple). I doubt their hardiness north of Washington, D.C.

Found in the wild in shady woods and well-drained soil, the second group consists of *F. atropurpurea* (dark purple), *F. coccinea* (scarlet and yellow), *F. lanceolata* (dark purple), *F. parviflora* (purple and green) and *F. recurva* (red and yellow). For these Purdy suggests a light, loose humusy soil, considerable shade, and shelter from

the wind. *F. pudica* (yellow) will take quite a lot of sun and does well in rock gardens. All worth trying in northern gardens.

F. camtschatcensis, the famous black- or chocolate-lily, is really more wine-purple, ranges from 6 to 18 inches, and is quite often available through bulb houses. Since it grows in Alaska, it ought to prove hardy in most gardens except the far south.

HYMENOCALLIS OCCIDENTALIS (spider-lily): this native cousin of the gorgeous Peruvian-daffodil (ismene) has white, fragrant flowers that are equally beautiful though not quite as large. It has been found growing in the wild as far north as Indiana and successfully winters in the ground at Philadelphia. While farther south it wants a moist but well-drained spot, in the north give it sheltered site which can have extra water in summer but remains as dry and warm as possible during the frosty months. Bulbs are available from southern dealers. Foliage is neater and shorter than that of the ismene. Southern gardeners treasure *H. coronaria* (basketflower), but I fear it cannot survive north.

HYPOXIS HIRSUTA (gold stargrass): few bulbs in the whole world have a longer flowering period than this little charmer. Native from Maine to Florida and Texas, it bears golden stars about the size of a nickel only a few

Few flowers bloom over a longer period than *Hypoxis hirsuta:* May into November.

inches high. If seed heads are removed, it may bloom from May to November.

The grassy leaves are never obtrusive, so give it a partially shaded spot where you can enjoy it. Plant the little bulbs an inch deep, adding peat since it prefers acid soil. Though often found in dry open woods, I have also seen it in low, grassy meadows which were literally wet in spring.

IRIS: a varying family of which there are some American members with outstanding garden value. This list is restricted to those which are generally available through houses which specialize in iris or wild plants.

They spread by creeping rhizomes which should be planted so the top is uncovered on a tiny ridge of soil while the roots from it are covered in the lower earth on either side. After a few years a healthy stand of iris will become too crowded. To get the best bloom, remove the extra rhizomes from the outside of the clump sometime after blooming but at least 6 weeks before frost. Each that has a fan of foliage can be reset in a new area and, if watered as for any transplanted perennial, will soon form the nucleus of a new grouping.

I. cristata (crested iris) is the most important native contribution for the garden, making a grand ground cover in almost any soil in sun or part shade. It seldom reaches even 6 inches and in spring has light-blue good-sized flowers with a yellow crest. Increase is good, and there is a rarer white form readily available too. Its wiry, creeping stems make thick patches quite quickly.

I. verna is even dwarfer though similar, but not recommended for any but the garden with very acid sandy soil and some shade.

I. prismatica (narrow-leaved iris) also insists that the soil be on the acid sandy side but is not quite as difficult as the preceding. While found along bog margins and wet lowlands, it will take drier situations. It has lavender-blue flowers with yellow markings on stalks as high as 24 inches.

Much more adaptable is *I. versi-*

136

color (blue-flag), which is happy in almost any soil as long as it remains moist. It is a good choice for the sunny margin of a lake or steam with lavender-blue flowers on stems to 36 inches.

For dry spots try *I. missouriensis* from the western states. It has lavender-blue flowers too on 15-inch stems, should go in full sun, and is reputed to stand summer drought very well. *I. douglasiana* is a species from California and Oregon that comes in shades from white to yellow and all those in the blue and purple range. Only a foot tall, it is hardy and will bloom in shade. It is on my order list.

From the southern states on both sides of the Mississippi comes *I. fulva* (Louisiana or copper iris), which has flowers in brown, red, and orange shades on 24-inch stems. It wants soil on the moist side, seems fairly adaptable to both neutral and acid soil, and is interesting iris breeders very much because of the startling color spectrum it offers for hybridizing. Currently I know only of seed sources, although rhizomes were offered by color a few years ago. I understand it has been successfully wintered in New England and Michigan.

LEWISIA REDIVIVA (bitter-root): every sunny rock garden should have a patch of this fine western plant, the state flower of Montana. In early spring pinkish flowers looking like tiny water-lilies are borne just above the ground. Don't despair when they wither and nothing remains. Mark the spot well against disturbance and wait until fall when small rosettes of foliage will appear. Fully hardy in the coldest states, this lewisia must have a hot dry summer spot to keep its fleshy root from rotting. Add pebbles to its planting area to give it a cool but sharply drained home. Since it looks best in quantity and transplants not too well (my early spring shipment flowered in the package), it will pay you to try it from seed, giving it a cool period first.

There are numerous other less

Iris cristata is the outstanding American member of its family.

137

dependable lewisias. It is named, incidentally, after the famous western explorer Meriwether Lewis. Some are evergreen and have clusters of small flowers. These demand the most well-drained spot you can provide in states with normal rainfall. Acid soil and considerable shade are also recommended. None is easy to locate or grow, but *L. tweedyi* with satiny blossoms of delicate peach is especially beautiful and available from rock-garden specialists.

Some forms of liatris have tall spires of flowers closely packed along the stem.

LIATRIS (blazing-star, button snakeroot, gayfeather): botanists tell me liatris tends to hybridize easily; only an expert can be sure of which species is what, but I never met one I didn't adore. Nothing is better for late-summer color in a dry sunny spot. Don't worry about which to plant, since all are good. Start with some seed and make selections later. Liatris will grow in almost any soil but avoid fertilizing. Given full sun, even the tallest types seldom need staking.

Most species come in both a pinkish-lavender and a white form, and I favor the latter simply because it combines so well with the gayer hues of chrysanthemums. From a single packet of "white" seed I now have short (3-foot) and tall (5-foot) forms as well as one which makes a fat spire of long branched racemes of flowers rather than the more common plain single spike. One or another bloom from mid-August until our late-October frost.

Liatris comes easily from seed with some bloom likely the second year. When you get a form you like, it is easily increased, for each plant produces numerous small offset corms which transplant most successfully in early spring. For showiest effects allow it to make big clumps before separating.

I have another liatris which was advertised as *L. spicata* Silver

Tips. It never exceeds 30 inches and begins blooming in early July. Placed at the top of my driest sunny garden, it showed no ill effects from the worst drought and slowly increased. It is more a thickly rooted perennial than cormous like the others, but it too can be pried apart for increase if you wish.

Individual liatris flowers have numerous thready petals which give a fluffy look, and those at the top of the spike open first. Butterflies and bees are frequent visitors, and so is the mature praying mantis, which often haunts my plants in search of other insects to eat.

LILIUM: although there are more than two dozen beautiful American lilies, only a few are adaptable enough for garden use. No less an authority than Jan de Graaff, the great Oregon lily hybridizer, deplores the senseless collecting of wild lilies, most of which have needs so specialized as to be considered impossible for ordinary gardeners. He is talking about those of the western states where there are a great many different kinds, most being found in a very limited area.

In the East our handful of species have hardly a wild nook left between roads and developments. Anyone who digs a flowering lily except in the track of a coming highway is criminally guilty. Buy your bulbs, please. There are some

This white liatris branches within the flower spire.

dealers who are propagating these lilies. Their chances of perpetuation depend heavily on their getting a foothold in our gardens, but not at the expense of the few wild stands left.

Several things should be kept in mind about lily culture. While the bulbs need moist loam, they must have perfect drainage. Moreover, although bulbs are sometimes found at very great depths in the wild, do not give them this treatment in your garden. Prepare the site well and deeply. Then if the lily wishes more moisture, it can draw itself downward. If you put bulbs too deep to begin with, that may be the last you ever see of them. If the bulbs you get are quite small, plant more shallowly than detailed below.

Lily bulbs are the favorite food of mice; rabbits and deer search out the foliage. One seasoned gardener who successfully grew American lilies in fairly wild country used liberal quantities of stone chips in the soil around her lilies to discourage mice. At Bowman's Hill we put wire baskets 5 feet tall around *L. superbum* plantings. This foils the rabbits, but deer often pluck the flower buds at the top just as they are opening. Most gardeners will not have to deal with deer, but rabbits are rapacious everywhere; these are special enough plants to warrant protection.

Lily bulbs are never really dormant and should be dug with as many roots as possible just after the foliage dies. They should never be stored any longer than necessary.

It is also often noted that wild lilies want partial shade. This is misleading, for I have found they will not bloom well or at all in too shady locations. What they want really is a cool root run but sufficient sun on the foliage to pump nutrition back into the bulb for storage against another blooming season. Rather than trying to find a spot with enough sun but some afternoon shade to prolong the life of the flowers, you do better if you shade just the lower part of the plant. This can be done by placing them behind a bush which will never grow taller than the lily or by giving them a thick, not too deeply rooted ground cover as a companion. Plant the bulbs out from the bush enough so they won't have to compete with its roots.

By far the easiest of the eastern types is the Canada lily *(L. canadense),* which has forms in all the shades from yellow to red. Although handbooks describe it as being found near water, it must not be a soggy site. Err on the side of dryness rather than wet. The many nodding flowers are borne on stems that vary from 5 to 10 feet in July. Pick a sunny spot with deep, moist soil that is well drained and plant bulbs no deeper than 6 inches, depending on size. If happy, they will produce wandering offsets, and you'll have a pretty colony. Soil for these may be either neutral or slightly acid. The midland lily *(L. michiganense)* is much like it but mostly reddish with more recurved flowers.

L. superbum (turk's-cap) is also worth trying, but the soil must be on the acid side. Because it may grow from 3 to 11 feet tall, it is harder to fit into the garden scheme. A well-grown clump, however, is a splendid sight in July or August with large candelabras of spotted-orange reflexed flowers. Yellow and red forms exist too. Add peat when planting and put the bulbs 5 to 6 inches deep. *L. michauxi (L. carolinianum)* is similar but somewhat shorter.

Unless you have very acid soil, do not even try *L. philadelphicum* (wood lily). It is dazzlingly beautiful with one to three upright orange chalices about 30 inches high toward the end of June, but it brooks no variation in its demand for a peaty, sandy, fairly dry site. Its nickname is misleading, for I have never seen it except on the sunny edges of woods. The most prolific planting I've ever known grew in an open field next my childhood home. The thick grass effectively shielded the bulbs from heat and built up a fine humus soil, but during most of the day the leaves got all the summer sun they needed. Bulbs should go about 5 inches deep.

Two bulbs from the West are in good enough supply and adaptable enough to consider. *L. kelloggi*

(West Coast martagon) grows 2 to 4 feet tall and has nodding fragrant turk's-caps in June or July. They open ivory to light pink, mature purple, and often have a yellow stripe on the petals. Give this moist, well-drained soil, plant 2 to 4 inches deep, and mulch the root run. *L. pardalinum* (leopard lily) varies from 2 to 8 feet, has many orange-crimson spotted turk's-caps in July, and multiplies quite rapidly by branching rhizomes. Depending on size, put the bulbs 2 to 5 inches deep and give a little afternoon shade.

A word here about hybrid lilies. This has been one of the great horticultural triumphs of this century, much of it the work of the aforementioned Jan de Graaff. Our lilies are not the only ones which are loathe to accept civilization. By crossing species from different parts of the world, a whole new race of hybrid lilies with great health and vigor has been created.

Unfortunately nothing concrete has yet been done with our eastern lilies, but there are a few good hybrids with the blood of western species. One is *L. pardalinum* Sunset, a strong grower which makes large clumps. It bears red-tipped recurved flowers 4 to 6 feet high in early July. Plant bulbs 4 to 5 inches deep.

The Bellingham hybrids also multiply well. They provide pyramids of many long-lasting flowers up to 6 feet high in June and July in shades ranging from yellow to orange-red,

most of them attractively spotted. Put them 5 inches deep and mulch in northern states against winter heaving of the rhizomes. For discriminating gardeners there are now some named selections of these hybrids, so you can grow clumps of a single color. Easiest to locate are Shuksan (orange-yellow), Buttercup (yellow), and Afterglow (crimson).

MERTENSIA VIRGINICA (Virginia bluebells): an outstanding native for garden use in neutral moist loam, these flowers are best treated as bulbs and moved in summer or fall when the big tubers are dormant.

In rich bottomlands of the East it may still be seen in the wild, covering lightly shaded spots with a

Mertensia clusters its blue bells on tall arching stems.

wave of ethereal blue in April. There are rare white, grayish-lavender, and pure-pink sports too, but the type has clusters of pinkish buds which open to all shades of blue on arching stems as high as 3 feet. Bloom will be much better if you plant it where it receives lots of early spring sun.

It will not care if there is deep shade later, for it quickly completes its season's growth and disappears entirely by the end of June. For this reason groups of ferns are a fine accompaniment, since they will take over decorating the spot in summer. Wild ginger is often found with mertensia too, liking the same conditions and providing a green ground cover until frost.

Mertensia may also be raised from seed. There are numerous species in western states which might be worth trying in gardens there, but I doubt any are more beautiful than their eastern counterpart, which has already proven itself a fine garden citizen.

MILLA BIFLORA (Mexican-star): native to Arizona and New Mexico, this is a fine subject for pot culture in northern states; or it can be put in the garden after the soil warms up in spring like other tender bulbs and lifted before frost. Give it a porous soil and a well-drained spot. Foliage is rushlike and never obtrusive. A succession of 2-inch flat white flowers with a delightful fragrance is produced on stems about 18 inches long. They have long

Not hardy, *Milla biflora* is decorative in pots.

tubes, and the buds are green-and-white-striped. Milla can be cut for bouquets too.

POLYGONATUM BIFLORUM (smooth Solomon-seal): the little pairs of hanging greenish-white bells in spring and the dark-blue fall berries are not particularly showy, but the arching summer foliage is a grand decoration for shady spots where the soil has plenty of humus and is slightly acid. It grows 2 to 3 feet tall. The oddly marked long creeping root, whose growth scars are responsible for the nickname, is

far more successfully moved in fall, but you can try very early spring transplanting too. Great Solomon-seal *(P. commutatum)* prefers slightly moister situations and may reach 8 feet, while the hairy Solomon-seal *(P. pubescens)* seldoms tops 2 feet.

SMILACINA RACEMOSA (false Solomon-seal, Solomon-plume, false spikenard): how handy that the alphabet allows us to place this immediately after its cousin. Though perhaps not as well known, smilacina wants the same situation and is an even better garden decorative. Its bears starry white flowers in a large terminal cluster about 2 or 3 feet high in spring. They are long-lasting and followed by showy speckled berries which turn red by

Berries of *Smilacina racemosa* are speckled most of summer, turn bright red in fall.

fall. Its arching stem provides an interesting focal point for the shady summer garden. Only about a foot high, starry Solomon-plume *(S. stellata)* does not have as showy a flowerhead but often spreads into patches, so it is a nice ground cover for the shady garden in acid soil. I have successfully moved the root in early spring before the leaves were much grown. There are several West Coast species.

STENANTHIUM ROBUSTUM (feather-fleece): if you can make your soil acid enough, this is a fine garden subject because its flowers come in late summer when bloom

Stenanthium's white plumes bring late-summer color to damp spots.

is scarce. It wants only the lightest shade in afternoon but must have moisture and may grow as high as 5 feet. The long erect panicles of tiny white and green flowers are well worth the extra effort. To make it happy in my garden I packed lots of acid sphagnum peat all around the bulb in a low spot which gets rain runoff but drains well. The developing flower head is evident from early summer on and droops in time of drought, which jogs me to let the hose run there for a while when necessary. *S. gramineum* is slightly lower in height, and its basal leaves are more grass-like than those of its larger relative.

STREPTOPUS ROSEUM (twisted-stalk, rosybells): rich, only moderately acid soil and shade suit the creeping roots of this diminutive plant, but it must have a cool situation to thrive. The small nodding pink bells are borne in late spring on stalks never higher than 2 feet, and red berries follow.

TRILLIUM (wake-robin): from coast to coast there are more than 20 American trilliums, many of them with color variations, and among them are some of the finest spring-time garden subjects. Give them all a spot with plenty of summer shade, deep soil rich in humus, and a leaf mulch to keep it cool. Some of the best will thrive where soil is neutral; most do well in the moderate acidity found in woodland soil. All are better moved in fall

and are usually offered by many dealers at that time. The sizes usually sold should go about 2 inches deep, but big tubers are often found at greater depths. Once established, they increase slowly.

To repeat, never pick the flowers since the single three-parted leaf is the only source to produce nourishment for subsequent seasons. If you are troubled by slugs, spread some metaldehyde bait under a piece of log.

Start with *T. grandiflorum* (great trillium), the easiest and the showiest. Its large white April flowers are up-facing and thus very noticeable. They slowly age pink on stems which can reach 18 inches. The Pacific Coast counterpart is *T. ovatum.* They take neutral to moderately acid soil. Every once in a while the angels create a double form of *T. grandiflorum.* Some resemble a gardenia, others are marked with a green stripe. Anyone who disturbs such a wonder should be ignominiously shot in the wee hours of the morning.

The darling snow trillium *(T. nivale)* is a miniature copy of *T. grandiflorum* and blooms here in late March. It will take dry neutral soil so is a good subject for a rock garden, but make sure it has summer shade. It makes a wonderful companion for *Hepatica acutiloba.* The western snow trillium is *T. rivale,* which has white flowers, often marked rosy-purple.

T. erectum (stinking Benjamin, wet-dog trillium) may come in white, yellow, or red forms, the latter being my favorite. I have never even noticed the rank odor which gave it the nicknames. The red form is wonderfully effective planted in front of the slightly taller *T. grandiflorum.* It wants cool soil on the acid side. *T. gleasoni* (midland trillium) is much similar but will take neutral soil; its flowers are white or pink.

Much less showy flowers are found on the toad trilliums *(T. sessile),* but their leaves are mottled with brown so a group is quite interesting. There are forms with purple, green, white, and yellow flowers. *T. luteum* is a southern variety with lemon-scented yellow blooms, and *T. recurvum* (prairie trillium) has brownish-purple blossoms.

T. cernuum (nodding trillium) has white or pink flowers in May, but does not make as good a display because they are often hidden by the leaves. It is most important for extending the season. In northern gardens the drooping *T. nervosum* (rose trillium) will be late too; it is often cataloged as *T. stylosum* or *T. catesbaei.* All these nodding species want soil definitely acid.

Which brings us to the loveliest of all. Paradoxically, *T. undulatum* (painted trillium) is also the most difficult. It absolutely demands a cold site with very acid soil. If you can support it, you'll have in late May a white erect flower with vivid rosy throat markings. If you don't have a permanently acid place for

it, don't encourage the rape of its native haunts by ordering any.

UVULARIA GRANDIFLORA (bellwort, great merrybells): nothing is prettier at the base of a tree trunk than a grouping of merrybells, and after the little yellow flowers go, you'll enjoy the perfoliate leaves all summer. It ranges from 12 to 24 inches tall and will grow almost anywhere but prefers woods soil and shade. Two other species *(U. sessilifolia* and *U. perfoliata)* want moderately acid soil.

XEROPHYLLUM ASPHODELOIDES (turkey-beard): difficult but a challenge for the advanced gardener, this plant wants strongly acid soil in sun or semi-shade where its grassy rosette of leaves can remain dry while its roots have moisture. Where successful, the reward is a dense head of small white flowers from 2 to 5 feet tall in late spring. I

Uvularia sessilifolia has typical yellow bells of the genus.

placed mine on a slope near a roof drain and added lots of sphagnum peat to already acid soil. Rainwater is directed so that it collects in a low spot below. My plant appears healthy but no sign yet of any flowers.

ZEPHYRANTHES ATAMASCO (zephyr-lily, cullowhee, rain-lily): southern gardeners know these well, and when I find a source of bulbs I shall try them here in a protected spot since I have already been able to carry over the related *Z. candida* from South America, which isn't supposed to be hardy either.

Where it can take the winters, the little bulb sends up a sparse clump of thin, bright-green foliage. Intermittently after rain there are small white lily-like flowers about a foot high. While it is found in damp meadows in the South, in the North it should have a much drier site in full sun, and this will help it winter over if you want to try. There are pink and yellow species also native to the warmer states which can be treated as tender bulbs for summer flowering if you can locate a source.

I am intrigued by a recent catalog listing a *cooperanthes,* which it describes as a hybrid between *zephyranthes* and *cooperia,* another tender bulb which no one seems to carry any more. Perhaps its hybrid vigor will give it a greater range than either of its parents; I have a protected warm spot all picked out for this one.

9 USEFUL NATIVE VINES AND GROUND COVERS

When you ice a cake, the hard work is over and it's almost time to sit back and enjoy it all. So too with the subjects of this chapter. They are finishing touches for your garden. Trees and shrubs go in first, then major bulbs and perennials. You can have a property without either vines or ground covers, but like an unfrosted cake, it will lack something.

VINES TO CLIMB AND COVER

Our ancestors appreciated vines more than we do. Cheap screens were unavailable, so they used living plants to shade their porches, garden houses, and gazebos. In the process they produced more graceful interruptions in the landscape. I would like to see some of those stark modern pre-fab toolhouses softened by some greenery too.

Without wandering horses and cattle to cope with, the fence went out of vogue too for a while, but the depredations of dogs and children are equally frustrating. As man seeks privacy on this crowded planet, the fence is staging a comeback,

and the vine is a natural accompaniment.

When planting a vine, you must remember that its climbing tendency is inherent and will be exercised at the expense of anything which gets in its way. A vigorous vine can smother a tree in time. It can grow many yards in a single season, so it is well to place one carefully. I do not recommend using vines as ground covers simply because it is too hard to keep them in bounds if you make a mistake.

Only the best American vines are included here. Most climb by winding tendrils or stems, but a few have clinging rootlets. These latter are capable of clothing masonry without any other help, but the others need some sort of support. This can be an arbor, trellis, or fence. Special nails to help smaller vines ascend smooth surfaces can be obtained at hardware stores.

Fences or arbors made of wood which does not need painting (like cedar) are ideal for vine ventures. Metal and plastic trellises are equally fine. Choose them to fit the

size of the building as well as the amount of vine you contemplate.

Vines can be a real nuisance on a surface which must be painted periodically. If you want one on a frame house, train it on a trellis fastened to the house in such a way that it can be lowered part way for the painter's convenience.

Almost all perennial vines benefit from some pruning. When they are still young, work to foster the growth of only a few main trunks so that they will not strangle themselves. Trying to prune an old overgrown vine can be pretty vexing, and too often it is necessary to sacrifice flowering branches to get it back in shape. Thus it pays to keep an annual eye on what's doing.

Such an inspection includes making sure our worst native vine (poison ivy) doesn't get a good start amidst another twiner. It is easy to remove the pest while still small, disastrous to allow it to proliferate.

There are some other very undesirable native vines which simply don't deserve space in a garden. These include the pesky bindweed *(convolvulus),* which you might think is a pretty morning glory until you have to try and root it out; ground-nut *(Apios americana),* also with dreadfully far-reaching underground roots; and moonseed *(Menispermum canadense),* which is just too hard to keep in bounds both above and below ground.

In the vines listed below maximum length is given only to acquaint you with a plant's natural tendencies. You can keep them much shorter. Indeed for their health, most will be better for the pruning. But by the same token you cannot hope to cover an entire pergola with a dainty thing like adlumia, nor can you keep a vigorous grape vine in miniature.

Remember too that eventually a vine will nearly cover its support if you have chosen it to conform with the vine's habits. So in selecting fencing or trellis for vines, stay with the simplest, most durable sort. An arbor made of fancy work is wasted effort when it is hidden by aristolochia. It also makes one of the most private, wonderful hideaways on a hot summer's day.

ADLUMIA FUNGOSA (mountain-fringe, Allegheny-vine, climbing fumitory): Zone 3*; to 15 feet; likes humusy acid soil, shades, and protection from the wind.

*Probably will need some protection within the zone.

Probably the daintiest vine available is *Adlumia fungosa.*

Among the burgeoning subjects of this chapter, this is the dainty lady. It seldom reaches over 10 feet, with small compound leaves and clusters of pink or white flowers all summer, which resemble wild bleedingheart (to which it is related). Its weak stems can be tied lightly to a support, or it can be allowed to festoon itself over a nearby bush or tree.

Unfortunately it is biennial, so you must employ a bit of ingenuity. Seed sown in early spring will make neat rosettes of clean foliage the first year. During the second it will lengthen and bloom. So you need to sow seed for two years running to make sure of an annual display. Once you do that, the vine will self-sow to provide a lovely spot, but you may have to do a bit of transplanting to keep it just where you want it. Place the new seedlings where they are to grow as early during their first spring as you can to give them a good root run before winter.

ARISTOLOCHIA DURIOR *(A. sipho,* Dutchman's-pipe): Zone 4; to 30 feet; good loam in sun or partial shade.

I know a shaded ell where two of these vines literally roof a patio as well as giving it privacy on the sides. After the vines had begun to cover the side trellises, a wood screen was fashioned over the top for it to clamber on. The last time I saw it, the twining stems of the vine were reaching into a nearby tree, calling for a bit of pruning. The big, dark-green, heart-shaped leaves are borne so close together that even rain is pretty much kept off the patio. During May and June the odd chartreuse flowers are the delight of neighboring children. They quite literally resemble a long-stemmed pipe and are often 4 inches long.

Since it enjoys a touch of lime, this vine is a natural for near the foundation of a house. With good pruning to keep it from going too high, it will make a porch screen so dense it cannot be seen through. For such use you can string wires from top to bottom of the porch with a few horizontals to make it stronger. There are several other native aristolochias, but this is the easiest to find in the trade.

CAMPSIS RADICANS (bignonia, trumpet-vine, trumpet-creeper): Zone 4; to 150 feet; rich garden soil in sun.

Frankly I've never seen a trumpet vine that long, but it is a vigorous

145

Vigorous trumpet vine has outgrown this short post.

plant which needs no attention after planting except to see that it doesn't strangle small children in second-story windows! The compound leaves are pretty of themselves, but the big midsummer attraction is trumpet-shaped orange or scarlet flowers 2 inches across at the lip and with tubes 3 inches long.

It climbs by means of aerial rootlets, so needs no support on masonry. If you have a frame house, train it up a big tree instead. An orange-yellow variety *flava* can be obtained but the type is showier.

146

CELASTRUS SCANDENS (bittersweet, waxwork): Zone 2; to 40 feet; any soil in sun or partial shade.

If you have winter birds, you'll soon have bittersweet (as well as poison ivy), and I do careful weeding spring and fall under favorite perching trees. The berries of both plants are good bird food, and evacuated seeds sprout like crazy.

You can buy plants too, but this is another one of those with male and female flowers on separate plants which nurseries do not bother to label. When you have the right mixture, the female plants will bear orange berries in fall which open to display a red fruit in the center. The best time to pick sprays for winter decoration is just before frost when the capsules have not yet opened. Strip the leaves off and arrange them so that when they open you'll not lose the drying

Bittersweet should be picked in fall after capsules turn orange but before they open to display red berry inside (top).

orange outer coverings. A few sprigs in a vase are a cheerful bouquet which stays neat all winter without water.

Unfortunately bittersweet along our roadsides has been badly overpicked by unthinking persons who cut off huge pieces of vines although they only need a little bit. This makes it difficult for a good fruiting female vine to recover.

Unfortunately, too, you must not put bittersweet in the garden itself. Give it a fence or a post or something all its own, and make sure it stays there. Allowed to climb on a tree, bittersweet will strangle its host, since it wraps itself ever more tightly around its support. It also suffers from scale infestations; treat with miscible oil as directed on the package spring and fall and keep away from lilacs and euonymus.

CLEMATIS VIRGINIANA (virginsbower): Zone 4: to 18 feet; moist, moderately acid soil, sun or partial shade.

Clusters of little white flowers can be expected on a mature specimen of this clematis from July to September. Later plumy seed heads are also decorative. The compound leaves are quite graceful, and the vine climbs by twisting leaf stalks. Since it likes acid soil, you may succeed with it where the fancier lime-loving clematis hybrids will not perform well. It needs a few years of growing to become really decorative.

Seldom reaching more than 10 feet, the related *C. viorna* (leather-flower) has single red-purple, urn-shaped flowers from May to August. It has a more southerly range. *C. texensis* (scarlet clematis) is well worth trying if you can find plants. It has urn-shaped red flowers and grows only 6 feet high. There are numerous other native clematis, but I have never seen them, nor do they appear in the trade hereabouts.

LATHYRUS MARITIMUS (*L. japonica*, beach pea): Zone 3; for neutral sandy soil or gravel near seashore.

While its purply flowers and trailing stems a few feet long may not be highly decorative, this is one of the few plants which will grow happily in the harsh climate of the beach. Those who live or summer there treasure it for its hardiness and ability to hold the soil against the wind. It is best started from seed.

LONICERA SEMPERVIRENS (trumpet honeysuckle): Zone 3; to 50 feet; garden soil in sun or partial shade.

Clusters of long-tubed flowers, scarlet or orange outside and often yellow within, make this a pretty twiner from May to August. In less rigorous climates it will be evergreen. It also attracts aphids so is better seen at a distance than on the porch. Prune in spring if it begins getting out of bounds. It needs a good strong support since it is a vigorous grower, but it is

Virginia creeper's five-parted leaflets easily distinguish it from poison ivy, which has only three.

not a strangling creeper like its Japanese counterpart *(L. japonica)*, which is rapidly overrunning our eastern woodlands, snuffing out whole forests in its path. Our native honeysuckle does not have the fragrance of the Asiatic, but its beauty and good manners make up for the lack. Do not ever plant a piece of Japanese honeysuckle; there is already far too much of this serious pest endangering the native flora.

PARTHENOCISSUS QUINQUEFO-

LIA (woodbine, Virginia-creeper): Zone 3; to 100 feet; humusy soil in sun or shade.

Tiny clinging disks allow this vine to cover masonry readily, and it has been used to decorate houses since colonial times. Five-parted compound leaves turn bright red in fall, and tiny bluish-black berries are eagerly sought by birds. All-in-all it is a fine subject for covering buildings or walls, and birds often nest in it too. It must not be used for a ground cover in cultivated areas because it layers far too readily and soon takes over.

PASSIFLORA LUTEA (passionflower): Zone 6; humusy soil in sun.

Only recently I met this hardier relative of the gorgeous passionflowers of the tropics. Its greenish-yellow flowers are not even an inch across and appear in late August. It climbs by tendrils but may be herbaceous and die down each fall. That is the habit of *P. incarnata* (Maypop) also. It has sweet-scented blue and white (sometimes pink) 2-inch flowers all summer as well as edible yellow fruits. It is ground-hardy at Philadelphia, making about 10 feet of growth each season before dying back with frost. Where hardy, a good selection to decorate a light standard or some other small object. Other passifloras are for southern states or greenhouse use only except in pots.

VITIS (grape): various zones, habits, and preferences.

Probably even before he left the trees, man found grapes delicious; no one knows how long he has been quaffing them in more or less alcoholic form. I know nothing of their culture and very little of their history. But I remember yet how impressed I was that my grandmother made jelly from her own fat Concords, which covered her backyard arbor so a little girl could dream all manner of delights away from the rest of the world. And I have elicited a grudging promise that my husband will make me a short piece of fencing to grow some seedless white grapes for the table.

Verbena bipinnatifida quickly covers dry, sunny areas with fine foliage and pink summer flower clusters.

I do know that most table grapes on the market today are from American stock. Even the famed wine grapes of Europe are often grafted on American rootstock to combat disease. And I have heard of the famous scuppernong of the South, enjoyed Catawbas, and seen a picture of the monument erected in Concord, Mass., to Ephraim W. Bull, the man who selected the first Concord grape vine from a planting of wild grape seeds during the early 1800's. No less an authority than Liberty Hyde Bailey says North America has more species than any other area of the globe.

Almost any size yard can support a couple of well-pruned grape vines, and it is a shame more people do not try. Contact your county agricultural agent for information on best varieties for your soil and climate. He will also have details on growing and pruning techniques.

GROUND COVERS TO MAKE LIFE EASIER

More and more gardeners are discovering how handy it is to plant a ground cover instead of constantly weeding or having wide expanses of rather uninteresting-looking mulch. To be effective, one must be leafy enough to hide the ground so weed seeds cannot get light. And it must increase fairly fast by stolons or creeping roots if you are to get good coverage.

Plants which do this vary from the tiniest mountain phlox, which never reaches more than a few inches, to bushes like symphoricarpus. Preference for sun or shade and soil acidity are also important when selecting a ground cover for a particular spot.

Remember, though, that the tendencies which discourage weeds act the same way on other garden subjects. The best use for ground covers is either to allow them sole sovereignty over a piece of ground or use them as secondary plants to cover spots where deeper-rooted early bulbs or perennials have bloomed and disappeared. Small ones can also be used to cover the earth under bushes. Shrubby ground covers are mostly used where erosion is a problem such as on steep banks.

There is much to recommend an evergreen ground cover since it will not leave a blank spot come frost. One which yields colorful flowers or fruit pays extra dividends.

Suggested native ground covers are listed here by site preference. Check the index for individual descriptions in the appropriate chapters. There are lots of weedier ones too. My list is limited to those considered most garden-worthy. Ferns as ground covers are discussed in the next chapter.

BEST NATIVE AMERICAN GROUND COVERS

SUN	SHADE
Antennaria, various	Asarum, various
Arctostaphylos uva-ursi	Convallaria majalis
• Comptonia peregrina	Cornus canadensis
• Diervilla lonicera	Dicentra eximia
• Eleagnus commutata	Galax aphylla
Heuchera villosa*	Gaultheria, various
Heuchera sanguinea*	Heuchera americana
Houstonia, various	• Leucothoe catesbaei
Iris cristata*	• Mahonia repens
• Juniperus horizontalis	• Pachistima canbyi
• Leiophyllum buxifolium*	Phlox divaricata
• Myrica pensylvanica	Phlox stolonifera
Phlox subulata	Polemonium reptans
• Shepherdia argentea	Sedum ternatum
• Symphoricarpus orbiculatus*	• Taxus canadensis
• Thuja occidentalis, dwarfs	Tiarella cordifolia
• Vaccinium angustifolium	Tradescantia virginiana
• Vaccinium vitis-idaea minus*	Viola, various
Verbena bipinnatifida	• Xanthorhiza simplicissima

(• = shrubby)   * Takes part shade.

Polemonium reptans contributes lush foliage all summer in rich, half-shaded spots.

10 FERNS FOR SUMMER INTEREST

Gardeners who concentrate solely on plants which flower miss the whole point of God's green world. Foliage display lasts much longer than any blossom period and can be equally decorative. High among the best greenery are the ferns, and our native kinds are hardy in a wide range of climates and exposures.

While ferns make superb ground covers, you should not limit their use to such a utilitarian purpose. Few other native plants do so much for the summer shady garden. Given adequate moisture and protection from the sun, most listed here can be used to create lovely cool pictures.

Ideally a summer patio is placed where the hot afternoon sun is minimal. Ferns add immeasurably to its attractiveness from the time the first fiddleheads show in spring. In places where all-season appearance is important, evergreen types are the best choices.

Deciduous ferns are good late-season plants for gardens where early spring bulbs have been planted in quantity. The bulbs do well on the edges of trees and woodlands, since they do most of their necessary growing before the trees leaf out. Groups of ferns behind the bulb plantings revel in the developing shade and help hide the bare ground where bulb foliage has withered away.

One word of caution: the word

Ferns are ideal for wettish places. Most unfold thusly from spring fiddleheads.

"moisture" must not be ignored. Almost all ferns must have it, particularly where they are hit by alternate periods of sunshine. Even those which live naturally on cliffs do so where seepage gives their roots a drink. If you want ferns in drier areas, you must water faithfully during drought. A good rule of thumb: the more sun a planting gets, the greater the need for extra moisture. Most ferns want humus in the soil, so add peat moss or leaf-mold freely when installing them.

Because of their natural habits, ferns are ideal for the north side of the house where lack of sunshine limits what you can plant. Even those too invasive for gardens can be used in spots with natural barriers such as those pesky narrow strips so often found along driveways.

Most ferns are perfect for low spots where water collects from downspouts. Use a few shrubs which like wet feet too, and you transform a problem area into a pretty oasis. Put the ferns on the

150

THE BEST NATIVE FERNS FOR GARDENS

Name	Max. height (in inches)	Situation in wild
Adiatum pedatum Maidenhair fern	18	lt. shade; moist humusy soil; likes limestone
delicately beautiful; creeping rhizome but not rampant		
• *Asplenium platyneuron* Ebony spleenwort	12	semi-shade; likes limestone ledges, woodsy soil
good for rock gardens, terrariums, foregrounds		
• *Asplenium trichomanes* Maidenhair spleenwort	6	semi-shade; moist but well-drained limestone cliffs
use in rock crevices; a darling for terrariums		
Botrychium virginianum Rattlesnake fern	30	shade; rich, moist woodland soil
succulent-looking; early foliage		
• *Camptosorus rhizophyllus* Walking fern	12	shade; dry limestone crevices
sloping rock gardens; tips of long, lancelike leaves root and start new plants		
Cystopteris bulbifera Berry bladder fern	36	moist shade; limestone crevices
rock gardens; long tapering, delicate fronds; reproduces by bulblets on underside of leaf		
Dryopteris cristata Crested shield fern	30	cool shade; moist acid woodland soil
excellent as background planting in woodland gardens		
Dryopteris goldiana Goldie's fern	60	cool shade; rich humusy soil, adequate moisture
golden-green fronds; use as a focal point		

(• = evergreen)   (Continued on next page)

Young maidenhair fern displays typical delicacy of genus.

shady side of the shrubs, of course.

Some ferns like a touch of limestone. They will be happy near the foundation where lime seeping out of the mortar creates a mini-world of basic soil even in naturally acid soil areas. In the rock garden you accomplish the same by a section formed with limestone rocks. And in the woodland garden you can help them along by burying most of a limestone boulder in the earth and placing the ferns around it. Water draining from the rock will give the ferns a limestone tonic for years.

Those which like crevices may be planted between two rocks, but make sure the spot is well-drained. A mulch of small rocks or even pebbles helps the surrounding soil stay moist and is a good trick to remember. Extra peat moss will help ferns which prefer acid soil.

Ferns which reach at least 36 inches under optimum conditions

151

Spleenwort from Christmas terrarium makes itself at home the next summer in shaded rock garden.

are valuable for providing focal points in shady gardens. Since they reach full development later in the season, ferns are also good companions for wildflowers which bloom in early spring; many of these mature their foliage quickly afterwards and leave a blank space the ferns help to cover.

Those with creeping rhizomes may be easily propagated by division. Even ferns which grow from crowns usually spread slowly and can be pried apart carefully. Do both jobs in early spring and water well afterwards. Some ferns grow outward naturally. The center of a clump eventually dies, but new plants form in an expanding ring around it.

Propagation of ferns by spores (they do not have seeds like flowering plants) is interesting, but I do not pretend to be a fern expert and have never done it. For me ferns are just one of many delightful native plants. I buy starts of those I want and increase them by division. Never purchase a fern without its

THE BEST NATIVE FERNS FOR GARDENS (continued)

Name	Max. height (in inches)	Situation in wild
• *Dryopteris marginalis* Marginal shield fern	20	full or part shade; deep humusy soil
leathery leaves; crown should be partially above ground		
• *Dryopteris spinulosa* Evergreen shield fern	30	full or part shade; rich, moist soil, neutral or slightly acid
lacy fronds often used by commercial florists		
Lygodium palmatum Climbing fern	48	shade; moist acid soil
vinelike growth; difficult and rare		
Osmunda cinnamomea Cinnamon fern	60	sun or shade; must have damp, acid soil
coarse; for bold effects in wet soil; odd fertile "sticks"		
Osmunda claytoniana Interrupted fern	60	shade; acid soil
coarse; adaptable to drier situations but will be smaller		
Osmunda regalis Royal fern	60	full to part shade; very wet, very acid soil
bold; fertile top resembles a flower		
Pellaea atropurpurea Purple cliffbrake	15	semi-shade; limestone pockets
leathery blue-green leaves; rock gardens; half-evergreen		
• *Polypodium virginianum (vulgare)* Common polypody	10	open shade; rocky ground; prefers lime
tolerant; slowly spreading rhizomes form dense mats; terrariums		

(• = evergreen)

152

THE BEST NATIVE FERNS FOR GARDENS (continued)

Name	Max. height (in inches)	Situation in wild
• *Polystichum acrostichoides* Christmas fern	36	full to part shade; any good soil
adaptable; spreads slowly; my favorite; other good forms in Northwest		
Polystichum brauni Braun's holly fern	36	cool shade; moist, woodsy soil
handsome glossy fronds; graceful arching habit		
Woodsia ilvensis Rusty woodsia	6	sun to open shade; loose, well-drained rocky slopes
turns brown in dry periods		
Woodsia obtusa Blunt-lobed woodsia	16	open shade; neutral soil
will grow in warmer sections than *W. ilvensis*		

INVASIVE FERNS (Keep out of gardens)

Athyrium filix-femina (lady fern): sun or semi-shade

Dennstaedtia punctiloba (hay-scented fern): sun or shade

Onoclea sensibilis (sensitive fern): sun or shade

Matteuccia pensylvanica (ostrich fern): sun or shade (*Pteretis nodulosa*)

Pteridium aquilinum (bracken): sun or semi-shade; poor soil
Thelypteris novaboracensis (New York fern): woodlands (*Dryopteris novaboracensis*)

All other *Thelypteris* species

Woodwardia virginica (Virginia chain fern): sunny swamps

(• = evergreen)

Walking fern wants dry limestone rock face.

Latin name, for the common names are all mixed up, and you can bring in one of the invasive kinds by mistake.

Those listed here are all native to the East Coast. Westerners should consult nearby nurseries to learn what does well under their conditions. In every case a tour of nearby woodlands gives a good picture of what luxuriates in your area. Use a field guide to identify the kinds that appeal most.

If this class of plants fascinates you, consult *The Gardener's Fern Book* (Van Nostrand Reinhold) by F. Gordon Foster. I have used it as my guide to nomenclature. For field guides nothing can beat Dr. Edgar T. Wherry's.

Finally, if you have a waste area, nothing could be prettier or easier than a planting of one of the invasive ferns. They are all rampant growers, though in sun most want some moisture to grow well. Their spreading rhizomes are strong enough to halt erosion and in time they will even smother most weeds.

11 ANNUALS AND BIENNIALS WITH A PATRIOTIC FLAVOR

It takes a little extra effort to have annuals and biennials every year, but it pays big dividends in summer color both in the garden and for bouquets. You will have to sow your own seed in most cases, for few of these are available as plants from garden centers. Generally they are so easy to grow it seems silly not to do it yourself. For new gardeners let's have a few definitions first.

An annual plant comes into bloom the same season the seed is sown and dies with frost or after it has produced seed to perpetuate the species. Keeping its flowers picked prolongs its blooming period. Half-hardy perennials which flower the first season are treated as annuals in the North since frost effectively cuts short their life but may live much longer in mild climates.

Biennials make only foliage their first season, often in rosette form. They bloom the second season but then usually die. Much biennial foliage is very susceptible to winter rot; give them well-drained sites. To have color from biennials every year it is necessary to start plants for at least two consecutive years. Many biennials self-sow, so that once you have done the planting twice, you may be able to depend on natural increase to keep a patch going. Inbreeding in time may weaken your strain. Periodically it is wise to start seed from a new source. This is true of self-sowing annuals too.

There are dozens more native annuals than are described here. I have tried to select those which are most decorative, not too weedy, adaptable enough for gardens in widely differing types of climate, and available from at least one of the larger national seed houses. Many were tested especially for this book.

APHANOSTEPHUS SKIRROBASIS (lazy daisy): perhaps this pretty 24-inch native of the southern states got that nickname just from toting around its botanical tag. At least it is noticeable that the pink buds bend over until the flower head is developed. They open to small white daisies with a gold center, which close each evening to show the pink tinge on the underside of the petals. The grayish foliage is clean, and the flowers free from any insect pests here. Seed sown in early May began flowering in late July, and bloom continued until frost. It will take partial shade but is more prolific in full sun.

Argemone's nickname is prickly poppy!

ARGEMONE (prickly poppy): though valuable for hot dry states where other plants may falter, argemone is of doubtful merit for climates with normal rainfall. The prickly, white-veined leaves are quite decorative when the plant is young, but they grow unkempt, and there is not enough bloom to compensate. I grew a blend which made plants 18 inches high with yellow or magenta flowers which lasted only a day or two. Seed sown in early May germinated poorly and began flowering August I. Give it the hottest, driest spot in thin soil. We had a wet summer, and I termed it a flop in our climate and acid soil.

ASTER TANACETIFOLIA (Tahoka daisy, machaeranthera): coming from the northern Plains states, this can be sown either in fall or as early as possible in spring in a well-drained sunny spot. Some plants act as biennials, but nearly

Aster tanacetifolia surrounds yellow disk with violet-blue rays.

all mine began to flower about 10 weeks after spring sowing and continued until hardest frost. Height ranges from 12 to 30 inches, foliage is fernlike with a very pungent odor when bruised, and the flowers are violet-blue with yellow centers. I plan to interplant it with xanthisma. It cuts well, but the flowers close up at night.

CALANDRINA CILIATA MENZIESI (C. speciosa, rock-purslane, red-maids): another western plant which proved disappointing here during a wet summer but might be fine in a sunny spot in drier states. The bright pinkish-red flowers were gay enough when they first opened the end of June, but the foliage was soon attacked by thousands of aphids. Most plants succumbed quickly. Before the disaster they were 3 to 6 inches high with leaves a cross between those of portulaca and spring-beauty, to each of which it is related. Germination from May-sown seed was very good.

CAMPANULA AMERICANA (star bellflower): although sometimes described as annual, these should be treated as biennials. Seed sown outside in late February gave wonderful germination, but only one of many dozens of plants bloomed the first year. Set the plants at least a foot apart since they make a big rosette of ground-hugging leaves the first year. During the second summer many small star-shaped, vivid blue or white flowers are

borne on stems ranging from 2 to 5 feet. It wants rich, well-drained soil in half shade and will self-sow. Seed of the true species is hard to come by; at least once I have been given some incorrectly labeled. There are many biennial campanulas. Our American entry is valuable because it will take some shade and also makes a more graceful plant than some of the bigger-flowered sorts.

CENTAUREA AMERICANA (basket-flower): here is a simply gorgeous garden ornament with fluffy heads 3 to 5 inches across when open. They resemble a soft thistle. Some flowers are pure white, others lavender or a combination of the two. Though described as reaching 6 feet, my plants ranged from 24 to 36 inches. They need full sun and can be planted as close as 6 or 8 inches since they do not branch much. Seed sown in early April began blooming in late July, but the plants did not last very long. It would be a beauty for cutting except that each flower folds up as the sun goes down. Since they do the same thing in a shaded room, they are useful inside only where there is much bright light.

CLARKIA: several different species of this showy little westerner named after one of the leaders of the Lewis and Clark expedition are offered, but the doubles are the real beauties. In some catalogs they are sold by color selection, and this is

155

a better idea than the mixture I planted which had every shade of rose and pink as well as white and some purples. Heights range from 6 to 24 inches; mine were around a foot.

Seed sown in mid-May began to flower in early July, lasted most of August. Because our summers are so hot, I gave them a site with plenty of morning sun but protection from the afternoon burn, and they prospered. They were never allowed to want for water, however. Farther north you could give them full sun, and they will probably do even better since they are definitely a plant which prefers a cool site. Another year I shall plant seed much earlier to get a longer period of color. It is best sown where the plants are to flower. Clarkia cuts well although mine were so short they were useful only for small bouquets. It is also grown under glass.

COLLINSIA HETEROPHYLLA (C. bicolor, Chinese-houses): oddly enough this California species has proved easier for me than C. verna (blue-eyed-Mary), which is native to the eastern woodlands. From spring-sown seed, Chinese-houses quickly make little mounds of blue, pink, or white no more than 18 inches high and should go only 6 inches apart in light shade for best effect. The flowers resemble tiny snapdragons.

Its blue and white eastern cousin blooms so thickly in the spring on lightly wooded slopes of our flower

preserve that it gives the illusion of a waterfall. Getting it established in cultivation is another thing. Pick a similar spot where the soil is rich with humus and sow the seed as soon in summer or fall as you can get it. Cover the area lightly with leaf mulch and don't disturb. Maybe you'll be luckier than I. This is really a winter annual and begins germinating in the fall. Once you get it started, it will resow nicely.

COREOPSIS TINCTORIA (calliopsis, tickseed, Philadelphia-breast-pin): few annuals are easier or more colorful than these bright westerners. The flat, small flowers range from yellow through all the orange and red shades to deep mahogany, some selfed, most a combination. Dwarf sorts are seldom more than a foot high, and planted 6 inches apart make a fine foreground carpet.

Tall calliopsis (it is almost always cataloged under that name in the annual pages) may reach 3 feet and shines for picking. A blend of mixed doubles sown in early May began flowering in mid-July. If kept from seeding, it provides bouquets all season. Given full sun, calliopsis will grow in almost any soil or climate and is ideal to interest a small gardener in the world of growing things. Other coreopsis are perennial.

ESCHOLTZIA CALIFORNICA (California poppy): the official flower of the Golden State has endeared it-

self to generations of gardeners by its adaptability and long blooming period. Single and double flowers exist in every conceivable shade from cream through yellow and orange to pinkish reds. Depending on the strain, they may be only a few inches high or nearly 18 inches with finely cut gray-blue foliage that is attractive of itself.

They ask only that they have full sun but do very well in dry spots, so I have always given them such a corner. Sow seed where it is to grow as early in spring as you can since the plants develop best in cool weather. Around five weeks later the first gay flowers will appear, and if you are good about snipping off the long narrow seed heads before they mature, you'll have color there until frost. Moreover they reseed themselves prolifically, so bloom will be even earlier the following year. Fresh blooms cut and remain lovely in bouquets for a day or two, something you cannot say about other poppies. For a really spectacular show, try sowing them in groups of a single color. Several houses carry a good selection, and they are just stunning handled this way. You can also sow seed the previous fall for early bloom.

GAILLARDIA PULCHELLA (G. drummondi, blanket-flower, gayflower): annual gaillardias which come in single, double, and quilled forms are more fun than the better-known perennials of the family. For one thing they're not quite as floppy, and the quilled forms make bright balls for summer cutting to contrast with the many flat daisy-like flowers of the season. You may find them listed as Lollipop or Tetra Fiesta gaillardias, and some houses offer them by separate colors. A mixture will range from lemon yellow to many oranges and reds, even maroon. Heights vary from 10 to 20 inches. Sow seed in April in a warm sunny spot in light, well-drained soil. They'll come quickly into flower and continue all summer if kept picked.

GENTIANA CRINITA (fringed gentian): if you have a moist sunny meadow with sterile, non-acid soil, you have a good chance of being able to establish a stand of this most capricious but beautiful native biennial. Seed is widely available. If you succeed, in September and October you'll have branching plants about 2 feet tall with vase-shaped blossoms of purest blue, their four petals delicately fringed.

To be honest I have not yet been able to raise this lovely successfully. I suspect it is our general soil acidity. But it could have been because the seed was not ripe or too old, or slugs could have eaten the baby plants. All these factors are important. So is keeping the growing medium moist but not so wet that the tiny seedlings mold or rot.

Some gardeners have raised it by sowing seed as soon as ripe in the fall in pots which were then plunged in a sheltered spot and left outside all winter. You can hope it will germinate naturally outside in the spring. Or you can bring the pots in during March and keep cool and damp in the house, then transplant the tiny seedlings to small pots and grow on until they can be safely put in a permanent site. Neither stratagem worked for me, but I have kept both pots watered lightly all summer because old seed sometimes germinates the following year.

Since fringed gentian is usually found in neutral grassy meadows, I shall now try liming the soil at the bottom of our property, fence it off against the mower, and sow fresh seed in place this fall. It may be that the protection of the grass and the natural bacteria in the soil will aid in germination.

The reason conservationists cringe whenever someone picks or uproots this gentian is that to be permanent a colony must successfully produce new seedlings every year. And failure in the wild is quite as common as it has been with my artificial attempts.

Just as ethereally lovely is the western or Rocky Mountain fringed gentian (G. thermalis), although it is a deeper blue and reputedly annual. It is the official flower of Yellowstone National Park, but I don't know where seed is available.

GILIA CAPITATA: (globe gilia): although there are many native gilias, only this form is recommended for summer cutting. It provides small fluffy balls of sky-blue in quantity on branching plants about 24 inches high some six weeks after sowing. Foliage is finely cut, and there is a white form too. Put in full sun.

Other gilias come in yellow, white, pink, or shades of blue, but they are mostly short, straggly plants and not good enough for the garden of anyone but a specialist even though the individual blooms are sometimes quite showy.

Two red forms are best treated as biennials. G. rubra (standing cypress) from the southern states can grow as high as 6 feet, has foliage so fine it is almost needle-like, and puts forth a showy ter-

Gilia capitata is an ideal cut flower.

Gilia rubra's red trumpets are speckled yellow within.

minal panicle of scarlet trumpet flowers with yellow throats. From an early-April sowing here about a third of the plants bloomed in September of that year, but they were less than 18 inches high. The flower heads are extremely showy even in the small size and make superb cut flowers. *G. aggregata* (scarlet or skyrocket gilia) from the western mountains sometimes has pink or white flowers, but the type is a cluster of bright-red salverform blooms on plants about 36 inches high. Seed is hard to find.

GODETIA (satin-flower, farewell-to-spring): if you live where summers are hot, godetia is not a good choice, but you can get it to bloom if you give it humusy soil in a cool spot which gets shade most of the

day, particularly after eleven a.m. Never let it want for water.

In such a position it will be a sprawly plant, but the rose chalices are quite unusual. Some of mine waited to flower until September when the days began growing cooler again. Many have petals edged in white to form a sort of star in the center. There are dwarf and double-flowered varieties offered too, sometimes by color selection. Most will be some shade of red or pink, but there are pure whites.

Sow seed as early in spring as possible where it is to grow for best results. In mild climates you can even sow it in fall for earliest spring flowers, and this is one way to get around its preference for cool conditions. In the north it can take sun and makes bushy little plants with heights depending on variety.

LAYIA ELEGANS (tidy-tips): neat yellow, white-tipped daisies for a well-drained sunny spot. Seed of this Californian germinated for me in a flat inside in three days, which is some kind of a record. The plants themselves seemed to stand still for weeks outside, possibly because I miscalculated the shade of a new tree so the layia got far less sun than anticipated. It makes somewhat sprawly plants about a foot tall, but is a bright note and cuts well. It seems to do much better in cool, damp weather, and another year I shall sow seed outside early where it is to grow.

NEMOPHILA MENZIESI (*N. insignis*, baby-blue-eyes): aptly nicknamed, this Californian provides numerous dime-size blooms of soft blue with white shading in the center. Plants seldom are more than 6 inches high and sometimes sprawl. Put them only a few inches apart in a spot shaded from hot afternoon sun, and you'll have an unusual summer ground cover. Seeds started in a flat and then transplanted did better than those sown in place, beginning to flower in a little over two months after early spring sowing. Mine did not last long, however.

Nemophila likes half-shady rich soil.

PAPAVER NUDICAULE (Iceland poppy): actually perennial, these poppies from far northern regions will flower the first season if seed is sown early and are better

158

treated as annuals since the plants are not long-lived, especially in warm climates. They will self-sow all over. It is easy enough to weed out the ones you don't want, but you can't transplant them successfully, so help nature along in the fall by sowing a few seed heads where you want them another year.

Although a mixture is very gay, most houses have a color selection, all the way from white through the yellows to pink and red. The silky flowers vary from 12 to 24 inches high, depending on variety; some are even double.

PHLOX DRUMMONDI (annual phlox): one horrible drought-ridden summer these brave Texans were the only annual that managed to flower in a sharply sloping sunny garden I used for spring bulbs. They will do much better with adequate water, but I have loved them ever since.

You can start them early inside and transplant or sow *in situ,* since they come quickly into bloom. If flowers are removed faithfully, they will keep right on all summer. There are a number of newish tetraploids which give bigger flowers as well as starred and fringed types in almost any color you can think of, often with a contrasting eye. Some of the taller ones bear their flower clusters as much as 15 inches high, but many more are dwarf. They are a wonderful plant to fill in the holes left in the foreground of a garden after little spring bulbs are through.

PROBOSCIDEA JUSSIEUI (martynia, unicorn-plant): while the individual flower is quite pretty, I can't conceive of anyone growing martynia except to get a good supply of the strange seed pods for winter arrangements. Or maybe to pickle the pods while they're still young. For one thing the 24-inch plants are just kind of ugly with a strange odor and big sticky leaves. They sprawl into a patch that resembles a non-creeping cucumber. Small heads of cream or purply-rose flowers are prominently displayed above the leaves but lack grace. The seeds, however, can be very cleverly used dried, even sometimes being painted to resemble birds about 4 or 5 inches long. Let them stay on the plant until they're completely ripe. After the thick outside pod is removed, the thin end of the seed capsule springs open. Your fall church fair will be able to make a mint selling them.

Proboscidea jussieui looks better than it smells.

Often used dried, seed pods of proboscidea split open when ripe to resemble exotic birds.

SALVIA FARINACEA (blue salvia, mealycup sage): in my southern Pennsylvania garden this Texan endured several winters, but it is better treated as an annual since it is only half-hardy in the north. It is most valuable for providing a tall bluish note in the late-summer garden. The 3-foot racemes can be floppy unless in full sun, and even then may need some staking. Individual flowers are much smaller than those of the more popular scarlet sage, but the head is longer. *S. azurea* and *S. pitcheri* are quite similar, the latter being the hardiest of this trio of tender perennials. *S. coccinea (S. rosea,* Texas sage) is a native coral-red species which is supposed to be quite quick to bloom from seed and sounds more interesting than the more commonly seen red salvias from Brazil. You might even get Texas sage to winter over with some protection.

THYMOPHYLLA TENUILOBA (*Hymenatherum tenuiloba,* Dahlborg daisy, golden-fleece): here is a real darling for the foreground of the sunny garden. Imagine 6-inch

159

mounds of fine ferny green covered with bright-yellow daisies about the size of a dime which seem not to care whether it is hot or cold, wet or dry, but just keep blooming their hearts out all summer. Actually they prefer a well-drained spot, and you should periodically remove the seed heads to encourage long blooming. Seed sown in early April began to flower in late June, and continued to frost. Another time I will start it earlier in the house just to have it that much sooner, and perhaps germination will be better, for this was my only complaint with my test planting; only a very small percentage of the seeds sprouted. What I really hope is that this year's plants will self-sow! Seed is available from several sources, and this is one annual I shall never be without again.

Bright flowers of *Verbesina enceloides* deserve the nickname of "butter daisy."

VERBESINA ENCELOIDES (butter daisy): only one seed germinated from my sowing of this southerner, but what a show it gave. A big branching plant 36 inches high and bearing all summer some fine yellow daisies much reminiscent of coreopsis but in clusters and with more interesting foliage. It wants full sun and begins blooming about 11 weeks after sowing.

XANTHISMA TEXANUM (star-of-Texas): the first pure yellow daisy of this happy-go-lucky annual opens about ten weeks after sowing. The plants produce more and more as the summer wanes (if seeds are removed) and there will still be some appearing even after the first frosts. Moreover it will seed itself, so the second year you will have bloom sooner. Xanthisma doesn't

Xanthisma's little bushes are studded with golden daisies until late frost.

mind transplanting, so you can just move the volunteer seedlings to wherever you want them early in the spring. A single packet of seed in my former garden was still supplying me with descendants when we moved five years later. Some plants may go over 3 feet, but most remain nearer 2. They branch some, but plant no more than a foot apart for solid display in full sun.

ZEA MAYS (Indian or ornamental corn): this is the only American vegetable included in this book, although such notables as beans, pumpkins, and squash are well-documented native contributions to our menus. No one knows the exact origin of the corn the Indians were growing when the first colonists arrived, but it was a staple crop for many tribes over a wide area. Today's table corn is a hybrid, far removed from Indian varieties. Ornamental corn is more closely related to the earlier types. It is for fun rather than eating, although the 2-inch red ears of so-called Strawberry corn can be used for popcorn if allowed to get good and ripe before picking. Other varieties widely offered are *gracilis,* which seldom grows over 4 feet and has green-and-white-striped foliage; Rainbow, with varicolored kernels; and Harlequin, with red ears and foliage striped green and red. They average about 100 days for ripening and are much prized for autumn arrangements and harvest fairs.

AMERICA CAN BE BEAUTIFUL 12

If by some magic I were allowed to pop back into the past, I would choose to sail up the Hudson River on a fine spring day before the European settlers arrived. Born and reared in that beautiful valley, I can remember little places that were still incredibly lovely even a few decades ago.

Imagine that great open sewer as it must have been: pure, fresh water teeming with fish. (When I was very young they still took shad from it, but in my teens even the roe was tainted with oil.) Along the litter-free shores the Indians gather luscious oysters. (Vaguely I can recall Mother mandating no more swimming at Croton Point because of the pollution count.)

In the marshes the red-winged blackbirds are chattering, but the herons and gulls are too busy looking for delicacies. (Even as children we were horrified when they started filling in the pretty inlets below Harmon with junk from somewhere.)

Early colonists wrote with awe of the great forests. (Alas, they were gone long ago; but my children, condemned to bulldozed develop-

ments, do not even have a giant tree to love like the great black birch at the top of my mother's garden in which I spent at least half the summer.)

In damp places among the rolling hills the spring-beauties are so thick one is transported by the fragrance. (Today it is fashionable to take one's trip with foolish weeds like pot, and the very air itself is hardly worth breathing.)

If it were April the deciduous woods would be carpeted with wild-flowers; in May the shade of the pine groves would prolong the ethereal beauty of the trailing arbutus; and if I had chosen June I might see grassy clearings ablaze with wood lilies. (I have never once found the vanishing arbutus in the wild but I have tripped over a thousand beer cans.)

What manner of animal are we that we have so polluted everything and thrown away treasures like these? Even the meanest tomcat makes an effort to cover his own excrement. We call ourselves *Homo sapiens,* affixing to our generic name a specific adjective, derived

from the Latin word for wisdom. I blush to remember we have already begun littering the moon too.

I am too old to believe I shall have that trip backward four centuries in the time machine, but what breaks my heart is that I cannot even show my children the glories I knew. Nevertheless, I am not yet willing to give up.

My home today is near the Delaware River, which in its day was quite as beautiful as the Hudson. Perhaps more so because here the flora of the southern states reaches up the temperate river valley, while that of colder climates to the north can survive in cool pockets.

Not long ago there was a great hullabaloo because a venturesome shad had been seen in the Delaware after protracted absence due to pollution. This was credited to the efforts of our conservationists in cleaning up the river. They have still a great way to go, but perhaps in old age I can say that I lived through the high-water mark of man's stupidity toward his environment.

Legislation already on the books

161

and sure to come will serve as guideposts to what must be done, but the turning point is public opinion. Already the pendulum may be swinging our way. Public indignation over flagrant cases of air pollution, fish kill, and rapacious development occurs daily. No longer dare the industrialist, the highway department, or the individual homeowner throw his refuse out the back door or carve up the landscape willy-nilly. Today someone may actually object. That is at least progress.

The pocketbook syndrome helps. I had a history teacher who stressed that economics was the key to understanding human action. It explains a great deal about practical politics too. Morally, emotionally, and socially there are good reasons to conserve our Earth. But the answer for action is cold cash.

Modern industry needs clean water to operate. However costly it may be to treat sewage and waste products, it becomes impossible to run a plant if the water which comes in is as bad as that which has been leaving. Common sense is beginning to convince even the pirates that something must be done about the latter if they are to be able to use the former.

There is not nearly as far a distance from the municipal dump to the wildlife sanctuary as first appears. I think it is time our women's clubs began making public trips to the first rather than the second. It ought not to take too long afterward for the first to become the second, and not for rats either.

Some farmers are already discovering that wildlife can be an ally. Gardeners can teach them a great deal more about how to treat the soil and about encouraging birds to do their dirty work. Watching a pair of mockingbirds feed their nestlings one kind of bug after another hour after hour, a gardener knows no spray can possibly keep up with their diligence. Rachel Carson went to her grave still being maligned by many, but just this year the terrible toxic residual effects of DDT and its hydrocarbon relatives are finally being recognized by persons of authority.

Somewhere soon the head of a highway department will realize that thickets of trees and bushes in medial strips not only help screen headlights but solve drainage problems too. Instead of planting afterward, he'll catch on that the whole job is easier if as little disturbance as possible is made to the original contour and its cover. God knows what catastrophe is needed to convince highway planners finally to keep their roads out of what is left of the river valleys and thus save eventual money needed to drain their mistakes. Highway departments are probably the most single dangerous element active today in ruining the landscape.

Builders whose monumental efforts with the bulldozer so often result in houses below street level are beginning to get the message, but zoning needs to get stricter. Those California houses which slid downhill in the rains might have been saved if the land had not been denuded of its original cover before building started.

So I close with a plea that each reader try to help his little piece of America stay beautiful. Keep the developer and the superhighway off the floodplains, where they cause nothing but endless problems. Do what you can to preserve the natural beauties still left, and let your monument on earth be a few pieces of greenery which you personally replaced and nourished.

Herein are the best of the growing things which are the heritage of all Americans. Developed in the New World over the millenniums through nature's trial and error, they are far better suited to our climate, soil, and topography than many of the exotics we spend so much time and money upon. Teach your children not to pick flowers but to sow them, and a whole new generation starts out with a fresh approach to nature. After you establish some in your garden, clear a few weeds away and scatter your extra seed along the roadside beyond the reach of the sickle bar. Baptisia, liatris, and butterfly-weed are far more lovely than beer cans. It would be nice to be able to say once again that they are more indigenous too.

Healthy tupelo leaves are brilliant green, blaze red in fall.

162

INDEX

Passing references to plants are not indexed. Hundreds of common plant names have been cross-indexed for convenience, but in the chapters of the book the genera considered are listed alphabetically by their botanical Latin names. Common names beginning with words like "false," "wild," and "Indian" are transposed so that they can be listed under the more meaningful part of the name: *indigo, false; senna, wild; pink, Indian.* However, hyphenated common names are usually not transposed: *star-grass.* Page numbers in plain type indicate discussion in the text, and numbers in italics indicate illustrations. If the only page number is in italics, both text and illustration are on that page.

164

168